The Bentley Collection Guide

J. PHILLIP INCORPORATED PUBLICATION

2006 • 2007

Acknowledgments

This 2006 Edition of The Bentley Collection Guide® is once again dedicated to all who love and enjoy collecting Longaberger Baskets and Products. We are so thankful to all who have helped contribute information, market values and baskets for photography. Once again, we thank Pam & Tom Thomas of Westerville, Ohio for allowing us back this year to wreck their home, pulling down baskets and disassembling beautiful displays in attempt to capture a glimpse of her collection in this Guide. Another successful photo shoot, and one we could not have done without you! There are so many others who consistently help us each year. The Bentley Guide is the most comprehensive and accurate listing available because of loyal customers and Collectors like you. Thank You!

A heartfelt thank you also goes to our staff, who dedicate countless hours towards putting this Guide together each year. Without all of you, The Bentley would not exist. You are special people and you set a standard of excellence unmatched by anyone. You are appreciated!

Please understand . . .

Our goal is to provide you with an accurate representation of the history of Longaberger products and to encourage the collectibility of these beautiful items. We continue to work hard to offer you the highest quality information and hope that through Bentley, you will find great joy in your collection.

This Guide is published by J. Phillip Inc. and is in no way affiliated with, authorized, endorsed or licensed by The Longaberger® Company. The Longaberger Company in no way sets, reviews, approves or determines the secondary market prices published in the Guide. All trademarks, including basket and collection names, are trademarks registered and owned by The Longaberger Company and J. Phillip, Inc. has no interest therein.

<u>Photographs by</u>:
Terry Thurston, *Morning Light Photography*
Andrew Korcok, *Lighthouse Photo Services*

Copyright© 2006 by J. Phillip, Incorporated
• 597 Sunbury Road • Delaware, Ohio 43015 •
• 1.800.837.4394   •   740.369.4100 •
• info.bg@bentleyguide.com
• www.bentleyguide.com

ISBN 0-9759815-1-X

All rights reserved. No part of this publication may be used or reproduced without the expressed written consent of J.Phillip, Incorporated.

Letter From the Editor

Welcome to our 2006 Edition!

We have often referred to this Edition as "Bentley Revamped"! This past year, we've looked at everything, no collection has been unturned. With the goal of creating efficiencies within the information provided and lowering printing costs for this growing collectible, this Bentley Edition has met the challenge and offers the Collector more than ever!

No longer is it necessary to match a picture from one page to its information on the opposite. With our new layout, all information is now in one spot, also making items easier to find. The Collectors Club section has taken on a completely new organization as subcategories have been created to better locate and view like items, placing Miniatures together, Renewals together, Ornaments together, etc... . The Incentive & Awards section has also been reorganized as existing subcategories have been streamlined and reordered to help make items easier to find. Another big change was implemented into the *Quick Find* which has been downsized to a one-page format, rather than two. While some repetitive information was pulled from those pages, the *Other Baskets Using Same Form* info was moved to the *Dimensional Search* to eliminate unnecessary flipping between those sections. We are very pleased with these changes and know that you will be, too!

Items from 1979 through April 2006 and the *Spring/Summer 2006 WishList*® are included in this edition of *The Bentley Collection Guide*.

As always, our objective is to provide a comprehensive and accurate listing of all baskets and products that have been produced by The Longaberger Company. Although we are not affiliated with the company, our goal is to promote and further the collectibility of Longaberger Products®. Therefore, with each new edition we make improvements and additions to the guide to provide more information and detail of the products.

Please keep in mind the current market values listed throughout this book should be used *only as a guide*. They are not intended to set prices, which vary from one section of the country to another. Secondary market prices vary greatly and are affected by many things, such as condition and demand. To better represent your specific market, we encourage you to report your results to us regularly.

We are hopeful you will enjoy the Bentley Guide. The Fun Facts, the photos of personal collections and the improvements in information are all for you, the collector. Through the *Bentley Collection Guide*, we hope to bring you many hours of happy collecting!

Your friends at Bentley

Table of Contents

INTRO PAGES
Why We Do What We Do 1
History of The Longaberger Company 2
Where to Find Longaberger Baskets 3
Directory of Secondary Market Resources 4
About Market Values—What You Need to Know .... 5 – 6
How to Use the Guide .... 7 – 9
Identifying and Valuing Your Baskets .... 10 – 14

COLLECTIONS
All-American® .... 15 – 16
Autumn Reflections™ 17
Bee® Baskets .... 18 – 19
Blue Ribbon™ 20
Booking™ & Promo Baskets .... 21 – 23
Christmas™ .... 24 – 26
Collectors Club® .... 27 – 34
Cookie Molds .... 35 – 36
Crisco® American™ 37
Easter .... 38 – 41
Employee Baskets .... 43 – 46
Father's Day™ .... 47 – 48
Feature Baskets (Baskets offered for a limited time only) .... 49 – 59
Foundry .... 60 – 64
Good Ol' Summertime™ 65
Heartland .... 66 – 67
Holiday Hostess™ .... 68 – 70
Horizon of Hope® 71
Hostess™ .... 72 – 76
Hostess Appreciation 77
Incentive & Award Baskets .... 78 – 98
J.W. Collection™ 99
J.W. Originals 100
May Series™ .... 101 – 102
Mother's Day™ .... 103 – 104
Pewter Ornaments .... 105 – 106
Pottery & Glass .... 107 – 120
Proudly American™ 121
Pumpkin Series™ 122
Retired Baskets .... 123 – 132
Regular Line Baskets .... Checklist
Shades of Autumn® 133
Special Events (Baskets made in honor of local or national events) .... 134 – 137
Sweetheart™ .... 138 – 139
Tour Baskets™ .... 140 – 142
Traditions® 143
Tree-Trimming™ 144
Wood Products .... 145 – 147
Woven Traditions® 148

SIGNATURES 150

FABRIC ID .... 151 – 156

FUN FACTS
Boyds Bee Bears 157
Boyds Bear Treasure Boxes 157
Cookbooks 159
Customized Baskets 158
Director Christmas Baskets 159
Form Number History 160
Hamper History 161
Harmony Kingdom pieces 162
Heisey Plates 162
Incentive/Award Jewelry 163
Insurance 164
Oak/Maple Handles 163
Original Weavers 167
Pottery History 165
Stain History 166
Weaving Techniques 167
White House Easter Egg Roll 168
Wood Loops 168

QUICK FIND .... 170 – 218

DIMENSIONAL SEARCH .... 219 – 234

Why We Do What We Do

Who is Bentley?
The staff at Bentley is a small family of five employees. Our publishing name is J.Phillip, Inc. and our office is located in Delaware, Ohio. We have been publishing *The Bentley Collection Guide* since 1993 and added *The Collectibles Database*® to our line-up of products in 1996. Our company is privately owned and not affiliated with The Longaberger Company in any way.

Our Goal
As fellow collectors of Longaberger Baskets, our goal is to further the collectibility of these beautiful items by educating collectors about the Secondary Market.

Our Commitment To You
We are dedicated to providing you, our customer, the highest quality product with the highest integrity of service.

We want you to be 100% satisfied with your *Bentley Experience*. Not because it's good business practice, but because it is what we would want as a customer. We want you to feel a part of our family and to look forward to getting your Bentley year after year!

Contact Us
If you have any questions about the Longaberger Secondary Market, our products or you would just like to talk about your collection, please do not hesitate to contact us! We would love to hear from you!

phone:	1.800.837.4394
fax:	614.568.7255
email:	info.bg@bentleyguide.com
website:	www.bentleyguide.com

May the God of hope fill you with all joy and peace as you trust in him, so that you may overflow with hope by the power of the Holy Spirit.

- Romans 15:13

History of The Longaberger Company

In the early 1900's, in the small town of Dresden, Ohio, John Wendell "J.W." Longaberger developed a love for hand-woven baskets. As a teenager, J.W. joined his father, Daddy John, at the Dresden Basket Company as a full-time weaver to help support the family. In 1927, J.W. married Bonnie Jean Gist and they had 12 children. In order to support his large family, J.W. worked at the Dresden Paper Mill during the day, and continued to make baskets at night.

In 1973, J.W. and his fifth child, Dave, began to teach others how to weave baskets. J.W. died that year but the quality and attention to detail he wove into his baskets were kept alive by Dave through The Longaberger Company. On March 17, 1999, Dave Longaberger passed away after a battle with cancer. His vision for what the Company could be and how it could positively impact people's lives is alive and well today through his daughters, Tami and Rachel.

Each basket is handmade from hardwood maple. Since 1978, each completed basket is dated and signed by the basketmaker. In 1982, the practice of burning the Longaberger name and logo into the bottom of each basket began, guaranteeing its authenticity.

The Company started selling through home parties in 1979. By 1981, they had 100 consultants and delivery of baskets took anywhere from eight to 12 weeks. Many changes have taken place since this humble beginning. From 1977 - 1991, the Company generated a total of $14 Million in sales, compared to their 2001 performance, in which reported earnings were close to $1 Billion. In 2005, nearly 60,000 Sales Consultants sold more than 15 million products, 3.1 million of those being baskets.

Along with its popularity among collectors, Longaberger has also been recognized nationally for its dedication to quality and excellence by many major sources. They have been spotlighted as one of the Top Ten Most Generous Companies in America by Newman's Own, Inc. They have also been listed among the top privately held companies by *Forbes Magazine* and *Working Woman* magazine recognized Longaberger as one of the largest woman-owned companies in the U.S.

The Longaberger Company has come a long way from the garage it once occupied more than 25 years ago. We encourage you to visit Dresden to fully realize the history and commitment behind Dave Longaberger's dream. If you are interested in touring the area, please contact the Dresden Village Association at 1-800-315-1809 or The Longaberger Company directly through Guest Relations, 740-322-5588.

Where to Find Longaberger Baskets

New Longaberger Baskets can be purchased only through Independent Home Consultants, usually at a basket home show. Baskets are ordered from the *WishList* and flyers, which feature products currently available from the Company, through consultants. If you are interested in a current Regular Line Basket and you do not know a consultant, please contact The Longaberger Company at (800) 966-0374 or visit www.longaberger.com to find one in your area.

Feature and specialty baskets are available for only a limited amount of time. For example, the 1992 Christmas Collection Season's Greetings® Basket was offered from only September through December 1992. After this time, the basket was no longer available from Longaberger.

Older, retired Longaberger Baskets can be obtained only on the Secondary Market, which is made up of people buying and selling these products. You may find retired items from a number of sources. The directory on the next page is a listing of the various sources we have found for collectors to buy and sell these unique, and sometimes rare, products.

Please understand . . .

The Directory of Secondary Market Resources is for **informational purposes only** and constitutes neither an endorsement nor a recommendation. The publisher does not assume responsibility for the selection, performance or use of these services. All understandings, agreements or warranties, if any, take place directly between the service providers and the prospective consumers. This listing of Secondary Market Resources is based on information available at the time of publication and J. Phillip, Inc. makes no warranties as to the completeness or accuracy.

To help better evaluate the services listed on the next page, we have included the number of years in which we have listed them within the Guide.

IT IS NOT A RATING SYSTEM

We do not charge these companies to be included in this publication. The only requirement is that they be in business for at least one year and consistently report their market results every month for at least two years. When dealing with any of these companies, we encourage you to let us know of your experience as we wish to continue providing you with quality information about the secondary market.

Directory of Secondary Market Resources

INFORMATION	TYPE OF SERVICE	YRS IN GUIDE
Basket Accessories 877.808.5437 www.basketaccessories.com	Dealer, PA	[1]
Basket City USA® 419.229.1285 www.basketcityusa.com	Internet	[7]
The Basket House wreidlr@adelphia.net www.baskethouse.com	Internet	[8]
Baskets Galore & More ebellew@columbus.rr.com www.dresdentraditions.com	Dealer, Dresden	[14]
Bay-Side Baskets **& Plastic Protectors** 888.754.1193 www.baysidebasketprotectors.com	Dealer, Dresden	[7]
The Bentley Guide 800.837.4394 www.bentleyguide.com	Internet	[14]
Dresden Transcript 740.754.1608	Newspaper, Dresden	[14]
Find A Basket® 740.687.6317 www.findabasket.com	Internet	[4]
Greg Michael, Auctioneer 574.686.2615 gmichael@ffni.com	Auctioneer, IN	[14]
The Online Auction Company 800.440.9848 www.theonlineauctioncompany.com	Internet	[2]
Plain City Auction, Inc. 1.888.249.2973 www.plaincityauction.com	Auctioneer, IN	[3]
Rebel Yell Auction Company 540.966.4656 www.rebelyellauctions.com	Auctioneer, VA	[7]
Williams Auction Company 217-636-8415	Auctioneer, IL	[6]

About Market Values

The prices provided in this guide are secondary market values obtained from various sources, such as dealers, auctioneers, collectors and Consultants. For the 2006 Edition, we have collected and confirmed over 25,000 transactions from all different markets.

The values shown are the *average* and the *highest* reported selling price for a particular product, *not* the asking price. By providing the selling price, the most accurate and reliable value is given for each basket. However, it is important to remember several points regarding this price guide:

TIME-SENSITIVE INFORMATION

It is the intent of the publishers to gather all pricing data up to the last possible moment before the Guide is published. However, some prices may have changed during the time it takes to publish and send the Guide.

LIMITED INFORMATION

The market values shown are not absolute. Increased demand in some areas may result in higher prices for particular baskets. It is impossible for us to be aware of every sales transaction; therefore, the market values listed may not be the absolute highest selling price during a particular time period. We encourage you to help us represent your market even more accurately by reporting to us all transactions that you participate in throughout the year.

SHIPPING COSTS CONSIDERED

Although some transactions reported to us may include shipping costs from seller to buyer, the prices reported in the Guide **do not include shipping and handling costs.** Even though shipping is often a part of a transaction, it is one cost associated with participating in the market and should not be considered part of a basket's value, except in the case of an eBay® transaction (see below). However, you may need to consider this additional cost when insuring your collection because most insurance agencies will only cover up to the insured value listed, regardless of whether or not there are additional costs to replace the item.

A WORD ABOUT EBAY

As market activity on eBay continues to increase, we felt it necessary to point out a few things to better understand this unique market. As with any auction environment, prices are strongly affected by supply and demand. Items that are abundant in supply tend to go for less than items that are in high demand. Successful auction prices are a result of many bidders wanting the same item and being motivated to bid higher. In contrast, common items tend not to be successful because there are fewer bidders interested. In general, it is usually a great environment to buy, but rarely to sell, unless you have a rare item. Also noteworthy is the fact that shipping is a profit center on eBay, which means that many sellers have shipping and handling fees that are higher than cost with the intention of making a small profit. This is a common, acceptable practice on eBay and most seasoned bidders will account for this fact when bidding. So when an item sells for $20, it is likely the buyer will spend just as much in shipping and handling fees. Therefore, that item really sold for $40. When in the market to buy or sell, eBay shipping and handling fees should be considered when comparing prices to tag sales, consignment shops or other person-to-person transactions.

RANGE OF VALUES DEFINED

The range of values listed throughout the Guide reflect the range of activity occurring in the Secondary Market.

Average Value is determined by taking a straight average of the values reported for an item during a specific period.

High Value is the highest value within the range of values reported. If a transaction is reported that is much higher than other results, we do not consider it to be a true reflection of the market and therefore will not report it until similar transactions are reported. It is important to note this definition of High is different from the one used in the Fourth Edition Guide, but is the same definition used in all other editions.

SOURCES FOR VALUES REPORTED

We try to collect a variety of information from several types of markets—Internet, person-to-person, dealers, stores and auctions. Please remember that your market could, and mostly likely is, very different from other markets. What is selling *hot* on the West Coast may be *dead* in Dresden, or vice versa.

If you have reported a value to us and you do not think it is reflected in the Guide it could be for the following reasons:

- It may have been out of range of the other values reported. For example, if we receive 100, 120, 115, 140 and then 500, we will not show 500 as the *High* until we have more values to support that activity.

- It is possible we did not receive your information. Please feel free to call for clarification.

REPRESENT YOUR MARKET—REPORT TO US!

- *Call*: 1.800.837.4394

- *Report Online*: www.bentleyguide.com

The Bentley Collection Guide and *Collectors Inventory Checklist* reflect what J. Phillip, Inc. considers current market values. J. Phillip, Inc. in no way warrants the prices therein. The publisher assumes no responsibility for loss that ensues as a result of consulting the Guide.

We have found that *The Bentley Collection Guide* is the most accurate and reliable reference tool available for valuing Longaberger Products.

How to Use the Guide

FINDING YOUR WAY THROUGH THE GUIDE

All collector series and feature items are listed categorically in the main body of the Guide. The order of the categories is alphabetical, starting with *All-American* and ending with *Woven Traditions*. Actual page numbers can be found in the Table of Contents.

We do not include Regular Line items in the Guide because we do not consider them to be a part of the Secondary Market since they are still available directly from the Company. For inventory purposes, however, they are listed in the *Quick Find* (page 170), the *Collectors Inventory Checklist* (see page 9) and also our *Bentley Guide Online* service. It is also a good idea to keep a copy of a current *WishList* with your Bentley to have pictures of these Regular Line baskets on hand.

The dimensions, form number(s) and quantities produced (when available) are listed directly under each product's picture. It is noted when a photo is not yet available for an item and with these few items, we are working to locate these items and hope to add them to a later edition.

READING NOTATIONS IN THE GUIDE

Due to space limitations, we have made use of many abbreviations and subscripted letters/dates to clarify details. In most cases, reading the description of the item will explain the abbreviations without any confusion. For example, if an item has multiple form numbers, subscript letters are used to distinguish which form number matches which color.

Spring (06)
1849112 SP/
1849121 SW/
1849122 BR
11L x 8W x 5.5H
Soft Pink, MedGreen, Soft White, Bold Blue & Bold Red.

1849112 is the form number for Soft Pink

10341G/10304WB/10327B
7.5RD 4.75H
Offered Leaf Green/dark trim, Warm Brown or Warm Brown/black trim

	Or	B	HIGH
B			75
CP/L	CP/L		79
FSC/Ld		FSC/Ld	139

Combo (C) included a protector & liner (P/L)

Each item in the Guide is listed by its title(s) and year, although in some collections, the year(s) are subscripted. Special characteristics may also be listed, such as swinging handles (sw/h), stationary handles (st/h), no handles (no/h), inverted bottom, etc. If the basket was originally sold with accessories, the following notations will distinguish which accessories were available: Protector **(P)**, Liner **(L)**, Lid **(Ld)** and Divider **(Div)**.

For baskets, values are listed for Basket only **(B)**, Combo **(C)** or Full Set **(FS)**. If values are listed for Combo or Full Set, the letters in parenthesis that follow identify what accessories are considered to be a part of that combination.

6.75L x 6.75W x 7.25H
Promoted with the 2000 Sweetheart Baskets

	Org$	AVG	HIGH
stand		33	56
+bskts	118	143	180

+bskts is showing the values for Stand + Sweetheart baskets

Should you have any questions with abbreviations that are being used, please do not hesitate to contact us for clarification.

APPLYING THE VALUES TO YOUR COLLECTION

At the bottom of each item cluster, the original price, if available, is listed, along with the range of values from the current market. If a value is not listed it is usually because either the item is too new to the market and no activity has yet been reported, or the item is so rare that not many transactions are available.

Before applying these values to your collection, it is important to fully understand how we determine the Average and High values throughout the Guide.

In most cases, the **High Value** represents an item in excellent or mint condition while the **Average Value** better represents an average product; however, without having seen each individual product, it is inappropriate for us to judge the condition of items reported to us. We encourage each collector to evaluate the condition of their collection before determining its market value. Please refer to page 11 to assess the condition of your collection.

Another aspect to consider when determining the value of your item is how its condition compares to other identical items in the market. For example, most baskets from 1996, or later, during the height of Longaberger collecting, many items were bought in multiples and stored in closets, thus making the 'average basket' from this time period one that is in Excellent or Mint condtion. For this reason, a basket that is in less than excellent condition from this time period may be valued below the Average value because the average basket is Excellent.

When valuing your collection for insurance purposes, the best option is to determine the unique value for each piece based on its demand, condition and other characteristics. If time is an issue, the **High Value** represents the potential of the collectible, and thus should be used as the potential replacement cost.

QUICK FIND INDEX

For those who may not know from which collection an item may belong, starting on page 170, all baskets are listed by name, not collection, in the *Quick Find* alphabetical index. For example, *J.W. Corn*® is listed under *Corn* and then lists *J.W. Collection* as a collection in which the basket was offered. It also lists the other collections that featured the Corn Basket. This tool is great for identifying the collections in which a basket or form was offered.

Next to the dimensions, the *Quick Find* index also lists the name of the form that was used for the basket, which is helpful when trying to locate an accessory to fit your item. An entire list of all baskets using that same form can be found under the corresponding dimension within the *Dimensional Search* tool.

How to Use the Guide

continued from previous page

This section is a reference tool that will help when trying to identify a basket by its dimensions. The baskets are divided into five categories—square, rectangle, round, oval, unique—and the dimensions are listed in numerical order under each appropriate heading.

Next to the dimension is a list of all the Baskets using that same form, which is helpful when trying to identify accessories, especially for retired items. Page 219 lists specific steps to take when using this handy tool to help identify items or locate an accessory for your retired item.

COLLECTORS iNVENTORY CHECKLIST

There is a supplemental booklet available to help you take inventory of your collection. The *Collectors Inventory Checklist* lists all items, including Regular Line. The Checklist enables you to indicate the quantity of baskets you have, as well as your original cost. If accessories were purchased with a basket, such as a liner or protector, it can be noted in the description column. Any unique characteristics of a basket should also be listed, such as special order color weave found in many earlier baskets.

When using the Checklist for insurance purposes, we give our customers permission to make <u>one</u> copy for their insurance agent or to place in a safety deposit box. Additional copies are not permitted unless expressed written consent is given by J.Phillip, Inc.

Collectors Inventory Checklists can be purchased individually, or in sets of 5 or 10 which can be used as Hostess gifts or for multiple collections.

Identifying & Valuing Your Baskets

The first step in identifying a Longaberger Basket is to look on the bottom for the Longaberger logo, which is burned into the basket. There have been six different logos used by the Company since 1982.

Longaberger Stamps – Through the Years

In 1982 this stamp first appeared on the Grandad's Sleigh Basket. Prior to that no stamp was used. This particular stamp appeared only for a short time because the machine broke!

Used only on several hundred baskets, this stamp was a temporary in 1983 until it was replaced by a permanent one.

This third stamp was introduced in 1983. The Company wanted the baskets to have Dresden, Ohio on them, so the stamp was replaced in 1989.

This stamp was used only for a short time from 1989 to 1990.

When replaced in March 2003, this was the longest running stamp—14 years.

Introduced in January 2003, this fully replaced stamp #5 on all products by March 2003 and is still in use today.

If a basket does not have a logo, that does not mean it is not a Longaberger Basket—the basket was probably made before 1982. In addition, the basketmaker will usually initial the basket and date it. This practice began in 1978, when the Company began selling baskets through home shows. These markings help identify the authenticity of a Longaberger Basket:

- Longaberger Stamp – starting in 1982
- Date – starting in 1978
- Weaver's initials – starting in 1978

There have been baskets produced by the Company that are missing any number of these markings, even all three. If your basket is missing any, we suggest having it authenticated by The Longaberger Company. If you are not able to take it to Dresden yourself, please contact your Consultant and she may be able to help you make arrangements or give you instruc-

continued on next page

continued from previous page

tions on how to ship it to the Company for authentication.

Baskets woven by J.W. himself, or J.W. Originals, most likely will not have any markings on them. If you believe you have one of these rare and unique baskets, we suggest you have it authenticated by a Longaberger family member. These baskets were made during the 1930s through the 1970s (before The Longaberger Company began operations) and do have some identifying trademarks on them that are commonly found on J.W.'s work. Please see page 100 for more information about J.W. Originals.

Value of a Basket Depends on Several Things:

Is the basket part of a collection or retired from the Regular Line?

Baskets which were part of a series, or were featured only for a short time, will generally increase in value faster than baskets still found in the Regular Line. A collection is a series of baskets produced either on a yearly basis or for a limited time. There are different trends occurring in the market all the time that will make different collections more sought after. In the past year, some of the more popular collections have been:

- Longaberger Pottery – page 107
- Various Feature Baskets – page 49
- Various Retired Baskets – page 123

What year was the basket made? Is the stain dark or light?

Baskets that were a part of the Regular Line, but later retired, tend to have higher values than those still in that line. However, older, darker stained Regular Line Baskets are beginning to become more popular. We continue to see collectors recognizing the added value older baskets have due to their age as well as because they have a stain that is no longer available.

If the older baskets have been maintained in good condition, they generally are worth more than newer baskets for the following reasons: (1) there were fewer made each year, (2) older baskets have a darker stain, which was discontinued in 1986, and (3) these baskets could be customized stained or unstained, with color weave and a variety of handles. Today, Longaberger rarely, if ever, offers this level of customization.

What is the condition of the basket?

The condition of a basket will significantly affect its value. A basket in excellent condition is worth much more than the same basket in poor condition. Determining the condition can be difficult and must ultimately be agreed upon by the buyer and seller. Please remember that Longaberger Baskets are all handmade; thus some inconsistencies in weave or stain are natural to the process and add to the uniqueness of the product.

There are some characteristics, however, that should be considered unnatural and may affect the value. Anything within the owner's control, such as obvious heavy wear, broken handles, missing or cracked splints or ink stained liners are just a few conditions that could lower the value of the basket.

Is the basket signed by a family member?

Generally, a Longaberger family member's signature can increase a basket's value, especially if the signature is either Dave's or Grandma Bonnie's. Baskets signed by Tami or Rachel have also garnered interest in the market because there are not many of them in circulation. A collector can have their basket signed by a family member by taking it to Longaberger Homestead™ or meeting up with the family at a Collectors Club Gathering or other Company sponsored event.

A few Longaberger family members can often be found at Longaberger Homestead. Wendy (#2), Jerry (#3), Larry (#4), Mary (#7), Judy (#8), Carmen (#11) and Jeff (#12) are regularly on hand at J.W.'s Workshop™, Monday through Saturday. Please see page 150 for more information on Longaberger family members as well as pictures of actual signatures.

The actual value of a signature depends on many factors. It often comes back to supply and demand. The harder-to-get signatures often add $50-$100 to a basket's value, but only if the buyer finds that signature of interest. We have had reports of baskets with Grandma Bonnie's signature doubling the value and others where it did not add anything additional. Why the added value is ultimately determined by buyer and seller we have many reports of Grandma Bonnie's and Dave's signatures adding an average of a $100 to any item. The other signatures usually do not add as much, unless there are multiple signatures.

The value of a signature can also depend on the circumstances surrounding the obtaining of it. For example, signatures on Bee Baskets, Tour Baskets, Employee or Incentive Baskets are more common because family members are more attainable during The Bee, in Dresden or to Consultants at other Company sponsored events. This does not mean that signatures on these baskets have no additional value, it just means they theoretically were easier to obtain and not as 'rare' as finding it on a different basket.

Product Tags

Another helpful tool in identifying your Longaberger Baskets and Products is the product card. If included, the product card can tell you not only the name of the item but also other fun information. While the original product tag does not always stay with the item all the way to the secondary market, there have been reports of items being valued higher when their original product tags and/or paperwork are included. While some collectors pay the premium for the fun of collecting the tags, many feel that having the original tags, paperwork and even the original shipping paper can add to the perception of a better quality item.

Yesterday...

Just as Longaberger Products have evolved over the years, so have the product cards that carry detailed information about the item. When first introduced, only a handful of baskets had product tags and they were not specific to each basket. Now, tags are included with baskets, pottery and wrought iron. The information contained in early product tags consisted of very basic information like how to care for the basket and a brief history of The Longaberger Company.

1ST GENERATION

Very first tags (left) were attached to baskets with pieces a jute or string

2ND GENERATION

... and Today

Through the years, the product tags have taken on many different stages of information. At one point the tags were specific to each item and offered care instructions as well as the inspiration behind the product and additional uses. Those cards were discontinued in 2004 when the company returned to providing only general product information. The only exception is *Collectors Club* which continues to provide detailed tags specific to each item.

3RD GENERATION

4TH GENERATION

Plastic Protectors

Baskets and protectors go hand-in-hand because they allow us to use our baskets without worrying about damaging them. When first introduced in 1989, protectors were simply molded plastic inserts that provided no-frills protection for a few select baskets. Now, protectors are available for every basket and are as innovative as the baskets they safeguard. In 2002 with the introduction of the 9" Bowl Basket, protectors became much more durable and versatile for today's lifestyles, now going from refrigerator to basket with ease. A partnership with Tupperware® also launched a new generation of lidded protectors that now make these accessories functional and beautiful enough to stand alone. A protector's role has certainly come a long way from simply protecting our heirlooms.

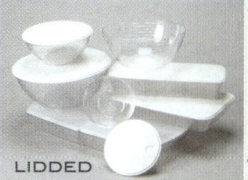
LIDDED

Styles of Longaberger Protectors:

BUNDLER

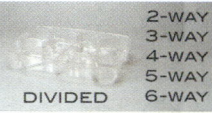
2-WAY
3-WAY
4-WAY
5-WAY
6-WAY
DIVIDED

INSULATED

Not pictured...

PROTECTOR/PLANTER INSERT:
Used with planters to permit easy drainage.
See *Window Box Basket*.

REGULAR

SEALABLE

STACKABLE

STAND-UP

CORD

RUFFLE

Fabric Liners

Fabric liners are great accessories that allow us to add personality to our baskets. Whether it is a bold floral or subtle solid, a fabric liner can add a splash of color and style to any room.

Liners first made their appearance in the *WishList* in 1984. The first collection series basket to feature the new liner accessory was the *1985 Christmas Cookie*™, with a traditional stand-up muslin fabric and lace trim (see page 24). There have been many different liner designs and fabric options throughout the years; and even more secondary vendor options, some even made from exclusive Longaberger fabrics. From the very beginning, authentic Longaberger liners have always carried an exclusive product label sewn right into the seam of the liner.

SPECIALTY

TOTE

ZIPPERED

OVER-THE-EDGE

BUTTONS

BOW TIES

FITTED

RUFFLE

Not pictured...

TAILORED BINDING:
See *Bagel Basket*

VELCRO

In the market, we have found that secondary vendor liners will sometimes add value to a basket. However, if it is your preference to own a 100% genuine Longaberger item, be sure to clarify what you are getting. When in doubt, look for the Longaberger label to insure authenticity.

14

All-American Collection™

1987 Medium Berry
1400-ABRS
7.5^L x 7.5^W x 3.5^H
Red/blue shoestring weave

	Org$	AVG	HIGH
B	19.95	77	130

1990 Small Spoon
10000-OBRS
5.5^L x 5.5^W x 6^H
First in All-Around Series

	Org$	AVG	HIGH
B	23.95	31	62

1987 Large Picnic
300-HBRS
17^L x 14^W x 11^H
Hostess only

	Org$	AVG	HIGH
B	64.95	258	385

1990 Medium Spoon
11000-OBRS
6.5^L x 6.5^W x 8^H
Second in All-Around Series

	Org$	AVG	HIGH
B	27.95	49	90

1988 Cake
100-GBRS
12^L x 12^W x 6^H
Riser included

	Org$	AVG	HIGH
B	39.95	73	120

1990 Mini Waste
12000-OBRS
7.5^L x 7.5^W x 10^H
Third in All-Around Series

	Org$	AVG	HIGH
B	35.95	49	113

1988 Small Picnic
100-HBRS
12^L x 12^W x 6^H
Riser included

	Org$	AVG	HIGH
B	65.95	87	175

1990 Small Waste
1800-OBRS
9.5^L x 9.5^W x 12^H
Hostess only. Fourth in All-Around Series.

	Org$	AVG	HIGH
B	45.95	60	70

1989 Stitching
5400-ABRS
7RD x 3^H

	Org$	AVG	HIGH
B	25.95	48	77

1991 Two-Quart
1000-CBRS
9.5^L x 5^W x 9.5^H
First year for accessories.

	Org$	AVG	HIGH
B	36.95	50	67
C^L	39.95	63	80

1989 Quilting
54000-ABRS
12RD x 5.75^H
Hostess only

	Org$	AVG	HIGH
B	46.95	66	110

1992 Small Market
10707
15^L x 9.5^W x 5.5^H

	Org$	AVG	HIGH
B	39.95	43	65
C$^{P/L}$	54.95	61	85

All-American Collection

1993 Liberty
14541
11.5^L x 5^W x 3^H
Napkin was used as its liner

	Org$	AVG	HIGH
B	36.95	41	52
C$^{P/L}$	36.95	65	72

1999 Blue Ribbon Bread
14346 | TO 36218[np]
10.5^L x 8.75^W x 4^H
Tie-On sold separately

	Org$	AVG	HIGH
B	39	47	75
C$^{P/L}$	49	61	90
TO	8	12	16

1994 Candle
11134
9^L x 5^W x 5^H

	Org$	AVG	HIGH
B	34.95	50	67
C$^{P/L}$	42.95	63	89

2000 Sparkler
18694 | TO 35483
11^L x 8^W x 5.5^H
Tie-On sold separately

	Org$	AVG	HIGH
B	48	56	85
C$^{P/L}$	67	76	129
TO	8	11	15

1995 Carry-Along
14656 | TO 31551
5.5^L x 5.5^W x 6^H
Tie-On sold separately

	Org$	AVG	HIGH
B	34.95	38	65
C$^{P/L}$	44.95	49	95
TO	6.95	17	25

2000 Star-Spangled Serving Tray
18091
20^L x 14^W x 3.75^H
Hostess only

	Org$	AVG	HIGH
B	98	99	100
C$^{P/L}$	139	100	140

1996 Summertime
18911 | TO 32891
7.75^L x 4.5^W x 2.25^{FH} x 4.5^{BH}
QTY: 146,951
2 protectors available

	Org$	AVG	HIGH
B	34.95	37	49
C$^{P/L}$	44.95	59	70
TO	5.95	13	19

2001 Strawberry
10141 | TO 74918
6.25^L x 6.25^W x 3.5^H
QTY: 150,197
Tie-On sold separately

	Org$	AVG	HIGH
B	34	40	50
C$^{P/L}$	39	51	89
TO	8	17	24

1997 Patriot
10651
7^L x 5^W x 3.5^H

	Org$	AVG	HIGH
B	32.95	42	59
C$^{P/L}$	46.95	47	65
FS$^{C/LD}$	59.90	62	90

2002 Casserole
12144
10.25RD x 3.5^H
Eagle Dish shown pg 116,..Shield Tie-On not shown.

	Org$	AVG	HIGH
B	59	67	79
C$^{P/L}$	79	83	99
TO	10	10	17

1998 Pie
12289 | TO 31950
12^L x 12^W x 4^H
Pie plate shown pg.110

	Org$	AVG	HIGH
B	55	64	75
C$^{P/L}$	72	72	99
FS$^{C/Ld}$	115	115	140
TO	8	11	15

2002 Block Party
12421
20.5^L x 12.5^W x 11.5^H
Hostess only

	Org$	AVG	HIGH
B	178	170	185
C$^{P/L}$	250	183	200

All-American Collection

Autumn Reflections™

2000 Small
Harvest Blessing
18058
15.25^L x 5.75^W x 2.5^H
Features 20th Century logo on bottom

	Org$	AVG	HIGH
B	42	50	79
C$^{P/L}$	54	60	92

2002 Tie Ons
Acorn: 20056
Pumpkin: 31732

	Org$	AVG	HIGH
acorn	10	14	16
pump	8	15	25

2000 Large
Harvest Blessing
14397
19.5^L x 8^W x 3.25^H
Features 20th Century logo on bottom

	Org$	AVG	HIGH
B	54	60	70
C$^{P/L}$	69	70	89

2003 Autumn Tote
10252 | TO 20819
8.5^L x 5.5^W x 9^H
Pumpkin tie-on sold separately

	Org$	AVG	HIGH
B	69	86	115
C$^{P/L}$	89	90	149
TO	8	12	15

2001 Small
Daily Blessings
11404
10^L x 7.25^W x 3.75^H
Liners: *Falling Leaves™, Orchard Park Plaid™ & Botanical Fields™.*

	Org$	AVG	HIGH
B	39	48	60
C$^{P/L}$	49	53	75

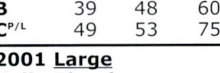

Fun Fact

Unlikely Leader . . .

Dave Longaberger inspired us all throughout his life with his determination, hard work and vision. But there is still more to his story that you may not know.

Very early in his life, Dave had many circumstances working against him. He grew up in a family with very little money, he stuttered so badly that he was difficult to understand, and he had epilepsy in a time when very little was known about it.

2001 Large
Daily Blessings
10656
12.75^L x 9.75^W x 5.25^H
Riser included

	Org$	AVG	HIGH
B	49	56	76
C$^{P/L}$	69	79	100

2001-02 Falling
Leaves Metalware
Dish:77508 | Tray:77224
Plate:77321 | Rings:77984
Tray: 14^{L}x10^W | Plate: 8RD

	Org$	AVG	HIGH
dish	29	29	39
tray	49	49	60
plate	24	24	27
rings	29	29	38

But his ambition outweighed the obstacles! He worked very hard and did many jobs in the small town, from shoveling snow to hauling garbage. Even though he struggled through school, he received his high school diploma at age 21 and started driving a bread truck for two local bakeries.

How many of us would have stopped at any one of his obstacles?

2002 Autumn Pail
10068^W / 12446^{WO}
8RD x 6.75^H
Available both with and without color accents

	Org$	AVG	HIGH
B	59	70	99
C$^{P/L}$	69	80	102
FS$^{C/LD}$	93	93	130

But, he pressed on and that drive continues to be an inspiration even years after he's been gone!

Truly born to lead!

Bee Baskets

1985 Potpourri
5^L x 5^W x 2.5^H
Director Sponsored. Booking Basket specially tagged "Proud to Be Me".

	Org$	AVG	HIGH
B		100	169

1991 Bee
1500-
8.5^L x 8.5^W x 5^H
"Imagine the Possibilities" – Teal/burgundy

	Org$	AVG	HIGH
B	19.91	29	65

1986 Forget-Me-Not
5RD x 4.5^H
Director Sponsored. Booking Basket specially tagged "Our Country Feeling".

	Org$	AVG	HIGH
B		74	81

1992 Bee
12335
14^L x 9^W x 4.5^H
"Discover the Vision" – Burgundy/teal/gold

	Org$	AVG	HIGH
B	20	30	65

1988 Decorated Peg
14000^S/10000^M/11000^L-AO
Small: 5^L x 5^W x 4.5^H
Bee Decorated Basket Contest award. 3 sizes given: Small, Med, Lg.

	Org$	AVG	HIGH
Sm	--	--	--
Md		--	--
Lg		--	--

1993 Bee
13501
13^L x 8^W x 5^H
"Making it Happen Together" – Pink/teal

	Org$	AVG	HIGH
B	25	46	62
C$^{P/L}$		70	104
tote		13	15

1988 Bee
3600-AO
Med: 13^L x 8^W x $5^{H\,[np]}$
Lg: 14^L x 7.75^W x 5.25^H
No tag, Stained over Med & Lg Easter Baskets, 4 colors: blue/green/lilac/pink

	Org$	AVG	HIGH
Md		109	150
Lg		106	125

1994 Bee
6.5^L x 6.5^W x 8^H
"Celebrate Your Success" – Rose pink/ purple. Attendees could buy one.

	Org$	AVG	HIGH
B	25	60	80
C$^{P/L}$		68	90
TO		15	20
tote		24	28

1989 Bee
5600-BRST/BGST
8.75^L x 4.75^W x 6.5^H
Red or green Christmas Memory Basket, including tag, with Bee theme/ logo on bottom.

	Org$	AVG	HIGH
B		180	260

1995 Bee
10^L x 6^W x 4^H
"It Begins with a Dream" – Purple/green. Attendees could buy two.

	Org$	AVG	HIGH
B	25	38	59
C$^{P/L}$	43	49	105
TO		15	18
tote		32	40

1990 Bee
3900-AO
7RD x 6.5^H
"Together We're on the Move" – Dusty rose and blue weave.

	Org$	AVG	HIGH
B	19.90	28	60

1996 Bee
8.5^L x 8.5^W x 5^H
"Light the Fire Within" – Gold/red/blue. Attendees could buy two.

	Org$	AVG	HIGH
B	25	34	41
C$^{P/L}$	43	51	91
TO		16	20
tote		17	25

Bee Baskets™

1997 Bee
5.5^L x 5.5^W x 6^H
"Bringing America Home" – Red/blue/green. QTY: ≈24,000

	Org$	AVG	HIGH
B	28	37	70
C$^{P/L}$	46	48	85
TO	7	11	15
tote		26	40

2003 Bee
9.25^L x 5^H x 6.25^H
"Love It! Live It! Share It!" – Dark blue/red. Attendee could buy 4.

	Org$	AVG	HIGH
B		55	62
C$^{P/L}$	59	74	125
TO	8	11	15
tote		27	45

1998 Bee
5.25^L x 5.25^W x 4^H
"Join our Celebration" – Blue/red. Attendees could buy 2.

	Org$	AVG	HIGH
B	25	42	50
C$^{P/L}$	41	54	99
TO	7	17	30
tote		16	28

2004 Bee
10.25^L x 8^W x 3.5^H
"Big Dreams, Bright Stars, Real Success" – Dark blue/red.

	Org$	AVG	HIGH
B		53	65
C$^{P/L}$	59	76	90
TO	8	8	11
tote	25	31	51

1999 Bee
7^L x 3.5^W x 4.75^H
"Building Tomorrow Together" – Green/rose/blue/purple.

	Org$	AVG	HIGH
B	29	35	66
C$^{P/L}$	45	55	75
TO	7	11	13
tote		30	35

2005 Bee
7.5RD x 5.5^H
"It all begins here. Laugh. Learn. Grow." – Navy, Natural & Sage.

	Org$	AVG	HIGH
B		--	--
C$^{P/L}$	59	72	109
TO	8	12	14
tote	25	24	32

2000 Bee
5.5RD x 4^H
"Unbeelievable" – Dark blue. Attendees could buy 2.

	Org$	AVG	HIGH
B		45	50
C$^{P/L}$	49	60	99
TO	7	10	12
tote		20	41

Fun Fact

PT CRUISER GIVEAWAY

During Bee 2005, the Company tried something unprecedented and allowed Consultants to earn entries into a random drawing for a key to a new *PT Cruiser*. 10 keys were drawn at all three Bees, with only 1 winning key per Bee.

2001 Bee
7.5^L x 4.75^H x 2.5^H
"Imagine – Believe – Achieve" – Sage/brown/blue.

	Org$	AVG	HIGH
B		47	60
C$^{P/L}$	49	54	94
TO	8	12	16
tote		38	45

At the end of the each Bee, all 10 Consultants were given the chance to sit behind the wheel and try their key!

Three very lucky Consultants drove home with a brand new *PT Cruiser* and some pretty amazing memories!

2002 Bee
7.75^L x 5.5^H x 4.5^H
"Proudly Longaberger" – Dark blue/red. Attendees could buy 4.

	Org$	AVG	HIGH
B		53	77
C$^{P/L}$	59	78	89
TO	8	14	19
tote		31	45

Bee Baskets

Blue Ribbon™

Each basket has this special logo burned into the bottom of the basket. Series completed in 2005.

2004 Crafting
10648
19.25^L x 11.75^W x 8^H
Jars sold in sets of 6

	Org$	AVG	HIGH
B	120	140	170
C$^{P/L}$	180	190	225
FS$^{C/LD}$	249	--	--
1/2pt ^{set6}	15	--	--
1pt ^{set6}	17	17	21

2003 Canning
10164 | jars: 96371
13.75^L x 5.75^W x 5^H
1qt canning jars were available from 2003-06

	Org$	AVG	HIGH
B	59	59	81
C$^{P/L}$	69	81	120
jars^{set3}	10	14	20

2004 Mending
10675 | TO 28594[np]
5.75^L x 5.75^W x 4.5^H
Blue Ribbon tie-on sold separately(not pictured)

	Org$	AVG	HIGH
B	50	--	--
C$^{P/L}$	69	74	95
FS$^{C/LD}$	88	95	110
TO	10	--	--

2003 Pride
10239 | TO 20251
3.25RD x 5.25^H
Berry candle offered in promotion for $12

	Org$	AVG	HIGH
B	39	65	79
C$^{P/L}$	54	77	100
FS$^{C/LD}$	67	--	--
TO	10	14	20

2005 Blue Ribbon Pie
10270^{WB}/10328^B |TO 20251
13.25^L x 13.25^W x 4^H
Warm Brown or Warm Brown with blue trim. 2 lids offered, tie-on not pictured.

	Org$	AVG	HIGH
B	59	--	--
C$^{P/L}$	80	93	100
FS$^{C/LD}$	125	125	136
TO	10	--	--

NATIONWIDE PHOTO WINNER

Marilyn Antol
Xenia, OH

What a Blue Ribbon display for her Blue Ribbon baskets! Marilyn loves changing her displays for the different seasons and including her grandchildren in her collecting!

Booking & Promo™

American Craft Originals Crock, 2Qt (05)
31076ᴾ/31077ᴵ/31079ᴮ
7ᴿᴰ x 7.25ᴴ / 76oz
Available in light paprika, light ivy (shown) or light cornflower

	Org$	AVG	HIGH
	35	40	74

Candle (84-90)
1100-AO
9ᴸ x 5ᵂ x 5ᴴ
Accessories sold separately.

	Org$	AVG	HIGH
B		30	70

Ambrosia (92-96)
10120
5.5ᴸ x 4ᵂ x 4ᴴ
3/8" weave, accessories sold separately.

	Org$	AVG	HIGH
B	22.95	25	49
Cᴾ/ᴸ	34.85	36	60

Chives (96-01)
15211
4ᴸ x 4ᵂ x 4ᴴ
Accessories sold separately.

	Org$	AVG	HIGH
B	25.95	25	37
Cᴾ/ᴸ	38.85	39	69

Baking Dish, 2Qt (06)
10 different colors
13.5ᴸ x 7.75ᵂ x 2.25ᴴ
Available in Woven Traditions blue, green, red & ivory or Solid colors cornflower, paprika, butternut, sage, eggplant & spice.

	Org$	AVG	HIGH
	45	--	--

Cilantro (03-04)
10301
5.5ᴸ 3.5ᵂ 1.75ᶠᴴ 3.25ᴮᴴ
Warm Brown only, accessories sold separately

	Org$	AVG	HIGH
B	27	28	35
Cᴾ/ᴸ	41	41	70
FSᶜ/ᴸᵈ	56	41	45

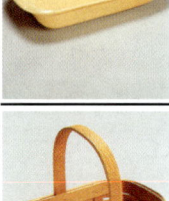

Blackberry (05-06)
10236
6.25ᴸ x 4.25ᵂ x 3.5ᴴ
Warm Brown only, accessories sold separately

	Org$	AVG	HIGH
B	32	42	47
Cᴾ/ᴸ	50	50	62

Forget-Me-Not (86-87)
3800-AO
5ᴿᴰ x 4.5ᴴ
Free to Hostesses with $150+ sales. Accessories sold separately.

	Org$	AVG	HIGH
B		36	45

Blueberry (04-05)
13060
6.5ᴸ x 6.5ᵂ x 3ᴴ
Warm Brown only, accessories sold separately

	Org$	AVG	HIGH
B	32	32	45
Cᴾ/ᴸ	50	50	53

Ivy (90-92)
13100-JOS
5.5ᴸ x 5.5ᵂ x 2.5ᴴ
3/8" weave. Accessories sold separately.

	Org$	AVG	HIGH
B		33	58
Cᴾ	2.95	40	75

Button (xx-84)
5400-JO
7ᴿᴰ x 3ᴴ
Regular line basket used as a promo item. Accessories sold separately.

	Org$	AVG	HIGH
B	6.43	58	65

Keepsake (88-90)
45000-IO
5.75ᴸ x 3.75ᵂ x 3ᴴ
Accessories sold separately.

	Org$	AVG	HIGH
B	16.95	34	60

Laurel (90-92)
17000-JOS
5.5RD x 3.75^H
3/8" weave. Accessories sold separately.

	Org$	AVG	HIGH
B		30	43
C^P	2.95	42	55

Parsley (99-02)
12882
6^L x 4.5^W x 2.5^H
Accessories sold separately.

	Org$	AVG	HIGH
B	27	27	49
C$^{P/L}$	40	40	55

Lavender (92-99)
10138
8^L x 4^W x 2^H
Accessories sold separately.

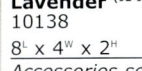

	Org$	AVG	HIGH
B	22.95	28	59
C$^{P/L}$	34.85	40	70

Potpourri (85-90)
13000-AO
5^L x 5^W x 2.5^H
Free to Hostesses with $150+ sales. Accessories sold separately.

	Org$	AVG	HIGH
B	3	35	49

Loganberry (04-05)
10011
5^L x 5^W x 4.5^H
Warm Brown only, accessories sold separately

	Org$	AVG	HIGH
B	32	--	--
C$^{P/L}$	50	--	--

Raspberry (05-06)
10234
5.25^L x 4.25^W x 1.75^{FH} x 3^{BH}
Warm Brown only

	Org$	AVG	HIGH
B	32	--	--
C$^{P/L}$	50	--	--

Measuring, 5" (xx-84)
3800-BO
5RD x 4.5^H
Dark Stain, Accessories sold separately

	Org$	AVG	HIGH
B		30	35

Rosemary (90-92)
45000-JOS
5.75^L x 3.75^W x 3^H
Accessories sold separately.

	Org$	AVG	HIGH
B		40	70
C^P	2.95	48	79

Mulberry (05-06)
10381
4^L x 4^W x 3.5^H
Warm Brown only, accessories sold separately

	Org$	AVG	HIGH
B	32	--	--
C$^{P/L}$	50	--	--

Sachet (92-95)
209581
Available in both Herbal Garden & Garden Splendor fabrics

	Org$	AVG	HIGH
	11.95	13	15

Oregano (98-01)
13145
5^L x 3^W x 3.5^H
Accessories sold separately.

	Org$	AVG	HIGH
B	27	27	45
C$^{P/L}$	40	36	60

Saffron (02-04)
12524 / 19090^{WB}
5.5RD x 2.75^H
Available in both Classic and Warm Brown.

	Org$	AVG	HIGH
B	27	27	45
C$^{P/L}$	41	41	48

Booking & Promo

Booking & Promo™

Sage (01-03)
19585 / 19152^WB
5.75^L x 5.5^W x 2.5^H
Available in both Classic and Warm Brown.

	Org$	AVG	HIGH
B	27	27	47
C^P/L	40	40	55

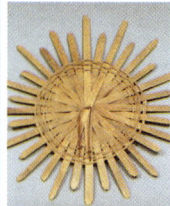

Sunburst (80)
7000-O
22RD

	Org$	AVG	HIGH
B	3.95	187	208

Spoon Rest
TH: 33472 | 32778^B / 32786^G / 32794^R / 33651^I
9.25^L x 3.25^W
Traditional Holly, Blue, Green, Red, Ivory

	Org$	AVG	HIGH
THolly	19	30	49
WTrad	20	33	56

Sweet Basil (92-94)
10146
5^L x 5^W x 2.5^H
3/8" weave

	Org$	AVG	HIGH
B	22.95	30	59
C^P/L	34.85	38	72

Spoon, Small (xx-84)
10000-OO
5.5^L x 5.5^W x 6^H
Regular line basket used as a promo item. Accessories sold separately.

	Org$	AVG	HIGH
B		60	65

Tarragon (01-04)
11830 / 19102^WB
5.5^L x 5.5^W x 2.5^H
Available in Classic and Warm Brown. Accessories sold separately.

	Org$	AVG	HIGH
B	27.00	31	45
C^P/L	41.00	--	--

Spring Booking (04-05)
10691
7.5^L x 4.25^W x 2.75^H
*Also the **Hostess Thank You Basket** ~ Renamed in Nov. 2004.*

	Org$	AVG	HIGH
B	32	32	35
C^P/L	50	38	40

Thyme (95-98)
19003
4.5^RD x 3^H

	Org$	AVG	HIGH
B	25.95	30	49
C^P/L	38.85	53	59

Star Dish, Small (03-04)
PA: 30507 | 30069^B / 30073^G / 30075^R / 30067^I
5.5^L x 2^H
Proudly American, Blue, Green, Red, Ivory

	Org$	AVG	HIGH
PA	24	26	38
WTrad	24	33	50

Totes
SDay (05) 4^W x 9^H
Khaki (05-06) 4^W x 6.5^H
Majolica Garden (06) 8^L x 6^H
Sunny Day, Khaki Tote & Majolica Garden

	Org$	AVG	HIGH
SD	15	18	22
K	15	--	--
MG	15	--	--

Sugar & Spice (88)
45000-AO
5.75^L x 3.75^W x 3^H

	Org$	AVG	HIGH
B		31	59

Votives, set of 2
AA: 35980 | TH: 36064
CC: 37508
3RD x 2^H
All-American, Traditional Holly & Candy Corn

	Org$	AVG	HIGH
AA	20	23	40
CC	20	26	39
TH	20	20	28

Christmas Collection™

1981 Candle
1100-R/G
9^L x 5^W x 5^H
QTY: 2000

	Org$	AVG	HIGH
B	14.95	654	925

1982 Grandad's Sleigh
4900-Z
9.25^L 5.5^W 2^{FH} 5.5^{BH}
QTY: 3200, Grandad with one 'd' was intentional misspelling.

	Org$	AVG	HIGH
B	19.95	628	1200

1983 Bell
4901-OO
6.5RD x 7^H
QTY: 3700, both red and green tag offered

	Org$	AVG	HIGH
B	22.95	493	679

1984 Holly
4600-AZ
15^L x 8^W x 2.25^H
QTY: 16,494, only available in red

	Org$	AVG	HIGH
B	24.95	181	282

1985 Cookie
5400-AR /AG
7RD x 3^H
Red or green, 1st year liner offered, only avail in muslin fabric

	Org$	AVG	HIGH
B	24.95	188	203
C^L	33.95	248	285

1986 Candy Cane
14000-ART /AGT
5^L x 5^W x 4.5^H
Red or green

	Org$	AVG	HIGH
B	26.95	138	220

1987 Mistletoe
700-ART / AGT
7^L x 5^W x 3.5^H
Red or green

	Org$	AVG	HIGH
B	19.95	63	75

1988 Poinsettia
3900-BRST / BGST
7RD x 6.5^H
Red or green

	Org$	AVG	HIGH
B	26.95	71	110

1989 Memory
5600-BRST / BGST
8.75^L x 4.75^W x 6.5^H
QTY: 129,651, available red or green

	Org$	AVG	HIGH
B	34.95	55	85

1990 Gingerbread
3400-ARST / AGST
10^L x 6^W x 4^H
QTY: 165,117, available red or green

	Org$	AVG	HIGH
B	32.95	45	75
C$^{P/L}$	50.85	65	100

1991 Yuletide Traditions
5100-CRST / CGST
13^L x 7.5^W x 3^{FH} x 8^{BH}
QTY: 147,247, available red or green

	Org$	AVG	HIGH
B	38.95	50	100
C$^{P/L}$	59.85	83	125

1992 Season's Greetings
10316^R / 10219^G
9.5^L x 6^W x 6^H
Red or green

	Org$	AVG	HIGH
B	44.95	51	95
C$^{P/L}$	53.95	70	100

Christmas Collection

Christmas Collection™

1993 Bayberry
11584[R] / 11592[G]
9[L] x 9[W] x 4.5[H]
Red or green

	Org$	AVG	HIGH
B	42.95	42	69
C[P/L]	49.95	55	98

1997 Snowflake
12645[R] / 12637[G]
10[L] x 9.25[W] x 6.5[H]
QTY: 507,000, available
red or green

	Org$	AVG	HIGH
B	49.95	58	88
C[P/L]	69.95	73	90
FS[C/Ld]	93.90	77	125

1994 Jingle Bell
17906[R] /17914[G]
TO: 31437
8RD x 6[H]
Red or green

	Org$	AVG	HIGH
B	47.95	58	75
C[P/L]	59.95	70	80
FS[C/Ld]	79.90	90	100
TO	6.95	16	20

1997 Tie-Ons
Christmas: 34738
2RD

Hanukkah: 34746
1.75[RD]

	Org$	AVG	HIGH
CTO	6.95	11	20
HTO	6.95	--	--

1995 Cranberry
19500[R] / 19518[G]
TO: 32441
8.5[L] x 8.5[W] x 7[H]
Red or green

	Org$	AVG	HIGH
B	47.95	50	70
C[P/L]	59.95	62	89
FS[C/Ld]	79.90	80	95

1998 Glad Tidings
12386[R] / 12394[G]
8.75[L] x 6[W] x 7.5[FH] x 9[BH]
Red or green

	Org$	AVG	HIGH
B	49	50	58
C[P/L]	69	70	84
FS[C/Ld]	91	93	120

1995 Tie-Ons
Christmas: 32441
2.5[L] x 1.75[H]

Hanukkah: 32450
2.5[L] x 1.75[H]

	Org$	AVG	HIGH
CTO	6.95	14	20
HTO	6.95	9	10

1998 Tie-Ons
Christmas: 33511

Hanukkah: 33529[np]

Kwanzaa(96-99): 33481[np]

	Org$	AVG	HIGH
CTO	8	13	30
HTO	8	--	--
KTO	8	--	--

1996 Holiday Cheer
18511[R] / 18520[G]
12[L] x 8[W] x 4.25[H]
QTY: 403,248, available
red or green.

	Org$	AVG	HIGH
B	47.95	50	75
C[P/L]	59.95	60	100
FS[C/Ld]	81.90	72	110

1999 Popcorn
15156[R] / 15351[G]
10.5[RD] x 5[H]
Avail red or green

	Org$	AVG	HIGH
B	59	60	74
C[P/L]	69	75	85
FS[C/Ld]	101	100	109

1996 Tie-Ons
Christmas: 31704
2RD

Hanukkah: 32301
2.25[RD]

	Org$	AVG	HIGH
CTO	6.95	13	22
HTO	6.95	8	10

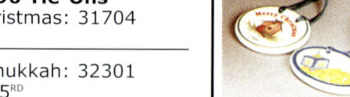

1999 Tie-Ons
Christmas: 36935
1.75[RD]

Hanukkah(99-01): 36943
2[W] x 1.5[H]

	Org$	AVG	HIGH
CTO	8	10	12
HTO	8	--	--

2000 Deck the Halls
17639^R / 17736^G
8.5^L x 8.5^W x 6^H
QTY: 269,523, available red or green

	Org$	AVG	HIGH
B	64	66	75
C^{P/L}	79	90	115
FS^{C/Ld}	106	100	119

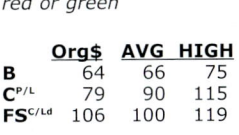

2000 Tie-Ons
Christmas: 33641

Pear: 36633

Kwanzaa⁽⁰⁰⁻⁰¹⁾: 36650^[np]

	Org$	AVG	HIGH
CTO	8	9	14
Pear	8	11	15
KTO	8	--	--

2001 Shining Star
10734^R / 10745^G
10.25^L x 11^W x 3.75^H
Red or green

	Org$	AVG	HIGH
B	59	61	79
C^{P/L}	75	81	99
FS^{C/Ld}	109	110	119

2001 Tie-Ons
Christmas 39438

American Holly^(01-P) 30602

	Org$	AVG	HIGH
CTO	8	15	30
AHTO	8	10	12

2002 Traditions
10008^R / 10018^G
9.75^L x 6.25^W x 4.5^H
QTY: 266,757, available red or green. 2 lids also offered.

	Org$	AVG	HIGH
B	59	59	79
C^{P/L}	79	83	115
FS^{C/Ld}	113	115	125

2002 Tie-Ons
Christmas: 20078

Menorah^(02-P): 20089

Kinara^(02-P): 20101

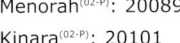

	Org$	AVG	HIGH
CTO	8	10	13
MTO	8	--	--
KTO	8	--	--

2003 Caroling
10465
7.5RD x 5^H
Only one color offered

	Org$	AVG	HIGH
B	59	59	77
C^{P/L}	75	83	90
FS^{C/Ld}	100	100	125

2003 Tie-Ons
Christmas: 27872

Nativity: 28067

	Org$	AVG	HIGH
CTO	8	--	--
NTO	8	--	--

2004 Get Together
10728^R /10729^G/10086^{WB}
12.25^L x 9.25^W x 5.25^H
Red, green or no color. 1st year to offer stained only, no color.

	Org$	AVG	HIGH
B	62	62	75
C^{P/L}	79	79	104
F^{C/Ld}	108	108	120
TO	8	--	--

2005 Silver Bells
10335^R/10336^G/10337^{WB}
11.5^L x 11.25^W x 4^H
Red, green or no color

	Org$	AVG	HIGH
B	62	75	103
C^{P/L}	79	--	--
F^{C/Ld}	113	--	--

2005 Tie-Ons
Christmas: 23174
25th Anniv: 23169
Special pewter tie-on offered to commemorate 25 years of the Christmas collection

	Org$	AVG	HIGH
CTO	8	--	--
25th	8	--	--

Christmas Collection

Collectors Club®

Membership Items

Membership, Charter (95-96)
Charter: 62839
9.5^L x 5^W x 9.5^H
QTY: 105,304, Charter Member is noted on tag.

	Org$	AVG	HIGH
B	75	75	119
C$^{P/L}$	104	110	135

Membership (97-03)
Non Charter: 62847
9.5^L x 5^W x 9.5^H

	Org$	AVG	HIGH
B	75	38	85
C$^{P/L}$	104	48	115

Membership II (03-06)
10205^{CM}/10085
15^L x 8^W x 7.25^H
Charter Member version has notation on tag

	Org$	AVG	HIGH
B	75	75	91
C$^{P/L}$	114	--	--

5yr Anniv, Charter (01)
Charter: 17345
6^L x 5^W x 8.25^H
Charter Member version has engraved lid

	Org$	AVG	HIGH
B	99	117	149
C$^{P/L}$	131	135	169

5yr Anniversary (02-06)
12020^C/18636^{WB}
6^L x 5^W x 8.25^H
Classic / Warm Brown, pin was given free with each renewal.

	Org$	AVG	HIGH
B	99	100	125
C$^{P/L}$	131	135	154

Membership Tie-On (96)
83089
2.5^W x 1.75^H
QTY: ≈95,000, sent free to all Members who joined thru May 1996.

	Org$	AVG	HIGH
B	free	41	75

Miniatures (all include box and certificates)

JW Mini Market (96)
150240 / 15024^{SIG}
5.75^L x 4^W x 3^H
Seal on box designates the basket came signed by a family member.

	Org$	AVG	HIGH
B	125	176	300
C$^{P/L}$	142	213	379

JW Mini Waste (97)
17797
3.75^L x 3.75^W x 4.75^H

	Org$	AVG	HIGH
B	99.95	110	185
C$^{P/L}$	117.85	124	215

JW Mini Apple (98)
13749
5.25RD x 3.25^H
Was offered with the same lid as the Banker's Waste, all accessories sold separately

	Org$	AVG	HIGH
B	139.95	140	165
C$^{P/L}$	156.85	160	200

JW Mini Two-Pie (99)
19356
4.75^L x 5^W x 4^H
Included divider stand

	Org$	AVG	HIGH
B	130	136	160
C$^{P/L}$	147	150	185

Mini 25th Anniversary Plates (99)
33537
3.25RD
Offered free to Members who purchased the Mini Two-Pie between Nov 21 – Dec 31, 1998.

	Org$	AVG	HIGH
	free	36	59

Mini Two-Pie Server & Mini Pie Plate (99)
76902 | Plates: 35581
4RD x 6^H | 3.25RD
1st miniature Foundry piece offered

	Org$	AVG	HIGH
Server	35	76	125
C^{plates}	80	90	155
Plate^2	45	55	110

JW Mini Bread & Milk [00]
13391
6.25[L] x 3.25[W] x 4.25[H]

	Org$	AVG	HIGH
B	130	140	150
C[P/L]	149	149	160

Mini Bowl Stand & Set of 3 Bowls [01]
75825 | Bowls: 31944
4[L] x 3[W] x 9[H]
Bowls only sold as set

	Org$	AVG	HIGH
bowls	59	60	91
stand	39	54	75
C[bowls]	98	110	179

JW Mini Banker's Waste [00-01]
16578
5.25[RD] x 5.25[H]
Lid could be earned
FREE for limited time

	Org$	AVG	HIGH
B	150	150	170
C[P/L]	169	169	190
FS[C/Ld]	184	184	220

JW Mini Cake [02-03]
11474
4.75[L] x 4.75[W] x 2.5[H]
Included cake stand.
Lid could be earned
free for limited time.

	Org$	AVG	HIGH
B	125	135	150
C[P/L]	142	150	189
FS[C/Ld]	157	158	200

JW Mini Gathering [00-01] **& Mini Baking Dish**
18941 | Dish: 37974
7[L] x 4.5[W] x 2[H] | 5[L] x 2.75[W]
Dish avail only as FREE
item with purchase

	Org$	AVG	HIGH
B	130	137	152
C[P/L]	149	150	180
D	free	38	89

Mini 8x8 Baking Dish & Pedestal Stand [02]
30456 | Stand: 77352
3.5[L] x 2.75[W] x 1[H] | 3[H]
Pieces sold separately,
dish designed to fit Mini
Cake

	Org$	AVG	HIGH
Dish	29	42	62
Stand	29	51	126

Mini Milk Pitcher [00]
36242
1.75[L] x 2.25[H]
Promoted along with
Mini Bread & Milk

	Org$	AVG	HIGH
P	30	50	99

JW Mini Original Easter & Eggs/Grass [03]
10046 | Eggs: 50089
6[L] x 3.5[W] x 2.25[H]
Eggs & grass were free
for limited time with
purchase

	Org$	AVG	HIGH
B	125	125	139
C[P/L]	144	150	169

JW Mini Berry [01-02]
10842
3.5[L] x 3.5[W] x 3[H]

	Org$	AVG	HIGH
B	85	90	145
C[P/L]	99	100	169

JW Mini Umbrella [03-04] **& Mini Umbrella Stand**
11933 | Stand: 70370
4RD x 6.5[H] | 8[H]
Stand could be earned
free for limited time

	Org$	AVG	HIGH
B	150	150	185
C[P/L]	169	169	204
Stand	39	40	50

JW Mini Corn [01-02]
11466
7.75[RD] x 4.25[H]

	Org$	AVG	HIGH
B	185	185	200
C[P/L]	204	210	245
FS[C/LD]	221	--	--

May Mini Geranium [05]
60245
4.5[L] x 3[W] x 3.5[H]
Silk flowers available
free when purchased
early, or avail separately

	Org$	AVG	HIGH
B	100	--	--
C[P/L]	118	125	134

Collectors Club

Collectors Club®

May Mini Peony (05-06)
& Mini Pots
10199 | Pots: 31311
5.75ᴸ x 2.75ᵂ x 1.25ᴴ
Mini Pots sold only as set of 2

	Org$	AVG	HIGH
B	90	105	126
Cᴾ/ᴸ	107	--	--
pots	29	--	--

2001-02 Renewal
10813 | Charter: 10273
5ᴿᴰ x 6ᴴ
Charter Member version noted on tag. Frame given free with each renewal.

	Org$	AVG	HIGH
B	45	53	65
Cᴾ/ᴸ	69	71	90
frame		17	25

May Mini Morning Glory⁽⁰⁶⁾
10349
3.75ᴸ x 3.5ᵂ x 2ᴴ
Silk flowers available free when purchased early, or avail separately

	Org$	AVG	HIGH
B	105	--	--
Cᴾ/ᴸ	123	--	--

2002-03 Renewal
12081
6.25ᴸ x 5ᵂ x 1.75ᴴ

	Org$	AVG	HIGH
B	39	39	58
Cᴾ/ᴸ	58	60	76

Renewal Baskets

1997 Renewal
105702
9ᴸ x 5ᵂ x 5ᴴ
Members could purchase within 90 days of membership renewal

	Org$	AVG	HIGH
B	39.95	44	75
Cᴾ/ᴸ	59.85	60	88

2003-04 Renewal
10116
4.5ᴸ x 3.25ᵂ x 4ᴴ

	Org$	AVG	HIGH
B	45	49	67
Cᴾ/ᴸ	66	70	82

1998 Renewal
13340
8.5ᴿᴰ x 4ᴴ

	Org$	AVG	HIGH
B	44.95	70	105
Cᴾ/ᴸ	68.85	85	110

2004-05 Renewal
10633
5.5ᴿᴰ x 4.75ᴴ

	Org$	AVG	HIGH
B	45	--	--
Cᴾ/ᴸ	67	72	80

1999 Renewal
12998
6.75ᴸ x 5.75ᵂ x 4.75ᴴ
Members could purchase within 90 days of membership renewal

	Org$	AVG	HIGH
B	42	46	63
Cᴾ/ᴸ	62	65	90

2005 Renewal
10029
6.75ᴸ x 3.75ᵂ x 4.5ᴴ

	Org$	AVG	HIGH
B	59	--	--
Cᴾ/ᴸ	85	--	--

2000-01 Renewal
18783
6.75ᴸ x 5.25ᵂ x 3.25ᴴ
New form. Members could purchase within 30 days of renewal.

	Org$	AVG	HIGH
B	44	62	70
Cᴾ/ᴸ	65	72	95

Ornaments

1996 Ornament
33758
3.5ᴿᴰ
Longaberger University – Edition 1996.

	Org$	AVG	HIGH
O	29.95	36	50

1997 Ornament
34207
3.5RD
Caroling in Dresden – Edition 1997

	Org$	AVG	HIGH
O	29.95	35	40

2003 Matthew Snowflake
28012
3.5^L x 3.75^W
Tami's son

	Org$	AVG	HIGH
O	32	32	34

1998 Ornament
32506
3.5RD
Shopping on Main Street – Edition 1998

	Org$	AVG	HIGH
O	30	22	50

2004 Ben Snowflake
20025
3.5^L x 3.75^W
Rachel's son

	Org$	AVG	HIGH
O	32	32	35

1999 Ornament
35599
3.5RD
Riding through the Snow – Edition 1999. Final ornament for this series.

	Org$	AVG	HIGH
O	30	32	40

2005 Rose Snowflake
23173
3.5^L x 3.75^W
Rachel's daughter

	Org$	AVG	HIGH
O	32	--	--

Pottery & Glass

2000 Kaitlyn Snowflake
36269
3.75RD
1st in the Snow Days series featuring snowflake designs by Tami's & Rachel's children. Kaitlyn is Rachel's daughter.

	Org$	AVG	HIGH
O	32	35	40

American Craft Originals 10" Bowl & Pie Plate⁽⁰⁴⁻⁰⁵⁾
30187 | Plate: 30185
9.5RD | 10.5RD

	Org$	AVG	HIGH
bowl	44	54	112
plate	35	35	46

2001 Dustin Snowflake
39365
3.5^L x 3.75^W
Rachel's son

	Org$	AVG	HIGH
O	32	32	35

American Craft Originals Tea Pot, Cream/Sugar⁽⁰⁴⁾
30683 | C/S: 30681
7.5^H | C: 3.75^H | S: 4^H
Pieces all sold separately. Tray Basket shown on page 34

	Org$	AVG	HIGH
teapot	89	89	119
c/s	74	74	99

2002 Claire Snowflake
31336
3.5^L x 3.75^W
Tami's daughter

	Org$	AVG	HIGH
O	32	32	35

American Craft Originals Tea Cups ⁽⁰⁵⁾
31183
4.5RD x 3^H
Set of 2 cups & 2 saucers

	Org$	AVG	HIGH
cups²	69	69	73

Collectors Club

Collectors Club®

Pottery & Glass con't

American Craft Originals Vase (05)
3.25RD x 7^H
QTY: 400, given free to Members who hosted the top 400 shows above $350.

	Org$	AVG	HIGH
vase	49	190	236

Gathering Event (03-04)
10576
6.5^L x 6.5^W x 8^H
Available to Members throughout 2004 at designated events

	Org$	AVG	HIGH
B	55	55	63
C^{P/L}	82	--	--

Bunny Dish, Mini (04)
30647
3.25RD x 3^H
Shown here to compare size with the larger version. Came in a Collectors Club box.

	Org$	AVG	HIGH
dish	29	29	43

Gathering Event (04-05)
10636
6RD x 4.75^H
Available to Members throughout 2004 at designated events

	Org$	AVG	HIGH
B	55	--	--
C^{P/L}	82	--	--
FS^{C/Ld}	100	--	--

Champagne Flutes (06)
90096
9.5^H
Set of 2. Given free with the purchase of Celebration Basket, shown on pg 32

	Org$	AVG	HIGH
flutes²	32	32	43

Gathering Event (05)
10028
5.5RD x 6^H
Available to Members throughout 2005 at designated events, same form as the Small Canister

	Org$	AVG	HIGH
B	55	75	120
C^{P/L}	82	--	--

Crocus Basket (06)
90125
8^L x 4.25^W x 6.5^H
Soft pink. Resin chocolate bunny was free with purchase for limited time.

	Org$	AVG	HIGH
dish	39	40	50

Gathering Event (06)
Charm Bracelet
23276
This bracelet replaced the Event baskets given in past years. Cupcake Charm was the first charm offered.

	Org$	AVG	HIGH
	14	--	--

Strawberry Jam Jar (06)
90065
4.75RD x 5.5^H

	Org$	AVG	HIGH
dish	35	35	38

Cupcake Basket (06)
5.5RD x 3.5^H
Available at the 10th Anniv Celebration Event, ceramic cupcake lid & other accessories sold separately

	Org$	AVG	HIGH
B	free	150	164
C^{P/L}	13	191	265
FS^{C/Ld}	35	300	406
TO	8	28	36
tote	20	48	60

Event Baskets

Gathering Event (01-02)
11222
12^L x 6.75^W x 3.5^H
Available to Members attending the Collectors Club Gathering Event

	Org$	AVG	HIGH
B	55	55	69
C^{P/L}	88	90	105

Heartwood Baskets

Binocular (05-06)
10388
10^L x 4.75^W x 7.25^H

	Org$	AVG	HIGH
B	229	--	--
C^{P/L}	263	--	--

Bowl, 10"
10385
11.25RD x 5^H

	Org$	AVG	HIGH
B	99	99	125
C^{P/L}	134	--	--

Family Legacy ⁽⁰⁴⁾
10718 / 10768^{w/inset}
15^L x 9^W x 5.25^H
Warm Brown. Lid came with every basket and was available with or without ceramic inset.

	Org$	AVG	HIGH
B^{Ld}	198	--	--
C^{P/L/Ld}	237	--	--

Serving Tray
10387
18.75^L x 11.25^W x 3.25^H

	Org$	AVG	HIGH
B	99	102	145
C^{P/L}	139	--	--

Flag, Miniature ⁽⁰²⁾
10128 / 10500
6.25^L x 3.25^W x 4.5^H

	Org$	AVG	HIGH
B	150	150	160
C^{P/L}	169	170	193

Vase
10403
7.25^W x 10.75^{FH} x 12.25^{BH}
Only sold with protector

	Org$	AVG	HIGH
C^P	159	--	--

Floral Vase ⁽⁰³⁻⁰⁴⁾
10264
7.5RD x 11^H
Came with 2-pc bouquet bundler protector

	Org$	AVG	HIGH
B		149	170
C^P	149	157	190

Feature Items (listed by alpha)

Celebration ⁽⁰⁵⁾
60611 | TO 23171
8.5RD x 8.5^H
Flutes given free with purchase, see pg 31

	Org$	AVG	HIGH
B	99	--	--
C^{P/L}	149	--	--
TO	10	--	--

Harbor ⁽⁹⁸⁾
10677
10^L x 8.25^W x 8.25^H
Made with first collapsible form

	Org$	AVG	HIGH
B	85	98	125
C^{P/L}	120	130	160
TO	148	150	175

Century Celebration ⁽⁰⁰⁾
15385 | TO 36196
10.5^L x 6.25^W x 4.75^H
Lid and Tie-On were not exclusive to members

	Org$	AVG	HIGH
B	59	94	100
C^{P/L}	85	85	120
FS^{C/Ld}	117	120	139
TO	8	12	16

Homestead Apple ⁽⁹⁹⁾
6609596 | TO 37541
10RD x 6.25^H
Sold only as a Combo. Club version has a tag. Tie-on not exclusive.

	Org$	AVG	HIGH
C^{P/L}	79	79	113
FS^{C/Ld}	106	107	120
TO	8	14	16

Compote ⁽⁰⁵⁾
10258
13.25RD x 6.75^H
Sold only with protector

	Org$	AVG	HIGH
C^{P/L}	159	160	185

Lightship ⁽⁰⁶⁾
10505
7.5RD x 5.75^H (w/lid)
Basket only sold with woven lid

	Org$	AVG	HIGH
B^{Ld}	129	129	136
C^{P/L/Ld}	156	--	--

Collectors Club

Collectors Club®
Feature Items con't

Proudly American Bowl, 9" (04)
10670
9.25RD x 4.75^H

	Org$	AVG	HIGH
B	90	100	128
C$^{P/L}$	123	--	--

Serving Tray, Small (96)
12629
11.5^L x 15.5^W x 3.75^H

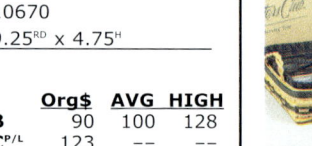
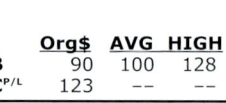

	Org$	AVG	HIGH
B	69.95	70	97
C$^{P/L}$	102.85	110	132

Proudly American Salt & Pepper (03)
10054 / 60162
5.75^L x 3.75^W x 3^H
Second form# is for new Members without a certificate.

	Org$	AVG	HIGH
B	39	54	61
C$^{P/L}$	56	61	65

Sewing Circle (01)
10575
8.5RD x 5.5^H

	Org$	AVG	HIGH
B	75	105	125
C$^{P/L}$	112	115	130
FS$^{C/Ld}$	145	145	165

Picnic, Family (99)
13561
20^L x 14^W x 9.5^H
Napkins ($10) & Place Mats ($20) sold separately

	Org$	AVG	HIGH
B	225	225	300
C$^{P/L}$	305	315	350
FS$^{C/Ld}$	364	370	400

#5
#4
#3
#2
#1

Series of five Shaker Baskets. All Baskets included the lid, protectors sold separately, no liners offered.

Shaker Harmony
No.1 (00)
19089
10.75^L x 9.75^W x 4.5^H

No.2 (01)
18988
9.75^L x 7.75^W x 4^H

No.3 (01)
16870
8.75^L x 6.75^W x 3.25^H

No.4 (02)
16861
7.5^L x 5.75^W x 2.75^H

No.5 (01)
18881
6.75^L x 4.75^W x 2^H

Saddlebrook, Large (00-01)
15776
9.5^L x 5.5^W x 9.25^H
Leather purse accessories were also offered

	Org$	AVG	HIGH
B	139	140	169
C^P	148	155	200

	Org$	AVG	HIGH
No1	95	95	165
C$^{P/Ld}$	107	107	178
No2	89	111	155
C$^{P/Ld}$	99	114	178
No3	79	79	88
C$^{P/Ld}$	85	85	158
No4	65	68	100
C$^{P/Ld}$	70	70	125
No5	40	47	52
C$^{P/Ld}$	59	60	75

Saddlebrook, Small (00-01)
15679
5.5^L x 3.5^W x 4^H
Leather purse accessories were also offered

	Org$	AVG	HIGH
B	79	88	129
C^P	83	115	135

Serving Tray (99)
15849
20^L x 14^W x 3.75^H
Unlike other Club items, this item <u>could</u> be purchased with Hostess benefits.

	Org$	AVG	HIGH
B	99	100	130
C$^{P/L}$	148	150	160

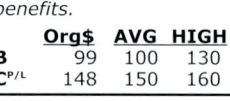

Spring Meadow (00)
17655 | TO 73326
16.25^L x 10.75^W x 4^H
Cottage Gate Tie-on given free to Members

	Org$	AVG	HIGH
B	95	95	120
C$^{P/L}$	130	130	165
TO	free	10	18

Collectors Club

Tea Tray (04)
10724
15.5L x 11.5W x 2.75H
American Craft Originals Pottery on pg 30

	Org$	AVG	HIGH
B	99	134	184
CP/L	135	169	200

Whistle Stop (01)
10303 | TO 73954
10.75L x 6.25W x 7.75H
First time for shaped tacks (stars)

	Org$	AVG	HIGH
B	89	100	115
CP/L	118	118	125
FSC/Ld	141	143	165
TO	10	14	18

Miscellaneous Items

Thyme (98)
19224
4.5RD x 3H
Free to Members who earned 2 bookings

	Org$	AVG	HIGH
B	free	31	42
CP/L	15	38	50

Book, 25 Years In Pictures (98)
85804
11L x 11W
Sent to all Members

	Org$	AVG	HIGH
	free	5	10

25th Anniversary (98)
12297 | TO 32492
16L x 8W x 11H
Tie-on given free to Members who redeemed certificate at a show

	Org$	AVG	HIGH
B	115	161	185
CP/L	173	180	205
TO	free	19	23

Cabinet, Display (03-04)
50857
36.25L x 9.25W x 22.25H

	Org$	AVG	HIGH
	500	450	525

Vase, Apology (05)
4.5RD x 4.5H
QTY 300, created and sent to Members who should have received the ACO Vase incentive, but did not

	Org$	AVG	HIGH
B	free	136	145

Handle Gripper (97)
Sent free to all Members. CHARTER MEMBER was embroidered for those who held that status.

	Org$	AVG	HIGH
	free	19	25

Ware Basket (04)
10058
9.5RD x 4.75H
Engraved lid

	Org$	AVG	HIGH
B	100	--	--
CP/L	128	--	--
FSC/Ld	167	--	--

Tapestry Throw (99)
71587
67L x 46W

	Org$	AVG	HIGH
	60	60	95

Welcome Home (97)
10464
15L x 9.5W x 5.5H

	Org$	AVG	HIGH
B	69.95	70	105
CP/L	102.85	103	120

Collectors Club

Cookie Molds (stands used for photography purposes only)

Santa Series

1990 Father Christmas
30066
8.5ʰ

Org$	AVG	HIGH
18.95	20	25

1994 Hope
31356
9ʰ

Org$	AVG	HIGH
19.95	11	20

1990 1st Casting
30066
8.5ʰ
QTY: 3200, front is the same as Father Christmas, back has "Longaberger Pottery – First Casting – Christmas 1990"

Org$	AVG	HIGH
18.95	32	36

1995 Love
32468
7.5ʰ

Org$	AVG	HIGH
19.95	13	20

1991 Kriss Kringle
30180
8.5ʰ

Org$	AVG	HIGH
18.95	12	25

1996 Joy
31721
9ʰ

Org$	AVG	HIGH
19.95	13	20

Easter Series

1992 Santa Claus
30457
7.25ʰ

Org$	AVG	HIGH
18.95	12	20

1994 Mama & Baby
31151 | Book 72079
6.25ʰ
Book offered with purchase. Only Hostesses could buy separately.

	Org$	AVG	HIGH
CM	18.95	9	20
BK	5.95	9	18

1993 St.Nick
31062
10.25ʰ

Org$	AVG	HIGH
18.95	11	20

1995 Grandpa & Herbie
31500 | Book 72796
6.25ᴸ x 4.75ʰ
Last year book was offered

	Org$	AVG	HIGH
CM	19.95	10	20
BK	14.95	10	15

Angel Series

1993 Peace
31071
7.5ʰ
1st year for this series

Org$	AVG	HIGH
18.95	12	24

1996 Rosemary Bunny
32182
6.5ᴸ x 4.25ʰ

Org$	AVG	HIGH
19.95	11	15

1997 Grandma & Lavender
32191
4.5^L x 6.5^H
_____

Org$	AVG	HIGH
19.95	10	23

Gingerbread Series

1995 Country Cottage
32476
9^L x 13.25^H
_____
First year for series

Org$	AVG	HIGH
29.95	14	20

1996 Country Cabin
33090
9^L x 13.25^H
_____

Org$	AVG	HIGH
29.95	15	20

1997 Holiday Home
34720
9^L x 13.25^{BH}
_____
Last year for series

Org$	AVG	HIGH
29.95	19	21

Snow Friends Series

1997 Chilly
34827
4.25^W x 7.5^H
_____
First year for series

Org$	AVG	HIGH
19.95	12	15

1998 Sleigh Belle
32484
6^W x 7.5^H
_____

Org$	AVG	HIGH
20	10	13

1999 Flurry & Snowball
36994
2.75^W x 4.75^H
_____
Sold only as a set of 2

Org$	AVG	HIGH
20	21	25

2000 Roger & Ginger
36536
4^W x 5^H
_____
Sold only as set of 2.
End of series and last
Cookie Molds to be
produced.

Org$	AVG	HIGH
20	12	20

Fun Fact

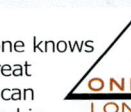

Everyone knows that great things can be found in an Attic! Why would we think it would be any different inside Longaberger's Attic?

Starting in 2004, Consultants have been exclusively treated through the new _Online Attic_, only accessible to Consultants through their mylongaberger.com account. Out of the blue, the sales force will be notified in their weekly company newsletter that certain items are available, all for a limited time and in limited quantities.

In many cases, these item are only overstock items, but in some very fun, rare occasions, something special will pop up, like one the following:

- Actual retired wood basket forms
- Medium Bushel Sleeve (pg 58)
- Autumn Basket (pg 97)
- At Home Garden Pail (pg 49)
- At Home 10" Sq Planter (pg 49)

More great reasons to become a Consultant ... or befriend one!

Cookie Molds

Crisco®American™

The Crisco American series started in 1991 when The Longaberger Company was invited to create the official Pie Basket for for the Crisco American Pie Celebration Bake-Off in New Orleans. Each of the 50 participants received the basket and then the Company made it available to customers for purchase. Although these baskets were sold during the All-American promotional season, they are not part of the All-American Series. They were, however, designed to compliment the collection.

Crisco® is a registered trademark of the Procter & Gamble Company.

1992 Cookie
10081
10RD x 4^H
QTY: 153,447

	Org$	AVG	HIGH
B	29.95	67	80
C^{P/L}	39.95	76	100

1992 Apron
20028
Not included in the Combo, sold separately

	Org$	AVG	HIGH
	13.95	23	50

1991 Pie
100-DBRS
12^L x 12^W x 6^H
Divider shelf was included

	Org$	AVG	HIGH
B	79.95	184	300
C^P	89.90	199	360

1993 Baking
14745
14.5^L x 7.5^W x 3.75^H
Liner is napkin-style

	Org$	AVG	HIGH
B	39.95	50	107
C^{P/L}	45.95	83	119

NATIONWIDE PHOTO WINNER

Julie Kokoszka
Issaquah, WA

What a beautiful display of spring! We just love the colors and the wonderful ways Julie finds to use her collection!

Easter Series

1987 Medium Chore
3500-CX

13^L x 8^W x 5^H

Easter Signature Series: Blue, red and green weave. All were signed by Dave, only 100 total were signed by Bonnie.

	Org$	AVG	HIGH
B	28.95	121	210

1987 Single Pie
2200-AX

12^L x 12^W x 4^H

Easter Signature Series: Blue, red and green weave. All were signed by Dave, only 100 total were signed by Bonnie.

	Org$	AVG	HIGH
B	28.95	100	180

1987 Small Gathering
2300-AX

14^L x 9^W x 4.5^H

Easter Signature Series: Blue, red and green weave. All were signed by Dave, only 100 total were signed by Bonnie.

	Org$	AVG	HIGH
B	28.95	158	199

1987 Spring
900-AX

11^L x 8^W x 5.5^H

Easter Signature Series: Blue, red and green weave. All were signed by Dave, only 100 total were signed by Bonnie.

	Org$	AVG	HIGH
B	25.95	107	180

1988 Easter Baskets were available in all four of these color options: blue, green, lilac, pink

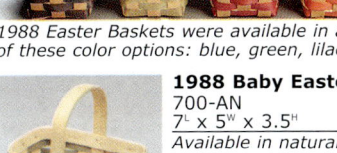

1988 Baby Easter
700-AN

7^L x 5^W x 3.5^H

Available in natural with blue, green, lilac or pink accent weave.

	Org$	AVG	HIGH
B	18.95	74	117

1988 Small Easter
3400-AN

10^L x 6^W x 4^H

Available in natural with blue, green, lilac or pink accent weave.

	Org$	AVG	HIGH
B	22.95	40	69

1988 Medium Easter
3500-AN

13^L x 8^W x 5^H

Available in natural with blue, green, lilac or pink accent weave.

	Org$	AVG	HIGH
B	28.95	46	99

1988 Large Easter
3600-AN

14^L x 7.75^W x 5.25^H

Available in natural with blue, green, lilac or pink accent weave.

	Org$	AVG	HIGH
B	32.95	81	115

1989 Blue Easter
5500-ABS/AO

10RD x 4^H

Available stained with pink or blue weave, or no color.

	Org$	AVG	HIGH
Stain	29.95	86	110
Blue	29.95	56	90

1989 Pink Easter
5500-APS

10RD x 4^H

Available stained with pink or blue weave, or no color.

	Org$	AVG	HIGH
Pink	29.95	35	75

1990 Medium Easter
40000-APVBS

8RD x 4.5^H

Available stained with Dresden Blue, violet and pink weave.

	Org$	AVG	HIGH
B	38.95	40	50

1990 Large Easter
41000-APVBS

9.5^{RD} x 5^H

Available stained with Dresden Blue, violet and pink weave.

	Org$	AVG	HIGH
B	43.95	44	65

Easter Series

Easter Series

1991 Customer
900-ATMS / ATMN

11^L x 8^W x 5.5^H

Available stained or natural with teal and mauve 3/8" accent weave

	Org$	AVG	HIGH
B	26.95	28	59

1995 Easter
18708 | TO 31518

10.75^L x 8.75^W x 5.25^H

QTY: 109,970 Available stained with rose pink and purple.

	Org$	AVG	HIGH
B	49.95	55	70
C$^{P/L}$	59.95	60	89
TO	6.95	9	15

1991 Hostess
700-ATMS / ATMN

7^L x 5^W x 3.5^H

Hostess only. Available stained or natural with teal and mauve 3/8" weave.

	Org$	AVG	HIGH
B	21.95	26	50

1996 Easter
12912^S/12939^N
TO 32271

7.5^L x 5^W x 6^H

QTY: 220,416, available stained or natural

	Org$	AVG	HIGH
B	39.95	40	60
C$^{P/L}$	49.95	50	75
TO	6.95	12	15

1992 Easter
34000-APVCNK

10.5^L x 7.5^W x 4.5^H

Available stained or natural with Dresden Blue, violet and pink weave

	Org$	AVG	HIGH
B	27.95	33	60
C$^{P/L}$	39.95	62	80

1997 Large Easter
13447^S / 13455^N
TO: 30007

12^L x 7^W x 4.5^H

Available stained or natural

	Org$	AVG	HIGH
B	42.95	55	60
C$^{P/L}$	52.95	61	76
TO	6.95	13	18

1993 Small Easter
10774^S / 10766^N

7^L x 5^W x 3.5^H

Available stained or natural with teal shoestring weave

	Org$	AVG	HIGH
B	24.95	25	49
C$^{P/L}$	35.95	40	69

1997 Small Easter
63541^S / 63550^N

8.5^L x 5^W x 3.5^H

Stained or natural. Only sold as Combo with purchase of Large Easter or any purchase of $42.95.

	Org$	AVG	HIGH
C$^{P/L}$	29.95	30	69

1993 Large Easter
13439^S / 13412^N

10^L x 6^H x 4^H

Available stained or natural with teal shoestring weave

	Org$	AVG	HIGH
B	27.95	28	40
C$^{P/L}$	38.95	40	95

1998 Large Easter
11851^S / 11860^N
TO 34100

9^L x 9^W x 4.5^H

Stained or natural

	Org$	AVG	HIGH
B	43.95	55	58
C$^{P/L}$	52.95	60	79
TO	6.95	13	18

1994 Easter
16926^S/-34^N/-00^{SC}/-18^{NC}

13.5^L x 8.25^W x 5.25^H

Heartland Blue with pink. Available stained, natural, stained with color or natural with color.

	Org$	AVG	HIGH
B	49.95	51	60
C$^{P/L}$	59.95	55	65

1998 Small Easter
11959^S / 11967^N

6^L x 6^W x 3^H

Stained or natural

	Org$	AVG	HIGH
B	32.95	33	41
C$^{P/L}$	29.95	50	55

1999 Large Easter
14061^S / 14265^U
TO 35637
7.5^RD x 3.75^H
Available stained or unstained, bunny divider given free with Combo

	Org$	AVG	HIGH
B	39	40	60
C^P/L	59	60	75
TO	8	14	16

1999 Small Easter
14052^S / 14168^U
5.75^RD x 3^H
Available stained or unstained, bunny divider given free with Combo

	Org$	AVG	HIGH
B	33	50	60
C^P/L	49	55	70

2000 Large Easter
19283^WW / 19186^S
TO 38644
12.5^RD x 6^H
Whitewashed with color or Classic with no color

	Org$	AVG	HIGH
B	65	70	79
C^P/L	79	84	119
FS^C/Ld	85	115	129
TO	8	13	15

2000 Jelly Bean
19488^WW | TO 38661
5.5^RD x 3.75^H
Small was offered only Whitewashed with color accents

	Org$	AVG	HIGH
B	34	40	65
C^P/L	42	48	100
TO	8	11	15

2001 Large Easter
10915^C / 11016^W
TO 39501 | Plate 35670
12.75^RD x 4^H
Classic or Whitewash w/ pink, green & lavender.

	Org$	AVG	HIGH
B	65	91	152
C^P/L	79	100	160
TO	9	12	18
plate	29	31	43

2001 Small Easter
10023^C / 10125^W
TO 39519
6RD x 2.75^H
Classic or Whitewashed. Bunny Divider sold separately ($9).

	Org$	AVG	HIGH
B	35	38	66
C^P/L/div	49	50	75
TO	7	10	16

2002 Large Easter
12233^C / 12411^W
TO:30108
12.5^L x 10.25^H x 4.25^H
Classic or Whitewashed

	Org$	AVG	HIGH
B	69	70	91
C^P/L	98	105	115
TO	8	13	15

2002 Small Easter
12093^C / 12111^WP / 12101^WG / 12123^WY
7.75^L x 6.25^W x 2.75^H
Classic or Whitewashed with pink, green or yellow accents

	Org$	AVG	HIGH
B	44	55	68
C^P/L	59	62	78

2002-03 Glass Hen
Hen:30098
7L x 5.75^W x 6^H
Pink glass, sold separately

	Org$	AVG	HIGH
hen	39	39	58

2003 Large Easter
10147^C / 10151^W
13.75^L x 10.75^W x 5.75^H
Classic or Whitewashed. Egg cups sold separately.

	Org$	AVG	HIGH
B	79	90	117
C^P/L	99	104	125

2003 Small Easter
10106^C / 10109^W
TO: 28691
10^L x 7.5^W x 4.25^H
Classic or Whitewashed

	Org$	AVG	HIGH
B	49	50	85
C^P/L	69	70	95
TO	8	12	23

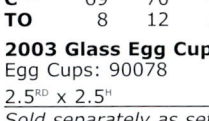

2003 Glass Egg Cups
Egg Cups: 90078
2.5^RD x 2.5^H
Sold separately as set of 2

	Org$	AVG	HIGH
cups	19	21	28

Easter Series

Easter Series

2004 Easter
10630^{WB} /10631^W
TO:28163
11^L x 8^H x 5.75^H
Warm Brown or Whitewash

	Org$	AVG	HIGH
B	69	73	87
C$^{P/L}$	89	100	110
TO	12	14	20

2005 Easter
10253^{WB} / 10249^S
TO: 23043
13^L x 8.5^H x 4^H
Warm Brown or Sun-washed w/color accents

	Org$	AVG	HIGH
B	59	61	85
C$^{P/L}$	79	85	123
TO	8	8	12

2004 Glass Bunny
Dish: 30577
6.5RD x 6^H / 22 OZ
Purple glass, shown here with the Collectors Mini version for size comparison

	Org$	AVG	HIGH
dish	39	39	42

2006 Picket Pail
10489-xx^{WB}
-12^{SP}/-11^{SPu}/-13^{SB}/-21^{SW}
7.25RD x 6^H
Warm Brown, Pink, Purple, Blue, White. See Pottery for Bunny Knob.

	Org$	AVG	HIGH
B	29	--	--
C$^{P/L}$	39	45	70
FS$^{C/Ld}$	58	--	--

Fun Fact

Heartwood joins the family

A new twist in the history of Longaberger design arrived when the beautiful *Heartwood* design made it's debut exclusively to Collectors Club Members in 2005. All collectors were soon thrilled to also be included in the new love affair!

Heartwood is from the very center of the maple tree and with its beautiful variations in color comes a lot of information about the tree from which it came, specifically the minerals from the soil in which it has been grown. It is a very resilient wood and packs a lot of punch in design!

The first four baskets to be introduced – Binocular, 10" Bowl, Vase, Serving Basket – were exclusive to Collector Club Members only and were created from exclusive original forms that were then retired at the end of January 2006.

The dual interpretation of the logo perfectly reflects the heart and soul behind this wood: focus on the open areas of the logo and see a heart in a circle, focus on the dark areas and see two upturned leaves with a flower in the center.

A perfect marriage between love of craft and love of nature, these are sure to be great collectibles!

Inventory Solutions

- Track your baskets
- Nothing to install
- Automatic back-ups
- Print or Email reports
- More frequent updates
- More user friendly
- Access from any computer
- MAC & PC compatible

New Online service that does all the work for you! **It's never been easier!**

Step 1: locate item

Step 2: add item

Step 3: repeat & enjoy!

1.800.837.4394
www.bentleyguide.com

Bentley Guide Online
42

Employee Baskets

Birthday Baskets | **Recognition Baskets**

Given to employees on their birthday. Characterized by red shoestring weave and trim, tags read: Longaberger Company Birthday Basket – Year – Employee Name. Number given is reported to be under 1000 pcs each.

Given to employees for years of service. Tag reads: Longaberger or Longaberger Company – Year – Achievement. Quantities produced are not reported.

1988 5" Measuring
3800-
5RD x 4.5^H

	Org$	AVG	HIGH
B		77	105

Sophomore[1yr], Junior[2yr] & Senior[5yr] Recognition (xx-97)
8.75^L x 4.75^W x 6.5^H
19xx-1997: Sophomore has no color, Junior has red and Senior has blue

	Org$	AVG	HIGH
Soph		67	75
Jr		79	85
Sr		85	125

1989 Sweetheart
45000-
5.75^L x 3.75^W x 3^H

	Org$	AVG	HIGH
B		76	95

Senior Employee(xx-97)
16^L x 9^W x 6^H
Given at <u>8 yrs</u> of service

	Org$	AVG	HIGH
B		320	425

1990 Potpourri
13000-
5^L x 5^W x 2.5^H
Tag did not include employee's name this year

	Org$	AVG	HIGH
B		87	112

Senior Employee II(97-P)
6.5^{RD} x 5^H
Given at <u>8 yrs</u> of service, lilac weave and double trim strip.

	Org$	AVG	HIGH
B		65	90

1991 Ivy
13100-
5.5^L x 5.5^W x 2.5^H

	Org$	AVG	HIGH
B		90	130

Master Employee(xx-97)
12.5^{RD} x 13.5^H
Given at <u>10 yrs</u> of service

	Org$	AVG	HIGH
B		232	275

1992 Tour
10022
8.75^L x 4.75^W x 6.5^H
Last year for the Birthday Basket to be given

	Org$	AVG	HIGH
B		62	85

Master Employee II (97-P)
10 yrs: 8RD x 6.5^H
15 yrs: 8RD x 9^H
20 yrs: 13RD x 8.5^H
Lilac weave and double trim strip

	Org$	AVG	HIGH
10		84	109
15		--	--
20		--	--

Charitable Champ(00-P)
9.5ᴸ x 5ᵂ x 9.5ᴴ
QTY: 32 given in 2000. Basket given for first year in charitable work program. Brass splints added for each participating year after.

	Org$	AVG	HIGH
B		--	--

Perfect Attendance(97)
7" Measuring
7ᴿᴰ x 6.5ᴴ
Red accents, accessories included

	Org$	AVG	HIGH
B		388	425

Conversion Baskets(92)
Mag: 16ᴸ x 8ᵂ x 11ᴴ
Cake: 12ᴸ x 12ᵂ x 6ᴴ
QTY: approx 160 total Special brass tag. Dave's signature is on the front of the basket, just below the tag.

	Org$	AVG	HIGH
magaz		--	--
cake		--	150

Perfect Attendance(98)
Large Peg
6.5ᴸ x 6.5ᵂ x 8ᴴ
Red accents, accessories included, first year award delivered to the employee's home, with box.

	Org$	AVG	HIGH
B		405	425

In 1992, Longaberger converted the weaving process at their Hartville facility. They moved to a piece rate method of payment. To compensate the weavers and the runners for the change, the company allowed each one to make their own Magazine or Cake Basket. Each was then tagged and personally signed by Dave.

Perfect Attendance(99)
Spring
11ᴸ x 8ᵂ x 5.5ᴴ
Red accents, accessories and box included

	Org$	AVG	HIGH
B		--	425

Perfect Attendance

Perfect Attendance(94)
Small Fruit
6.5ᴿᴰ x 5ᴴ
QTY: ≈200, lilac trim and shoestring weave around bottom. First Employee Basket to include accessories.

	Org$	AVG	HIGH
B		433	475

Perfect Attendance(00)
Bread
14.5ᴸ x 7.5ᵂ x 3.75ᴴ
Red accents, featured 1 stationary handle, accessories & box included

	Org$	AVG	HIGH
B		--	325

Perfect Attendance(95)
Pansy
7ᴿᴰ x 4.5ᴴ
Lilac accents, accessories included

	Org$	AVG	HIGH
B		425	475

Perfect Attendance(01)
Envelope
12ᴸ x 5.25ᵂ x 3.75ᶠᴴ x 5ᴮᴴ
Red accents, accessories and box included

	Org$	AVG	HIGH
B		--	--

Perfect Attendance(96)
Candle
9ᴸ x 5ᵂ x 5ᴴ
QTY: ≈309, Lilac accents, accessories included

	Org$	AVG	HIGH
B		400	425

Perfect Attendance(02)
Large Gatehouse
6.5ᴿᴰ x 10.5ᴴ
Warm Brown, dark brown leather trim with dark brown accents, one leather loop, box. Last year for this award.

	Org$	AVG	HIGH
B		269	300

Employee Baskets

Employee Baskets

Employee Christmas

Identified by the red and green alternating shoestring weave and no color on trim. Tags read: Merry Christmas (or Happy Holidays) – Year – The Longaberger Company.

1992 5" Measuring
3800-
5RD x 4.5^H

	Org$	AVG	HIGH
B		89	123

1987 Medium Market
500-
15^L x 10^W x 7.5^H
First year.

	Org$	AVG	HIGH
B		125	150

1993 Button
5400-
7RD x 3^H

	Org$	AVG	HIGH
B		99	125

1988 Cake
100-
12^L x 12^W x 6^H
Did not include riser.

	Org$	AVG	HIGH
B		98	150

1994 Tea
700-
7^L x 5^W x 3.5^H

	Org$	AVG	HIGH
B		102	125

1989 Candle
1100-
9^L x 5^W x 5^H

	Org$	AVG	HIGH
B		100	140

1995 Ambrosia
10120
5.5^L x 4^W x 4^H
First year for the tag to read: Happy Holidays.

	Org$	AVG	HIGH
B		75	95

1990 Small Gathering
2300-
14^L x 9^W x 4.5^H

	Org$	AVG	HIGH
B		143	195

1996 Cracker
4500-
11.5^L x 5^W x 3^H

	Org$	AVG	HIGH
B		65	95

1991 Tall Key
1000-
9.5^L x 5^W x 9.5^H

	Org$	AVG	HIGH
B		62	90

1997 Chives
4^L x 4^W x 4^H

	Org$	AVG	HIGH
B		115	130

1998 Small Berry
6.5^L x 6.5^W x 3^H

	Org$	AVG	HIGH
B		73	85

2001 Small Boardwalk
9.25^L x 5^W x 6.25^H

	Org$	AVG	HIGH
B		62	100

1999 Tissue
6.5^L x 6.5^W x 6.25^H
Did not come with the lid, but many employees did choose to add one to the basket

	Org$	AVG	HIGH
B		69	110

2002 Tiny Tote
6^L x 5.5^W x 7^H

	Org$	AVG	HIGH
B		87	95

2000 Holiday Cheer
12^L x 8^W x 4.25^H
Liner was made available to purchase separately

	Org$	AVG	HIGH
B		65	99

2003 Back Porch
13.25^L x 9.5^W x 3^H
Last year Christmas Baskets were given

	Org$	AVG	HIGH
B		72	100

DESIGNING FOR THE SEXES

Diana Wood
Cardington, OH

While Diana's approach to decorating may not be for everyone, we love her creative solution to the age-old question: *How do I mix his idea of decor with mine?*

Answer: Go with his idea of decor and <u>your</u> idea of compromise!

Employee Baskets
46

Father's Day™

1991 Spare Change
1300-JCWS

6.5^L x 6.5^W x 3^H

Liner was not originally offered – available for the first time in 1995, in new fabric.

	Org$	AVG	HIGH
B	21.95	45	80
C$^{P/L}$	32.95	70	125

1996 Address
12611

8.25^L x 6.25^W x 3.75^H

QTY: 173,381, Combo included prot, address cards and card holder$^{(CH)}$. Lid and liner sold separately.

	Org$	AVG	HIGH
B	29.95	42	80
C$^{P/CH}$	42.90	56	90
FS$^{C/L/Ld}$	61.85	65	95

1992 Paper
16000

7.5^L x 5.5^W x 2^{FH} x 3.5^{BH}

Included note paper. Liner made available in 1995.

	Org$	AVG	HIGH
B	23.95	70	95
C$^{P/L}$	33.95	90	98

1997 Personal Organizer
13137

14^L x 6^W x 3^H

Combo included divided protector. Regular protector avail for $5.95.

	Org$	AVG	HIGH
B	39.95	40	79
C$^{P/L}$	54.95	55	85
FS$^{C/L}$	77.90	78	92

1993 Pencil
15000

4RD x 4.25^H

Liner made available in 1995

	Org$	AVG	HIGH
B	20.95	44	65
C$^{P/L}$	29.95	50	70

1998 Finder's Keeper
12777

6^L x 6^W x 4.25^{FH} x 5.25^{BH}

	Org$	AVG	HIGH
B	34	48	70
C^P	37	60	80
FS$^{C/L/Ld}$	67	68	100

1994 Tall Tissue
18490

6.5^L x 6.5^W x 6.25^H

No liner offered

	Org$	AVG	HIGH
B	29.95	44	60
C$^{P/L}$	39.95	60	98

1999 Tee
14940

5.25^L x 5^W x 3^H

Combo included 50 Longaberger golf tees.

	Org$	AVG	HIGH
B	29	30	45
C$^{P/L}$	39	46	50

2000 Basket was not offered

1994 Business Card
17477

4.75^L x 3.75^W x 2.25^H

Hostess only

	Org$	AVG	HIGH
B	22.95	35	60
C^P	25.90	35	60
FS$^{P/L}$	34.85	41	70

1995 Mini Waste
11266

7.5^L x 7.5^W x 10^H

Lid and liner sold separately. First year for new fabric.

	Org$	AVG	HIGH
B	46.95	61	81
C^P	49.95	71	85
FS$^{C/L/Ld}$	83.85	90	100

2001 Tic-Tac-Toe
10346 | Games TO 74772$^{[np]}$

7.5^L x 7.5^W x 2.75^H

1st year for leather
(No basket given in 2000)

	Org$	AVG	HIGH
B	44	63	85
C$^{P/L}$	59	70	97
FS$^{C/L}$	82	92	125
TO	10	13	16

2001 Checkerboard
10036 | Dad TO 74756
Chess Set 74748

15^L x 15^W x 6^H

	Org$	AVG	HIGH
B	139	140	200
C$^{P/L}$	182	200	250
F$^{SC/Ld}$	198	240	300
TO	8	10	12
Chess	198	207	227

2002 Daddy's Caddy
11854 | TO 77267
8^L x 6.75^W x 5.25^{FH} x7^{BH}

	Org$	AVG	HIGH
B	49	53	59
C$^{P/L}$	69	89	100
TO	8	11	12

2004 Valet
10679 | TO 28157
Valet Bag 28623155
10^L x 6.75^W x 3.75^H

	Org$	AVG	HIGH
B	49	64	85
C$^{P/L}$	72	--	--
FS$^{C/Ld}$	87	89	112
TO	8	--	--
bag	24	--	--

2003 Pocket Change
10035 | TO 20062
5.25^L x 4.75^W x 3^H

	Org$	AVG	HIGH
B	39	56	68
C$^{P/L}$	55	65	72
FS$^{C/Ld}$	70	70	85
TO	8	11	15

NATIONWIDE PHOTO WINNER

Becky Miller
New London, NC

25 years is a long time and no one knows that better than Becky! The entire Christmas Collection is represented here – all 25 of them!

Many collectors collect more than one item and we love how Becky has incorporated many of her interests in this display – not only showing her love for Santa's, but also a few J.W.'s peeking in at the top.

Well done!

Father's Day

Feature Baskets

At Home Garden Collection (alpha)

At Home Garden Blooms (05)
10168
22.25^L x 11^W x 2.75^H

	Org$	AVG	HIGH
B	90	90	110
C$^{P/L}$	132	132	139

At Home Garden Blossoms (05)
10257
13^L x 6.5^W x 2.25^H
See page 114 for info on the 2 vases that were promoted along with this basket.

	Org$	AVG	HIGH
B	54	66	79
C$^{P/L}$	80	80	90

At Home Garden 2005 Pail
8RD x 6.75^H
QTY: ≈1000, available only to Consultants through online Longaberger Attic

	Org$	AVG	HIGH
B	49.95	--	--

At Home Garden 2006 Planter, 10"Square
835714
Available only to Consultants through online Longaberger Attic

	Org$	AVG	HIGH
B	49.95	--	--

Happy Halloween Hostess (04)
10716 | Lg TO 28575
8.5RD x 4.5^H
Lg Tie-on is also a pin

	Org$	AVG	HIGH
B	90	90	100
C$^{P/L}$	120	120	130
FS$^{C/Ld}$	149	150	165
TO	12	12	17

Happy Halloween (04)
10709 | TO 28571
5.75RD x 3.5^H
See pg 118 for info on Ghost knob.

	Org$	AVG	HIGH
B	49	50	67
C$^{P/L}$	59	69	85
FS$^{C/Ld}$	81	81	85
TO	8	9	11

October Fields (00)
16951 | TO 73393
6.5RD x 9^H
QTY: 129,583. Has 1 swinging handle

	Org$	AVG	HIGH
B	59	83	100
C$^{P/L}$	79	99	127
FS$^{C/Ld}$	101	107	130
TO	10	14	18

Pumpkin Patch (01)
10621
6.5RD x 6.75^H

	Org$	AVG	HIGH
B	49	62	95
C$^{P/L}$	69	82	110
FS$^{C/Ld}$	109	110	130

Halloween/Fall Themed Features (alpha)

Boo (04)
10987
11^L x 8^W x 5.5^H

	Org$	AVG	HIGH
B	34.95	40	50
C$^{P/L}$	44.95	47	80

Candy Corn (99)
14354 | TO 36676
7.75^L x 4^W x 3.75^H
Unique form is shaped like a piece of candy corn

	Org$	AVG	HIGH
B	29	53	70
C$^{P/L}$	39	60	99
TO	8	10	15

Holiday Themed Features (alpha)

Frosty (00)
10242
10RD x 4^H
Promoted along with the Small Snowman Stand (see Foundry)

	Org$	AVG	HIGH
B	43	47	54
C$^{P/L}$	69	70	95

Frosty Jr (00)
10230
7RD x 3^H

	Org$	AVG	HIGH
B	33	35	60
C$^{P/L}$	53	53	70

Holiday (con't)

Holiday Helper (03)
10530
4.75^L x 4.75^W x 2^H
Post-It note pad sold separately, 270 sheets

	Org$	AVG	HIGH
B	34	38	49
C$^{P/L}$	39	41	59

Holiday Helper (04)
60043xxx
7.75^L x 3.75^W x 4.5^H
Only available as a combo with napkins, could choose four different fabrics.

	Org$	AVG	HIGH
B		31	40
C$^{P/L}$	39	39	57

Holiday Helper (05)
60560166
5.5RD x 3.5^H
Sold only as a Combo, included the Mini Zesty Tuscan Olive Mix

	Org$	AVG	HIGH
C$^{P/L}$	39	--	--

Little Elf (02)
19279
3.75RD x 3.75^H

	Org$	AVG	HIGH
B	29	33	55
C$^{P/L}$	46	60	76

Little Star (01)
12202^R/12214^G
7.5^L x 8^W x 3^H
Available red or green

	Org$	AVG	HIGH
B	49	51	75
C$^{P/L}$	69	75	108
FS$^{C/LD}$	88	90	125

Noel Bell (00)
16845
5.5RD x 5.5^H
Sold by itself or combined with tassel tie and hanger

	Org$	AVG	HIGH
B	43	48	59
C$^{tas/hang}$	59	65	79

santa's helper

little elf

Santa's Helper (02)
10053
4.25RD x 6.25^H

	Org$	AVG	HIGH
B	36	51	60
C$^{P/L}$	56	60	75

Sleigh
Dash Away(98) **(Medium)**
13943
7.75^L 4.5^W 2.25^{FH} 4.5^{BH}
Full Set include runners

	Org$	AVG	HIGH
B	36	43	66
C$^{P/L}$	50	51	86
FS$^{C/run}$	69	69	94

Sleigh
Holiday(97) **(Large)**
16811
13^L x 7.5^W x 3^{FH} x 8^{BH}
This unofficial collection ran from 1997-1999

	Org$	AVG	HIGH
B	47.95	50	76
C$^{P/L}$	59.95	74	110
FS$^{C/run}$	85.85	86	120

Sleigh
Santa's Little Helper(99)
19721
5.75^L 3.75^W 1.5^{FH} 3.5^{BH}

	Org$	AVG	HIGH
B	30	55	60
C$^{P/L}$	42	67	75
FS$^{C/run}$	55	70	85

Naturals/Whitewash (alpha)

Berry, Large (99)
19844
8.5^L x 8.5^W x 5^H
Natural. January Sale 1999

	Org$	AVG	HIGH
B	28	33	43

Berry, Small (00)
17841
6.5^L x 6.5^W x 3^H
Natural. January Sale 2000

	Org$	AVG	HIGH
B	22	30	35

Feature Baskets

Feature Baskets
Naturals/Whitewash (con't)

**Bread,
Woven Traditions**[00]
18031
14.5^L x 7.5^W x 3.75^H
Natural. January Sale 2000

	Org$	AVG	HIGH
B	33	--	--

Gathering, Medium[87]
2400-C
18^L x 11^W x 4.5^H
Hostess only. Available Natural or Natural with red, blue, green or brown accents.

	Org$	AVG	HIGH
B	41.95	74	85

Cake[98]
10481
12^L x 12^W x 6^H
Natural. Riser included. January Sale 1998.

	Org$	AVG	HIGH
B	43.95	48	55
C$^{P/L}$	78.85	80	95

Gathering, Small[98-00]
12572
14^L x 9^W x 4.5^H
Natural. Offered in Jan 1998, Feb 1999 and again in Jan 2000

	Org$	AVG	HIGH
B	39.95	65	100

Card File[05]
10247
7.25^L x 6^W x 4^H
Whitewash, no handles

	Org$	AVG	HIGH
B	39	--	--

Market, Medium[87]
500-
15^L x 10^W x 7.5^H
Hostess only. Available Natural or Natural with red, blue, green or brown accents.

	Org$	AVG	HIGH
B	41.95	50	99

Carry Along[05]
10043
15.5^L x 9^W x 5.5^H
Whitewash, 1 st/h

	Org$	AVG	HIGH
B	64	64	76
C$^{P/L}$	90	90	104

Market, Medium[98]
10588
15^L x 10^W x 7.5^H
Natural. January Sale 1998. 2 sw/h.

	Org$	AVG	HIGH
B	53.95	63	76

Darning[99]
19640
10RD x 4^H
Natural, both a regular and divided protector were offered.

	Org$	AVG	HIGH
B	31	32	50

Picnic, Large[99]
19755
17^L x 14^W x 11^H
Natural. January Sale 1999, included riser.

	Org$	AVG	HIGH
B	89	104	125
C$^{P/L}$	140	--	--

Fruit, Small[00]
17671
6.5RD x 5^H
Natural, January Sale 2000

	Org$	AVG	HIGH
B	25	37	39

Picnic, Small[00]
18040
12^L x 12^W x 6^H
Natural. January Sale 2000. Shown here with Sm.Fruit and Sm.Berry baskets.

	Org$	AVG	HIGH
B	59	75	89

Pie (99)
19441
12^L x 12^W x 4^H
Natural. Jan-Feb 1999.

	Org$	AVG	HIGH
B	39	41	67

Vegetable Baskets
Large(99) 19551
16^L x 9^W x 3.5^{FH} x 9^{BH}
Medium(00) 18333
13^L x 7.5^W x 3^{FH} x 8^{BH}
Natural.

	Org$	AVG	HIGH
Lg	48	48	53
Md	37	43	62

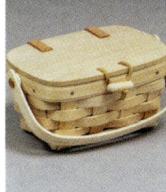

Purse, Kiddie (98)
10898
7^L x 5^W x 3.5^H
Natural. January Sale 1998.

	Org$	AVG	HIGH
B	27.95	48	60
C$^{P/L}$	51.85	60	70

Wash Day, Medium(05)
10248
18.75^L x 18.25^W x 9.5^H
Whitewash stain, available Feb 2005. 2 leather handles.

	Org$	AVG	HIGH
B	169	169	190

Spoon, Medium (99)
19658
6.5^L x 6.5^W x 8^H
Natural. January Sale 1999. Accessories sold separately.

	Org$	AVG	HIGH
B	28	37	43
C$^{P/L}$	51	--	--

Waste, Medium (98)
11789
13.5^L x 13.5^W x 16^H
Natural. January Sale 1998.

	Org$	AVG	HIGH
B	71.95	--	--

St.Patrick's Day theme (year)

Spoon, Small (98,00)
10871
5.5^L x 5.5^W x 6^H
Natural. Offered Jan 1998 and then again in Jan 2000.

	Org$	AVG	HIGH
B	19.95	26	41
C$^{P/L}$	39.85	--	--

1990 Basket O'Luck
17000-AGS
5.5RD x 3.75^H
Hostesses only could earn this basket at the $300+ show level.

	Org$	AVG	HIGH
B		105	130

Spring (98, 99)
10880
11^L x 8^W x 5.5^H
Natural. Offered Jan 1998 and then again in Feb 1999.

	Org$	AVG	HIGH
B	29.95	35	46
C$^{P/L}$	51.85	--	--

1990 Shamrock
13000-HGS
5^L x 5^W x 2.5^H

	Org$	AVG	HIGH
B	19.95	58	119

Tea (98)
10847
7^L x 5^W x 3.5^H
Natural. January Sale 1998.

	Org$	AVG	HIGH
B	19.95	29	45
C$^{P/L}$	37.85	--	--

1999 Lots of Luck
18465 | TO 36056
4.25^L x 4.25^W x 3^H
Often associated with Dave Longaberger's death due to his passing on 3/17/99

	Org$	AVG	HIGH
B	29	50	100
C$^{P/L}$	39	76	145
FS$^{C/Ld/HT}$	58	93	163
TO	6	25	45

Feature Baskets

Feature Baskets

St. Patrick's Day theme (con't)

2002 Lucky You
11911 | TO 30542
4.75^RD x 3^H
QTY: 167,434

	Org$	AVG	HIGH
B	34	52	59
C^P/L	44	57	82
FS^C/Ld	59	70	99
TO	8	12	20

2006 Lucky Twist
10498
5.75^L x 5.75^W x 3^H
Lid included both wood and Shamrock knob

	Org$	AVG	HIGH
B	39	39	56
C^P/L	49	49	78
FS^C/Ld/HT	68	68	91

Seasons (alpha)

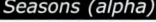
Soft Pink | Med Green | Soft White | Bold Blue | Bold Red

Bread (06)
17231-12^SP/-19^MG/-21^SW/
-16^BB/-22^BR
14^L x 7.5^W x 3.75^H

	Org$	AVG	HIGH
B	39	--	--

Cake (06)
17300-12^SP/-19^MG/-21^SW/
-16^BB/-22^BR
12^L x 12^W x 6^H
Soft Pink, Med Green, Soft White, Bold Blue & Bold Red.

	Org$	AVG	HIGH
B	69	--	--

Spring (06)
18491-12^SP/-19^MG/21^SW/
-16^BB/-22^BR
11^L x 8^W x 5.5^H
Soft Pink, Med Green, Soft White, Bold Blue & Bold Red.

	Org$	AVG	HIGH
B	46	--	--

Tea (06)
1860312^SP/1860319^MG/
1860321^SW/1860316^BB/
1860322^BR
7^L x 5^W x 3.5^H
Soft Pink, Med Green, Soft White, Bold Blue & Bold Red

	Org$	AVG	HIGH
B	29	--	--

Tissue, Tall (06)
68757-12^SP/-19^MG/-21^SW/
-16^BB/-22^BR
6.5^L x 6.5^W x 6.25^H
Soft Pink, Med Green, Soft White, Bold Blue & Bold Red

	Org$	AVG	HIGH
B	50	--	--

Three Color Promotion (alpha)

Berry, Medium (96-97)
16241^B/55^R/33^G
7.5^L x 7.5^W x 3.5^H
Available blue, red and green

	Org$	AVG	HIGH
B	29.95	37	66
C^P/L	36.43	53	73

Key Baskets (94)
Med: 9^L x 5^W x 5^H
Sm: 7^L x 5^W x 3.5^H
Tall: 9.5^L x 5^W x 9.5^H
Available in red, blue or green accent weave

	Org$	AVG	HIGH
Med	29.95	43	67
Sm	27.95	36	55
Tall	40.95	52	75

Market, Large (96-97)
16641^B/24^R/32^G
16^L x 11^W x 9^H
Available in red, blue or green accent weave

	Org$	AVG	HIGH
B	77.95	94	120
C^P/L	92.43	115	138

Pantry (96-97)
16446^B/20^R/38^G
14^L x 9^W x 4.5^H
Available in red, blue or green accent weave

	Org$	AVG	HIGH
B	46.95	48	74
C^P/L	55.93	56	90

Remembrance (96-97)
16748^B/21^R/30^G
10.5^L x 9^W x 8^H
Available in red, blue or green accent weave. Hostess only.

	Org$	AVG	HIGH
B	99.95	115	158
C^P/L	112.93	121	165

Spoon, Medium [96-97]
16349[B]/22[R]/31[G]
6.5[L] x 6.5[W] x 8[H]
Available in red, blue or green accent weave

	Org$	AVG	HIGH
B	36.95	53	63
C[P/L]	44.93	62	75

Bakery [87]
4700-JO
14.5[L] x 7.5[W] x 3.75[H]

	Org$	AVG	HIGH
B	19.95	48	55

Vegetable, Large [96-97]
16543[B]/27[R]/35[G]
16[L] x 9[W] x 3.5[H] x 9[H]
Available in red, blue or green accent weave

	Org$	AVG	HIGH
B	61.95	62	79
C[P/L]	72.43	85	95

Basket Splint Candle [03]
69119
4.5[RD] x 5[H]
Real splints in wax. Candle was recalled during production period so a limited number were produced.

	Org$	AVG	HIGH
	39	68	81

Miscellaneous Features (alpha)

All-Star Trio [93]
64408
5.75[L] x 3.75[H] x 3[H]
Sold only as a 3-piece combo. Product card shows form number 14494 for basket only.

	Org$	AVG	HIGH
B	29.95	38	54

Bed [89]
4500-AO
11.5[L] x 5[W] x 3[H]
See Breakfast for info on the Bed/Breakfast set

	Org$	AVG	HIGH
B	18.95	36	45
C[L]	29.95	44	66

American Craft Original Baking Dish [03-04]
10586
11.5[L] x 8[W] x 2[H]

	Org$	AVG	HIGH
B	59	59	75
C[P/L]	86	86	100

Breakfast [89]
4700-AO
14.5[L] x 7.5[W] x 3.75[H]
Set= Bed and Breakfast

	Org$	AVG	HIGH
B	24.95	42	54
C[L]	37.95	64	83
Set	43.90	89	150
C[L]	67.90	152	165

American Craft Original Casserole [03-04]
10585
9[L] x 7.5[W] x 3[H]

	Org$	AVG	HIGH
B	59	59	70
C[P/L]	86	86	92
FS[C/Ld]	109	109	125

Berry, Small [85, 88]
1300-AO
6.5[L] x 6.5[W] x 3[H]
The only time Small Berry was offered with 1 stationary handle

	Org$	AVG	HIGH
B	16.95	50	55

Baguette [05]
10296
20.5[L] 6.5[W] 2.75[H]
Warm Brown with brown trim strip

	Org$	AVG	HIGH
B	59	61	70
C[P/L]	78	79	99

Berry, Medium [85, 88]
1400-AO
7.5[L] x 7.5[W] x 3.5[H]
The only time Medium Berry was offered with 1 stationary handle

	Org$	AVG	HIGH
B	17.95	53	58

Feature Baskets

Miscellaneous Features (con't)

Berry, Large (85, 88)
1500-AO
8.5^L x 8.5^W x 5^H
The only time Large Berry was offered with 1 stationary handle

	Org$	AVG	HIGH
B	18.95	58	65

Card Keeper (01)
12195
10.75^L x 9^W x 5^{FH} x 7^{BH}

	Org$	AVG	HIGH
B	54	58	90
C$^{P/L}$	69	99	120
FS$^{C/Ld}$	103	103	125

Biscuit (04)
10009
7.5^L x 4.75^W x 2.5^H
Only offered Sept 1 – Dec 31, 2004

	Org$	AVG	HIGH
B	29	--	--
C$^{P/L}$	39	58	81
FS$^{C/Ld}$	55	60	95

Cheers (00)
18945 | TO 36196
7.5^L x 4.5^W x 3.5^H
Shown with the natural Hostess Appreciation

	Org$	AVG	HIGH
B	39	50	71
C$^{P/L}$	49	53	88
FS$^{C/Ld}$	72	72	100
TO	8	12	16

Bread & Milk Grandma Bonnie's (81)
2100-
16^L x 8^W x 11^H
First basket to ever be tagged

	Org$	AVG	HIGH
B		430	631

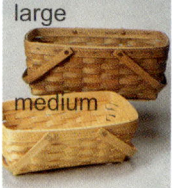

large

medium

Chore Baskets
Large(86) 3600-CO
14^L x 7.75^W x 5.25^H
Medium(85-86) 3500-CO
13^L x 8^W x 5^H
Small(86) 3400-CO
10^L x 6^W x 4^H

	Org$	AVG	HIGH
Lg	23.95	68	85
Md	18.95	53	69
Sm	17.95	45	55

Bushel, Medium (05)
10342^G/10302^{WB}/10329^B
12RD 7.75^H
Offered Leaf Green/dark trim, Warm Brown or Warm Brown/black trim

	Org$	AVG	HIGH
B	79	81	95
C$^{P/L}$	120	120	139
FS$^{C/Ld}$	154	154	215

Info for the Large Bushel can be found on page 72, within Hostess

Bushel, Small (05)
10341^G/10304^{WB}/10327^B
7.5RD 4.75^H
Offered Leaf Green/dark trim, Warm Brown or Warm Brown/black trim

	Org$	AVG	HIGH
B	54	54	75
C$^{P/L}$	67	70	79
FS$^{C/Ld}$	89	89	139

Cradle, Doll (91)
2500-LO
19^L x 12^W x 6^H
Muslin liner and protector sold separately

	Org$	AVG	HIGH
B	69.95	143	185
C$^{P/L}$	97.85	--	--

Crocus (06)
10434^{WB} / 1043421^{SW}
14^L x 10.5^W x 6^H
Offered Warm Brown or Soft White

	Org$	AVG	HIGH
B	79	79	92
C$^{P/L}$	99	103	140

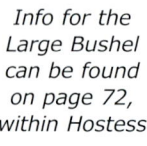

Cake (83-84)
100-CO
12^L x 12^W x 6^H
Featured 2 swinging handles, eventually moved to regular line

	Org$	AVG	HIGH
B	20.95	--	--

Daisy (86, 87)
5500-AO/5500-AN
10RD x 4^H
In 86, available stained and natural. In 87, only offered stained.

	Org$	AVG	HIGH
Stain	25.95	68	95
nat	27.95	63	70

Feature Baskets

Founder's Basket⁽⁰⁰⁾ Dave Longaberger
18791

15ᴸ x 10ᵂ x 7.5ᴴ

Made in memory of Dave Longaberger

	Org$	AVG	HIGH
B	189	231	295
Cᴾ/ᴸ	249	275	310

Homestead Apple⁽⁹⁹⁾
13871 | TO 37541

10ᴿᴰ x 6.25ᴴ

2 versions: one for all customers & one for Club members only(has tag)

	Org$	AVG	HIGH
B	59	84	109
Cᴾ/ᴸ	79	95	126
FSᶜ/ᴸᵈ	113	120	140
TO	8	14	16

Friendship ⁽⁸⁹⁾
13100-JO

5.5ᴸ x 5.5ᵂ x 2.5ᴴ

Features 1/2" weave

	Org$	AVG	HIGH
B	21.95	48	65

Hostess Two-Pie⁽⁰³⁾
19219

14ᴸ x 13ᵂ x 7.75ᴴ

Included riser. First time for reinforced center trim strip.

	Org$	AVG	HIGH
B	98	104	113
Cᴾ/ᴸ	138	138	164
FSᶜ/ᴸᵈ	186	186	210

Hamper, Large ⁽⁸⁶⁾
1600-OO

16.5ᴸ x 16.5ᵂ x 21.5ᴴ

Available only to Hostesses as their half-price purchase. No lid. First time for hand slots.

	Org$	AVG	HIGH
B	79.95	223	295

Ice Bucket⁽⁰³⁾
10363 | TO 28073

9.25ᴿᴰ x 8.5ᴴ

Regular and insulated protector both offered. Tie-On sold separately.

	Org$	AVG	HIGH
B	69	108	115
Cᴾ/ᴸ	99	116	150
FSᶜ/ᴸᵈ	123	133	165
TO	8	10	10

Hamper, Large ⁽⁹³⁻⁹⁴⁾
11622

16.5ᴸ x 16.5ᵂ x 21.5ᴴ

	Org$	AVG	HIGH
B	179.95	235	275
Cᴾ	185.95	225	280

Inverted Waste Large⁽⁸⁷⁾
2000-BO

14ᴿᴰ x 16ᴴ

	Org$	AVG	HIGH
B	59.95	71	82

Hamper, Large & Small Shades of Autumn⁽⁹¹⁾
1600-DSᴸᵍ | 1700-DSˢᵐ

Sm:12ᴸ x 12.25ᵂ x 16.25ᴴ

	Org$	AVG	HIGH
Lg	149.95	227	295
Cᴾ	169.90	--	--
Sm	99.95	153	165
Cᴾ	113.90	160	180

June Hostess Bonus⁽⁰⁴⁾
10016

5.75ᴸ x 3.75ᵂ x 3ᴴ

Free to June Hostesses with $250 in guest sales.

	Org$	AVG	HIGH
B	34	34	46
Cᴾ/ᴸ	51	--	--

Herb & Garden⁽⁸⁶⁾
4500-AOᴴ | 4600-AOᴳ

Herb: 11.5ᴸ x 5ᵂ x 3ᴴ

Gard: 15ᴸ x 8ᵂ x 2.25ᴴ

Originally sold only as a set

	Org$	AVG	HIGH
herb		59	75
garden		78	85
Set	32.90	--	--

Laundry, Oval⁽⁰¹⁾
10893

21.25ᴸ 14.25ᵂ 10.5ᴴ

	Org$	AVG	HIGH
B	159	160	200
Cᴾ/ᴸ	198	200	250
FSᶜ/ᴸᵈ	281	--	--

Feature Baskets

Feature Baskets
Miscellaneous Features (con't)

Memory (88-91)
5600-BBS
8.75ᴸ x 4.75ᵂ x 6.5ᴴ
Sold only as a combo of book and basket.

	Org$	AVG	HIGH
B		60	95
Cᴮᴷ	39.95	78	110

Planter, Fern Large⁽⁸⁸⁾
3200-RO
13ᴿᴰ x 8.5ᴴ

	Org$	AVG	HIGH
B	42.95	168	170

Pantry⁽⁸⁵⁾
2300-JO
14ᴸ x 9ᵂ x 4.5ᴴ

	Org$	AVG	HIGH
B	21.95	62	70

Planter, Fern Small⁽⁸⁸⁾
2900-RO
8.5ᴿᴰ x 7.5ᴴ

	Org$	AVG	HIGH
B	35.59	128	145

Peg, Shaker⁽⁸⁴⁾
10000-AO
5.5ᴸ x 5.5ᵂ x 6ᴴ

	Org$	AVG	HIGH
B	14.95	45	60

Planter, Patio⁽⁸⁴⁾
6000-R
10ᴿᴰ x 5.5ᴴ

	Org$	AVG	HIGH
B	21.95	90	135

Picnic, Old Oak Lid⁽⁸²⁾
12ᴸ x 12ᵂ x 6ᴴ
Less than 2500 were made. Lid is solid oak. Included riser.

	Org$	AVG	HIGH
B		477	615

Pocket of Gold⁽⁰²⁾
11903
19.75ᴿᴰ x 12.5ᴴ
Hostess only. New form.

	Org$	AVG	HIGH
B	198	198	215
Cᴾ/ᴸ	278	278	298
FSᶜ/ᴸᴰ	357	357	375

Pie, Single⁽⁸⁵⁾
2200-AO
12ᴸ x 12ᵂ x 4ᴴ
Most baskets from 1985 wil appear darker than the one pictured.

	Org$	AVG	HIGH
B	19.95	--	50

Red Pottery Thank You⁽⁹³⁾
190xx
11ᴸ x 8ᵂ x 5.5ᴴ
QTY: 7478, sent as a Thank You to customers who waited for the Traditional Red Pottery production difficulties.

	Org$	AVG	HIGH
B		63	70

Pie, Small⁽⁰⁶⁾
10780ᴿᴺ/17092ᶜᴺ/10807ᵂᴮ
7ᴿᴰ x 2.25ᴴ
Available three ways: Red & Natural, Cherry & Natural or Warm Brown.

	Org$	AVG	HIGH
B	39	--	--

Resolution⁽⁸⁷⁾
3800-ABS
5ᴿᴰ x 4.5ᴴ
Offered Dec 1987

	Org$	AVG	HIGH
B	16.95	46	63

Round Serving (04)
10684^{WB}/10713^I
10717^P/10714^S
12RD x 3.75^H
Available in four colors: Warm Brown, Indigo, Paprika & Sage

	Org$	AVG	HIGH
B	56	56	83
C^{P/L}	78	78	99

Serve-Around(05)
10202
13.75RD x 4.25^H
Accessories offered included bowl, lidded protector, protector egg tray insert and liner.

	Org$	AVG	HIGH
B	69	104	119
C^{P/L}	99	--	--

Saddlebrook, Med(01)
12306
7.25^L x 4.5^W x 6.5^H
Hostess Only

	Org$	AVG	HIGH
B	109	110	130
C^{P/L}	116	120	160

Sewing, Round(85,87)
3200-EO
13RD x 8.5^H
No stand included

	Org$	AVG	HIGH
B	37.95	207	218

Scalloped Boutique(06)
1044612^{SP}/1044621^{SW} /
1044619^{MG}
14^L x 6.5^W x 3.5^H
Available Soft Pink, Soft White and Medium Green

	Org$	AVG	HIGH
B	54	--	--
C^{P/L}	81	--	--
FS^{C/Ld}	101	--	--

Sleeve, Bushel Medium (05)
12RD x 7.75^H
Leaf Green only, available to Consultants through Longaberger Attic only

	Org$	AVG	HIGH
B	24.95	58	68

Scalloped Pocket Large(06)
1044912^{SP}/1044921^{SW} /
1044919^{MG}
12.5^L x 5.5^W x 6.5^H
Available Soft Pink, Soft White and Medium Green

	Org$	AVG	HIGH
B	69	--	--
C^{P/L}	96	--	--

Strawberry, Large(05)
10267^{WB} / 10265
7RD x 7.25^H
Available Warm Brown and Warm Brown with red upsplints

	Org$	AVG	HIGH
B	64	64	88
C^{P/L}	89	104	123
FS^{C/Ld}	111	--	--

Scalloped Pocket Small(06)
1044712^{SP}/1044721^{SW} /
1044719^{MG}
7.75^L x 4.25^W x 4.5^H
Available Soft Pink, Soft White and Medium Green

	Org$	AVG	HIGH
B	49	--	--
C^{P/L}	69	--	--

Strawberry, Small(05)
10266^{WB} / 10262
4.5RD x 4.5^H
Available Warm Brown and Warm Brown with red upsplints

	Org$	AVG	HIGH
B	49	58	70
C^{P/L}	65	65	80
FS^{C/Ld}	79	80	85

Scalloped Waste(06)
1045012^{SP}/1045021^{SW}/
1045019^{MG}
12RD x 12.5^H
Diagonal upsplints. Available in Soft Pink, Soft White and Medium Green.

	Org$	AVG	HIGH
B	99	--	--
C^{P/L}	142	--	--

Two-Pint (06)
10508^{RN} / 10779^{CN}
8.25^L x 5^W x 3.75^H
Available Red with Natural and Cherry with Natural

	Org$	AVG	HIGH
B	44	--	--
C^{P/L}	64	--	--

Feature Baskets

Feature Baskets

Miscellaneous Features (con't)

Two-Pie Grandma Bonnie's[98]
19241
12L x 12W x 10H
Created in celebration of Grandma's 90th birthday

	Org$	AVG	HIGH
B	95	95	128
CP/L	124	130	170
FSC/Ld	182	163	200

Two-Quart[85,87]
1000-CO
9.5L x 5W x 9.5H

	Org$	AVG	HIGH
B	28.95	74	85

Vacation Keepsake[03]
10244
10.25L x 8W x 3.5H
2 lids offered: chalk board or solid wood

	Org$	AVG	HIGH
B	39	69	80
CP/L	63	75	90
FSC/Ld	54	82	115

Weekender[87,88]
200-YO
10.5L x 9W x 8H

	Org$	AVG	HIGH
B	54.95	96	165

Window Box[02]
16977
21.25L x 9W x 5H
Will hold 34 CDs, 3 flower pots or 3 One-QT crocks.

	Org$	AVG	HIGH
B	89	96	125
CP/L	118	118	141

NATIONWIDE PHOTO WINNER

Diana Wood
Cardington, OH

Diana has been collecting for years, as may or may not be evident in her entry! We love that she always shows us a different look into her collection.

What did we like about this photo entry?

EVERYTHING, of course!

Foundry Collection

Basket Tree

Hanging

Table

Basket Tree [95-97]
74012[Tree] | 70084[Hang]
4'7"[H]
Made up of the Hanging Tree [top] and Table Top Tree [lower]

	Org$	AVG	HIGH
tree	120	120	210
hang	70	75	105

Table Top Tree [95-97]
70068
24[H]

Org$	AVG	HIGH
65	94	140

Finials
Leaf: 74039 [(95-97)]
Hook: 70254 [(96-97)]
Sold separately

	Org$	AVG	HIGH
leaf	12.95	10	15
hook	10.95	--	--

Herb Markers

Herb Markers [(96-97)]
Basil/Chives: 32905
Parsley/Thyme: 32808
Dill/Cilantro: 33006
Sage/Oregano: 33014

Org$	AVG	HIGH
19.95	17	29

Stands

Basket Rack, 5-Tier [(99-06)]
76805
15.25[L] 10.75[W] 37.75[H]
Shelves sold separately for $38 each, or set of 3 for $114

	Org$	AVG	HIGH
+shelf[2]	180	218	290
	218	243	306

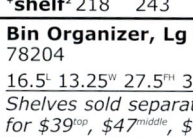

Bin Organizer, Lg [(00-03)]
78204
16.5[L] 13.25[W] 27.5[FH] 34.5[BH]
Shelves sold separately for $39[top], $47[middle], $49[bottom] or set of 3 for $135

Org$	AVG	HIGH
99	160	290

Bin Organizer, Little [(00-03)]
78085
8.5[L] x 8.5[W] x 13[H]
Shelves sold separately for $18 each, or set of 2 for $39

Org$	AVG	HIGH
64	79	193

Cafe, Dogwood [(06)]
chair(2): 71272
table: 71271
Chairs were sold in set of 2

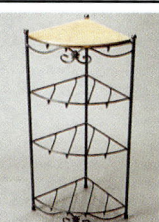

	Org$	AVG	HIGH
chair	350	--	--
table	150	--	--

Corner Stand [(02-06)]
77456
15[L] x 9.5[W] x 29.25[H]
Shelves sold separately for $30 each

Org$	AVG	HIGH
129	129	223

File Basket Stand [(99-02)]
75906
20[L] x 17.25[W] x 22.5[H]

Org$	AVG	HIGH
189	251	305

Generations Stand [(97-04)]
71463
16.5[L] x 10[W] x 24.5[H]
Designed to hold the Generation Baskets. Wood shelves sold separately.

Org$	AVG	HIGH
149.95	149	180

Hope Chest Stand [(98-03)]
72621
26.5[L] x 15[W] x 20[H]
Top shelf sold separately for $69

Org$	AVG	HIGH
179	208	260

Foundry Collection

Foundry Collection

Newspaper (01-05)
77887
17.5^L x 12.75^W x 18^H
Shelf sold separately
for $45

	Org$	AVG	HIGH
	79	89	135
†shelf	134	134	143

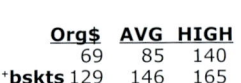

Snowman, Small (00)
77691
11^W x 12^D x 22^H
Shelves sold separately.
Designed to hold Frosty &
Frosty Jr. baskets.

	Org$	AVG	HIGH
	69	85	140
†bskts	129	146	165

Plant Stand, Medium (05)
At Home Garden
71210
11.75RD x 10.25^H
Features leaves, vines,
floral pattern, bronze
accents,

Org$	AVG	HIGH
69	--	--

Treasure Stand (96-01)
70327
24^L x 14^W x 15^H
Wood top sold sepa-
rately for $49.95

Org$	AVG	HIGH
149	155	221

Quilt Rack (04)
70392
29^L x 15^W x 36^H
Hostess only

Org$	AVG	HIGH
130	148	200

Umbrella Stand (00-04)
76899
12.5RD x 23^H
Shelf sold separately
for $29

Org$	AVG	HIGH
89	106	140

Side Table (00-02)
76473^W / 76481^G
19^L x 19^W x 24^H
Choice of solid wood or
glass tabletop

Org$	AVG	HIGH
229	229	289

Window Box Stand (05)
At Home Garden
71212
21.5^L x 9.25^W x 4.5^H
Features leaves, vines,
floral pattern, bronze
accents,

Org$	AVG	HIGH
89	--	--

Side Table, Ceramic (04-05)
71140
17^L x 17^W x 21.5^H
Hostess only

Org$	AVG	HIGH
198	--	--

Tabletop Items

Buffet Server (05-06)
71229
16.75^L x 10.75^W
Top holds mugs while
bottom accommodates
plates up to 9.25" in
diameter.

Org$	AVG	HIGH
59	--	--

Snowman, Large (99)
75795
17^W x 13.25^D x 31.5^H
Shelves sold separately.
Designed to hold the '99
Christmas baskets.

	Org$	AVG	HIGH
	99	108	165
†bskts	299	276	390

Caddy, Baguette (05)
71232
28^L x 7^W x 3.5^H
Designed to hold the
Baguette Basket

Org$	AVG	HIGH
49	49	120

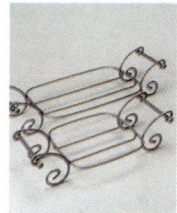

Caddy, 8x8 Baking(04-06)
70321 | 16^L x 8.5^W x 4.5^H
Caddy, 9x13 Baking(04-06)
71155 | 20.5^L x 9^W x 4.5^H
Designed to hold the 8x8 and 9x13 Baking Dishes

	Org$	AVG	HIGH
8x8	42	--	--
9x13	46	--	--

Countertop Corner(03-05)
70339
7^L x 9.25^W x 10^H
Shelves sold separately for $18 each, or set of 2 for $36

	Org$	AVG	HIGH
stand	59	88	116
+shelf^2	95	--	--

Caddy, Convertible(04-06)
71132
15.75^L x 8.75^W x 4.75^H

Org$	AVG	HIGH
49	--	--

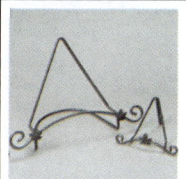

Easels
Large(00-02) 77992
12.75^L x 7.5^W x 9.5^H
Small(98-02) 75604
5.5^W x 4^H

	Org$	AVG	HIGH
large	32	32	47
small	19	20	32

Caddy, Dessert(03-05)
70332
14^L x 9.5^H
Designed to hold four Small Dessert Bowls

Org$	AVG	HIGH
49	49	63

Halloween Lantern(04-05)
71537
6.5RD x 9.5^H
Will hold pint size candle

Org$	AVG	HIGH
39	39	42

Caddy, Swivel(03-05)
71233
18.5^L x 18.5^W x 11.25^H
Wood shelves sold separately

Org$	AVG	HIGH
39	--	--

Heart to Heart Stand(00)
78221
6.75^L x 6.75^W x 7.25^H
Promoted with the 2000 Sweetheart Baskets

	Org$	AVG	HIGH
stand		33	56
+bskts	118	143	180

Candle Stand, 3-tier (03-06)
70386
20^L x 4.5^W x 4.25^H
Originally called the Decorative Stand

Org$	AVG	HIGH
39	39	55

Holiday Stand(05-06)
71236
13.5^L x 12.75^W x 16.25^H
Shelves sold separately for $14^{top} and $29^{bottom}

	Org$	AVG	HIGH
stand	59	--	--
+shelf^2	102	--	--

Christmas Tree (04)
71562
7^W x 11.5^H
Candle holder

Org$	AVG	HIGH
19	19	43

Mixing Bowl Stand(02-04)
77309
12^L x 10.25^W x 18.5^H
Shelves sold separately

Org$	AVG	HIGH
79	95	138

Foundry Collection

Foundry Collection

Mug Rack[99-02]
75892
9.75[W] x 16[H]

Org$	AVG	HIGH
54	54	69

Pedestal, Star[01]
Large: 76732
13.25[W] x 4.25[H]
Medium: 76635
10.25[W] x 6.5[H]
Small: 75931
7.25[W] x 6.25[H]

	Org$	AVG	HIGH
Lg	59	60	65
Md	49	50	53
Sm	39	40	42

Mug Tree[04-06]
71511
7.5[RD] x 14[H]

Org$	AVG	HIGH
49	--	--

Pie Server, Single[01-03]
76996

11.5[L] x 9.5[W] x 11.5[H]
Shelf sold separately

Org$	AVG	HIGH
49	49	53

Paper Tray[99-04]
75809
13[L] x 14[W] x 15.5[H]
Shelves sold separately
for $47 each or set of 2
for $94

	Org$	AVG	HIGH
	64	79	84
+shelf²	173	--	--

 98-04

Pie Server, Two[95-98]
95-98: 74004
98-04: 72630
10.5[RD] x 14[H]
In 1998, only the top
finial was changed

	Org$	AVG	HIGH
95-98	60	60	90
98-04	70		

Pedestal Stand[00-06]
78280
11RD x 3.5[H]
Holds Pasta Bowl or
11" round shelf/lid

Org$	AVG	HIGH
32	32	48

Pillar Candle Holder[04-06]
Large: 70003
6.75[W] x 11[H]
Medium: 70002
5.5[W] x 8.25[H]
Small: 71529
4.5[W] x 6[H]

	Org$	AVG	HIGH
Lg	27	--	--
Md	24	--	--
Sm	19	--	--

Pedestal, Divided[03-04]
70205
16[L] x 7.5[W] x 3[H]
Shown with Divided
Dish. Dish and shelf
sold separately

Org$	AVG	HIGH
39	39	45

Table Lamp[02-03]
77287
6.5[RD] x 31[H]
Hostess only

Org$	AVG	HIGH
329	310	329

Wall Hangings

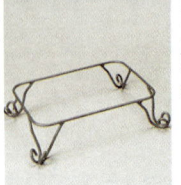

Pedestal, Rectangle[04-06]
77526
11.5[L] x 7.75[W] x 3.5[H]
Shelf sold separately
for $27

Org$	AVG	HIGH
39	39	69

Envelope Rack[99-05]
76091
13[L] x 4.75[W] x 22.5[H]
Shelf sold separately

	Org$	AVG	HIGH
	79	79	92
+shelf	125	--	--

Foundry Collection

Hanging Lantern & Bracket, Dogwood(06)
71274 | bracket 71270
5.75ᴸ x 5.75ᵂ x 10.75ᴴ
Bronze accents, 4 sides of glass, Dogwood floral pattern

	Org$	AVG	HIGH
lantern	29	--	--
bracket	19	--	--
set	43	--	--

Shelf, Wall(03-06)
70092
32ᴸ x 9.25ᵂ x 10.5ᴴ
4 hooks and hanging hardware included

Org$	AVG	HIGH
99	--	--

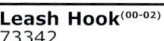

Leash Hook(00-02)
73342
2ᵂ x 3ᴴ
Pewter hook featuring the checkerboard and puppy design from the Mulligan line.

Org$	AVG	HIGH
12	--	--

Spice Rack(97-98)
71307
17ᴸ x 3.5ᵂ x 8.5ᴴ
Mug rack included four S-hooks

	Org$	AVG	HIGH
rack	75	112	150
+mug	105	105	110
+shelf	140	132	178
set	170	210	250

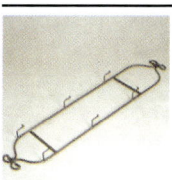

Plant Hanger(96-98)
70271
18ᵂ x 16ᴴ

Org$	AVG	HIGH
39.95	45	81

Trellis, Dogwood(06)
71273
23.25ᴸ x 1ᵂ x 29ᴴ
Dogwood designs with bronze accents

Org$	AVG	HIGH
89	--	--

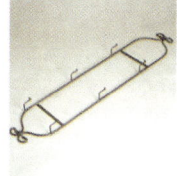

Plate Rack, 3-Tier(01-03)
76295
7.75ᴸ x 2ᵂ x 39ᴴ

Org$	AVG	HIGH
89	94	138

Wall Arch(96-98)
70297
15.5ᵂ x 11.5ᴴ
Hanging hardware included

Org$	AVG	HIGH
29.98	33	45

Quilt Hanger(04)
71243
38ᴸ
Includes solid rod to hang quilts

Org$	AVG	HIGH
24	25	35

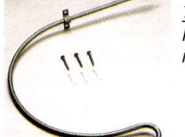

Wall Hook(98-06)
72664
2ᵂ x 6.75ᴴ

Org$	AVG	HIGH
19	19	30

Shelf, Utility (01-06)
76821
15.5ᴸ x 7ᵂ x 13.75ᴴ
Wood shelf sold separately for $29

Org$	AVG	HIGH
79	--	--

Wall Sconce(04-06)
71515
10.25ᵂ x 15ᴴ

Org$	AVG	HIGH
35	--	--

Foundry Collection

Good Ol' Summertime

1998 Picnic Pal
18643
9.5ᴸ x 9.5ᵂ x 2.75ᴴ
Red and blue trim strip

	Org$	AVG	HIGH
B	37	50	65
Cᴾ/ᴸ	51	53	70

2001 Boardwalk Medium
10552
12.5ᴸ x 6.75ᵂ x 8.5ᴴ

	Org$	AVG	HIGH
B	89	89	119
Cᴾ/ᴸ	115	120	145

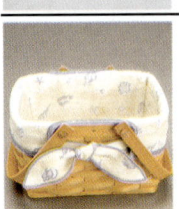

1999 Seashell
15296
7.75ᴸ x 5.75ᵂ x 5ᴴ
One of 2 baskets offered to everyone in 1999

	Org$	AVG	HIGH
B	39	60	70
Cᴾ/ᴸ	49	64	75
FSᶜ/ᴸᵈ	69	74	105

2001 Boardwalk Small
11393 | TO 30088
9.25ᴸ x 5ᵂ x 6.25ᴴ
Surf's Up Tie-on sold separately

	Org$	AVG	HIGH
B	59	67	80
Cᴾ/ᴸ	79	82	100
TO	8	12	18

1999 Beachcomber
15342 | TO 36561
10.5ᴸ x 9ᵂ x 8ᴴ
One of 2 baskets offered to everyone in 1999

	Org$	AVG	HIGH
B	67	71	89
Cᴾ/ᴸ	97	100	135
FSᶜ/ᴸᵈ	127	141	175
TO	8	13	16

2002 Back Porch
12381 | Pin 77320
13.25ᴸ x 9.5ᵂ x 3ᴴ
Bumblebee pin was also featured with the Window Box Basket

	Org$	AVG	HIGH
B	59	60	69
Cᴾ/ᴸ	79	85	110
Pin	8	10	14

2000 BBQ Buddy, Lg
16284 | 36234
12ᴸ x 5.25ᵂ x 3ᴴ
BBQ Buddy/Table Toppers Tie-on sold separately

	Org$	AVG	HIGH
B	49	59	90
Cᴾ/ᴸ	59	64	100
TO	10	11	16

Photo Search

We invite you to share your collection with us!

Each year, we ask Collectors to send us pictures of their Longaberger collection and we select the best ones to publish within our next edition. It's a great way for you to share your decorating ideas , as well as your love for collecting!

Be it a beautiful display, or something crazy, we've seen it all and now we want to see what YOU have!

Go to our website or call us for details and tips on what type of pictures we are seeking.

800.837.4394
www.bentleyguide.com

2000 Shaker Taker
17469 | TO 35700
7.5ᴸ x 3.75ᵂ x 2.75ᴴ
Salt & Pepper/Spice It Up Tie-on sold separately

	Org$	AVG	HIGH
B	39	45	67
Cᴾ/ᴸ	49	50	95
TO	8	13	18

2001 Boardwalk Large
10564 | TO 39551
17.75ᴸ x 10.5ᵂ x 12ᴴ
Sand Dollar Tie-on sold separately

	Org$	AVG	HIGH
B	129	130	140
Cᴾ/ᴸ	169	169	180
TO	8	12	22

Heartland Collection®

All Heartland Baskets have this burned-in logo on the bottom, authenticating the collection.

The Dresden Blue® shoestring weave will sometimes look like different variations of colors, depending on what it is next too: gray, green, steel blue, black.

Chore, Small (89-97)
13404
10^L x 6^W x 4^H

	Org$	AVG	HIGH
B	22.95	25	45

Bakery (90-01)
14711
14.5^L x 7.5^W x 3.75^H

	Org$	AVG	HIGH
B	30.95	37	60

Darning (96-01)
15598
10RD x 4^H

	Org$	AVG	HIGH
B	36.95	44	56

Button (94-01)
15423
7RD x 3^H

	Org$	AVG	HIGH
B	22.95	33	50

Getaway (90)
300-CCS
17^L x 14^W x 11^H
Hostess only

	Org$	AVG	HIGH
B	65.95	107	140

Cake (99-00)
15148
12^L x 12^W x 6^H
Included a wood riser

	Org$	AVG	HIGH
B	62	65	85

Key, Medium (88-97)
11118
9^L x 5^W x 5^H

	Org$	AVG	HIGH
B	26.95	35	54

Chore, Medium (88-97)
13528
13^L x 8^W x 5^H
One of the first in the series

	Org$	AVG	HIGH
B	36.95	40	60

Key, Small (94-97)
10782
7^L x 5^W x 3.5^H

	Org$	AVG	HIGH
B	21.95	30	45

Chore, Mini (89-97)
10758
7^L x 5^W x 3.5^H

	Org$	AVG	HIGH
B	19.95	26	34

Key, Tall (88-97)
11061
9.5^L x 5^W x 9.5^H
One of the first in the series

	Org$	AVG	HIGH
B	34.95	39	56

Heartland Collection

Heartland Collection®

Market, Medium (89-97)
10545
15^L x 10^W x 7.5^H

	Org$	AVG	HIGH
B	43.95	50	98

Spoon, Small
11096
5.5^L x 5.5^W x 6^H

	Org$	AVG	HIGH
B	23.95	49	65

Muffin (90-00)
14516
11.5^L x 5^W x 3^H

	Org$	AVG	HIGH
B	25.95	36	55

Spring (90-97)
10936
11^L x 8^W x 5.5^H

	Org$	AVG	HIGH
B	34.95	48	75

Pantry (98-00)
13951
14^L x 9^W x 4.5^H

	Org$	AVG	HIGH
B	53	53	75

Vegetable, Med (97-99)
16713
13^L x 7.5^W x 3^{FH} x 8^{BH}

	Org$	AVG	HIGH
B	50.95	54	75

Peg, Large (89-97)
11177
6.5^L x 6.5^W x 8^H

	Org$	AVG	HIGH
B	28.95	43	65

Purse, Small (88-98)
10839
9.5^L x 6^W x 6^H

	Org$	AVG	HIGH
B	36.95	50	69

Recipe (98-01)
10596
8^L x 5.5^W x 4.5^{FH} x 6^{BH}
Hostess only

	Org$	AVG	HIGH
B	39	43	50

Fun Fact

From 1995 to 2005 the *Horizon of Hope* campaigns have sold over 3.1 million baskets, raising more than $11.7 million dollars for breast cancer research!

Thank you!

Holiday Hostess™

1987 Tray
2300-JGRS
14^L x 9^W x 4.5^H

	Org$	AVG	HIGH
B	32.95	76	126

1989 Large Fruit
3200-BGRS
13RD x 8.5^H

	Org$	AVG	HIGH
B	49.95	74	81

1988 Tall Key
1000-IRGS
9.5^L x 5^W x 9.5^H

	Org$	AVG	HIGH
B	30.95	82	125

1989 Magazine
2100-CGRS
16^L x 8^W x 11^H

	Org$	AVG	HIGH
B	53.95	102	180

1988 Weekender
200-YRGS
10.5^L x 9^W x 8^H
Tie-On sold separately

	Org$	AVG	HIGH
B	65.95	71	125

1990 13" Measuring
4200-CGRS
13RD x 12.5^H

	Org$	AVG	HIGH
B	69.95	79	100

1988 Large Market
600-ARGS
16^L x 11^W x 9^H

	Org$	AVG	HIGH
B	49.95	60	81

1990 Large Gathering
2500-CGRS
19^L x 12^W x 6^H

	Org$	AVG	HIGH
B	65.95	70	125

1988 Small Laundry
2600-ORGS
24^L x 17^W x 10^H

	Org$	AVG	HIGH
B	67.95	93	100

1991 Tree Trimming
1900-BRGS/BGRS
12.5RD x 13.5^H
Available in red or green

	Org$	AVG	HIGH
B	79.95	99	135
C$^{P/L}$	92.90	153	225

1989 Medium Gathering
2400-AGRS
18^L x 11^W x 4.5^H

	Org$	AVG	HIGH
B	40.95	65	90

1992 Gift Giving
12700^R / 12718^G
20.5^L x 15^W x 10.5^H
Available in red or green

	Org$	AVG	HIGH
B	124.95	92	128
C$^{P/L}$	169.85	118	165

Holiday Hostess

1993 Homecoming
12084^R / 12092^G
15^L x 15^W x 7.5^H
Red or green, accessories sold separately. Combo included protector, liner & lid.

	Org$	AVG	HIGH
B	109.95	120	160
C$^{P/L/Ld}$	145.90	160	185

1999 Pinecone
15253^R / 15164^G
13RD x 6.25^H
Red or green. Lid available with red or green knob. Two piece protector.

	Org$	AVG	HIGH
B	99	74	100
C$^{P/L}$	129	93	129
FS$^{C/LD}$	174	120	140

1994 Sleigh Bell
14427^R / 14435^G
16.5RD x 11.5^H
Red or green, lid with red or green knob. Accessories sold separately, Combo included protector, liner & lid.

	Org$	AVG	HIGH
B	139.95	145	169
C$^{P/L/Ld}$	175.90	152	178

2000 12 Days of Christmas
17833^R / 17931^G
13^L x 13^W x 8.75^H
Red or green. Lid available with red or green knob.

	Org$	AVG	HIGH
B	139	111	150
C$^{P/L}$	189	133	180
FS$^{C/LD}$	234	154	215

1995 Evergreen
19607^R / 19615^G
15.5^L x 15.5^W x 12.25^H
Red or green, lid with red or green knob. Accessories sold separately, Combo included protector, liner & lid.

	Org$	AVG	HIGH
B	139.95	123	179
C$^{P/L/Ld}$	179.90	134	194

2001 Shining Star
10753^R / 10761^G
13.5^L x 14.5^W x 4.75^H
Red or green. Offered a 2-piece, 5-way divided protector.

	Org$	AVG	HIGH
B	109	63	115
C$^{P/L}$	149	90	125
FS$^{C/LD}$	198	130	180

1996 Yuletide Treasures
18619^R / 18627^G
20.25^L x 13.75^W x 7.5^H
Red or green, accessories sold separately. Combo included protector, liner & lid. Lid also fits the Treasure Stand.

	Org$	AVG	HIGH
B	129.95	86	119
C$^{P/L/Ld}$	199.95	164	215

2002 Treasures
10030^R / 10041^G
19^L x 11.25^W x 8.75^H
Red or green. Liners avail in 3 fabrics.

	Org$	AVG	HIGH
B	169	115	149
C$^{P/L}$	229	153	200
FS$^{C/LD}$	298	189	210

1997 Snowflake
12661^R / 12653^G
14^L x 12.75^W x 11.5^H
Red or green. 3-level protector and lid with or without a knob.

	Org$	AVG	HIGH
B	129.95	80	120
C$^{P/L}$	159.95	100	149
FS$^{C/LD}$	204.90	105	180

2003 Joyful Chorus
10501
12RD x 7.5^H
Fabric lid cover was available in 3 fabrics.

	Org$	AVG	HIGH
B	129	85	129
C$^{P/L}$	170	134	185
FS$^{C/LD}$	198	172	200

1998 Winter Wishes
12483^R / 12491^G
12.5^L 8.25^W 10.5^{FH} 12^{BH}
Red or green. Lid available with red or green knob. 2 liners offered.

	Org$	AVG	HIGH
B	95	62	90
C$^{P/L}$	115	75	135
FS$^{C/LD}$	149	92	160

2004 Greetings
10730^R / 10733^G
18^L x 14^W x 8^H
Red or green. Liner was available in 4 fabrics.

	Org$	AVG	HIGH
B	135	--	--
C$^{P/L}$	178	153	188
FS$^{C/LD}$	247	192	222

2005 Garland
10338[R]/10339[G]/10366[WB]

16.75[L] x 16.25[W] x 6.5[H]
Red, green or Warm Brown

	Org$	AVG	HIGH
B	110	--	--
C[P/L]	153	130	179
FS[C/LD]	222	185	200

NATIONWIDE PHOTO WINNER

Kim Wright
Parkersburg, WV

Such a great use of a very small place – that's what caught our attention with Kim's entry. We have received many entries featuring Christmas trees, but not many so heavily adorned with as much Longaberger bling!

As far as we can count, Kim has every Longaberger ornament represented! What a fun display of more than a decade of Ornaments!

Holiday Hostess

Horizon of Hope®

Since its inception, Longaberger, in partnership with the American Cancer Society®, has raised more than $11 million dollars for the fight against breast cancer through these Horizon of Hope baskets.

2000 Horizon of Hope
17787[C]/19194[W]
TO 37036
7.5[L] x 4.25[W] x 2.75[H]
QTY: 361,027, Classic or Whitewash.

	Org$	AVG	HIGH
B	32	48	75
C[P/L]	49	58	95
FS[C/Ld]	65	71	100
TO	8	11	15

1995 Horizon of Hope
17124
5.75[L] x 3.75[W] x 3[H]
QTY: 181,506

	Org$	AVG	HIGH
B	28.95	58	105
C[P/L]	41.85	70	145

2001 Horizon of Hope
10591[C]/11605[W]
TO 77429 | Votive 74985
5.25[RD] x 4.25[H]
QTY: 332,258, Classic or Whitewash.

	Org$	AVG	HIGH
B	34	46	79
C[P/L]	52	55	84
FS[C/Ld]	68	68	99
TO	8	12	14
votive	15	16	25

1996 Horizon of Hope
15911
6.75[L] x 4.75[W] x 2.25[H]
QTY: 226,292, Set of 12 recipes given with each basket

	Org$	AVG	HIGH
B	28.95	62	70
C[P/L]	41.85	71	89

2002 Horizon of Hope
17213[C]/17311[W]
TO 31730
4.75[RD] x 4.5[H]
QTY: 239,229, Classic or Whitewash.

	Org$	AVG	HIGH
B	34	38	79
C[P/L]	51	56	89
FS[C/Ld]	68	68	95
TO	8	12	18

1997 Horizon of Hope
18724
5.75[L] x 4[W] x 4[H]
QTY: 278,689

	Org$	AVG	HIGH
B	28.95	37	70
C[P/L]	41.85	52	79

2003 Horizon of Hope
10546[C]/10547[W]
TO 20231
5.5[L] x 4.5[W] x 2[H]
QTY: 318,679, Classic or Whitewash

	Org$	AVG	HIGH
B	34	36	69
C[P/L]	51	51	89
FS[C/Ld]	67	67	105
TO	8	13	18

1998 Horizon of Hope
10472 | TO 33677
4[L] x 4[W] x 5.5[H]
QTY: 372,941

	Org$	AVG	HIGH
B	31	50	70
C[P/L]	44	67	99
TO	8	13	20

2004 Horizon of Hope
10660[WB]/10661[W]
TO 28578
5.25[L] x 4[W] x 5.5[H]
QTY: 228,582, Warm Brown or Whitewash

	Org$	AVG	HIGH
B	36	56	69
C[P/L]	56	75	80
FS[C/Ld]	75	83	92
TO	8	8	10

1999 Horizon of Hope
14150 | TO 36625
6.25[L] x 5.25[W] x 3[H]
QTY: 368,719

	Org$	AVG	HIGH
B	31	43	60
C[P/L]	47	50	79
FS[C/Ld]	62	80	88
TO	8	12	16

2005 Horizon of Hope
10280[WB] / 10295[W]
TO 23125 | Mugs 31410
6.75[L] x 3.75[W] x 3.5[H]
QTY: 201,074, warm Brown or Whitewash

	Org$	AVG	HIGH
B	36	46	57
C[P/L]	56	58	80
FS[C/Ld]	72	72	89
TO	8	8	12
mugs[2]	24	27	35

Hostess Collection

Banker's Waste (99-02)
14761
12.5RD x 13.5^H
$500 show level

	Org$	AVG	HIGH
B	119	119	125
C^{P/L}	168	--	--
FS^{C/Ld}	214	154	180

Corn (95-99)
14443
17RD x 11.5^H
$500 show level

	Org$	AVG	HIGH
B	139.95	147	190
C^{P/L}	193.85	212	265

Bowl, 13" (02-04)
10722
13.25RD x 6.5^H
Shown with the 11" for size comparison

	Org$	AVG	HIGH
B	129	--	--

Corner Hamper (03)
10333
17.25^L x 17.5^W x 20.75^H
Introduced into Hostess collection, but then moved to Regular Line in 2004

	Org$	AVG	HIGH
B	65.95	125	210

Bowl Stand (03-04)
70348
21^L x 16^W x 41^H

	Org$	AVG	HIGH
B	139	--	--

Cradle, Doll (86-90)
2500-LO
19^L x 12^W x 6^H
Liner sold separately

	Org$	AVG	HIGH
B	44.95	120	185

Bushel, Large (05)
10396^{LG}/10397^{WB}/10398^B
18RD x 11.25^H
Leaf Green, Warm Brown or Warm Brown with Black Trim

	Org$	AVG	HIGH
B	189	--	--
C^{P/L}	228	263	276
FS^{C/Ld}	297	--	--

Cradle, Large (86-90) (Infant)
2800-M
30^L x 20^W x 10.5^H
Available stained, natural, or natural with color. Stain offered from 80-84, and 89-90.

	Org$	AVG	HIGH
B	109.95	350	465

Butcher Block (02-04)
50831
20.5^L x 20.5^W x 34.5^H
$1000 show level

	Org$	AVG	HIGH
	499	499	650

Craft Keeper (02-04)
12535^C / 18954^{WB}
18^L x 13.75^W x 9.25^H
Classic or Warm Brown.
$500 show level.

	Org$	AVG	HIGH
B	169	195	285

Canister Set (98-02)
Various form numbers
4QT, 3QT, 2QT, 1.5QT
Offered in all 4 Woven Tradition colors(99-02) and five Solid colors(02)

	Org$	AVG	HIGH
WTrad	249	273	410
Solid	269	317	350

Ficus (04-06)
10681
16.25RD x 11.5^H
$250 show level

	Org$	AVG	HIGH
B	120	120	130
C^{P/L}	264	162	172
FS^{C/Ld}	343	211	221

Hostess Collection

File (99-03)
12769
20^L x 17.5^W x 12.5^H
$750- $1000 show level

	Org$	AVG	HIGH
B	189	199	288
C^{P/L}	264	275	330
FS^{C/Ld}	343	305	330

Harvest (90-92)
3700-AOS
16^L x 9^W x 6^H

	Org$	AVG	HIGH
B	54.95	96	122
C^P	66.90	118	150

Gathering, Large
Version1 96-99: 12564
Version2 05-06: 10256
19^L x 12^W x 6^H
Retired in '99 and brought back in '05 with new reinforced design.

	Org$	AVG	HIGH
V1	89.95	103	130
V2	120	--	--

Hat Box (04-06)
60092
13RD x 6^H
Warm Brown only, basket included lid

	Org$	AVG	HIGH
B	160	--	--
C^{P/L}	211	--	--

Gourmet Picnic (92-95)
10413
13.25^L x 11.25^W x 9^H
$250 show level

	Org$	AVG	HIGH
B	99.95	100	120
C^{P/L}	132.95	140	180

Hearthside (90-92)
42000-AOS
11.75RD x 6.5^H
3/8" weaving

	Org$	AVG	HIGH
B	59.95	87	130
C^P	68.90	105	140

Hamper, Large (86-90)
1600-DO
16.5^L x 16.5^W x 21.5^H
$1000 show level

	Org$	AVG	HIGH
B	109.95	165	243

1986-90

Heirloom (90-92)
500-HOS
15^L x 10^W x 7.5^H
3/8" weaving

	Org$	AVG	HIGH
B	87.95	90	114

Hamper, Large
95-01: 11631
01-04: 11362^C/19055^{WB}
17^L x 17^W x 22^H
Revamped in 2001 with new lid and reinforced body. Warm Brown introduced in 2002.

	Org$	AVG	HIGH
95-01	220	246	275
01-04	259	306	335

1995-01

Homecoming (99-02)
13081
15^L x 15^W x 7.5^H
$250 show level

	Org$	AVG	HIGH
B	99	97	165
C^{P/L}	158	116	185

Hamper, Medium (86-90)
1700-DO
12^L x 12.25^W x 16.25^H

	Org$	AVG	HIGH
B	69.95	184	281

Hope Chest (98-03)
18431
23^L x 14^W x 11.25^H
$1500 show level

	Org$	AVG	HIGH
B	189	303	355
C^{P/L}	254	310	370
FS^{C/Ld}	323	314	378

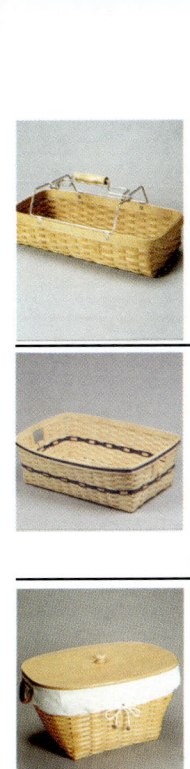

Household Caddy (04-05)
10693

18.25^L x 8.5^W x 4.25^H
Stainless steel handle and solid wood bottom

	Org$	AVG	HIGH
B	100	--	--
C$^{P/L}$	140	85	120

Picnic, XLarge Oval (03-04)
10007

21^L x 12.25^W x 11.25^H
Included lid

	Org$	AVG	HIGH
B	259	259	300
C$^{P/L}$	344	--	--

Laundry, Large (86-90)
2800-O

30^L x 20^W x 10.5^H
Classic, natural, or natural with color. Available Stain offered 80–84, and then again 89-90.

	Org$	AVG	HIGH
B	96.95	165	200

Remembrance (90-92)
200-YOS

10.5^L x 9^W x 8^H

	Org$	AVG	HIGH
B	79.95	125	175
C^P	88.90	134	179

Laundry, Oval (02-03)
10893^C/18989^{WB}

21.25^L x 14.25^W x 10.5^H
Classic and Warm Brown

	Org$	AVG	HIGH
B	159	204	238
C$^{P/L}$	222	--	--
FS$^{C/Ld}$	281	--	281

Serve It Up (02-06)
60895^C/18784^{WB}

23^L x 13.25^W x 3.75^H
Classic and Warm Brown

	Org$	AVG	HIGH
B	105	110	138

Mail (92-96)
10600

12^L x 8^W x 11.5^H

	Org$	AVG	HIGH
B	79.95	80	100
C$^{P/L}$	106.85	107	133

Serving Tray (92-02)
60011^C/68586^W

20^L x 14^W x 3.75^H
Classic$^{(92-02)}$ and Whitewash$^{(01-02)}$

	Org$	AVG	HIGH
Classic	74.95	80	129
C$^{P/L}$	116.85	120	179
WWash	95	--	--
C$^{P/L}$	146	--	--

Odds & Ends (95-02)
18902

18.75^L 9^W 12.75^{FH} 5.25^{BH}
$500-$1000 show level

	Org$	AVG	HIGH
B	149.95	224	249
C$^{P/L}$	204.85	234	279

Sewing (95-00)
13234

13RD x 8.5^H
$500 show level

	Org$	AVG	HIGH
B	89.95	96	140
C$^{P/L}$	129.85	137	160

Picnic, Family (06)
10509^{RN}/10777^{CN}

21^L x 11.5^W x 9.75^H
Available in Red/Natural or Cherry/Natural

	Org$	AVG	HIGH
B	225	--	--
C$^{P/L}$	260	--	--

Shopping Cart (04-05)
10344

17^L x 14.75^W x 38.5^H

	Org$	AVG	HIGH
B	300	250	410
C$^{P/L}$	399	--	--

Hostess Collection

Hostess Collection

Shoulder Bag (04-06)
Longaberger Signature
10705

10^L x 4^W x 6^H

Warm Brown with black leather details. Shown here with l/A larger version for size comparison.

	Org$	AVG	HIGH
B	300	182	215

Large
Small

Teapot, Large (95-99)
32069^R/32042^B/32051^G/33782^I

40oz

Red, blue, green or ivory. Shown here with the small version for size comparison

	Org$	AVG	HIGH
	59.95	68	70

Side Table (04-05)
71140

17^L x 17^W x 21.5^H

Features bronze highlighting

Org$	AVG	HIGH
198	--	--

Treasure (98-01)
18716

20.25^L x 13.75^W x 7.5^H

$1500 show level

	Org$	AVG	HIGH
B	119	120	190
C$^{P/L}$	164	180	210
FS$^{C/Ld}$	223	200	223

Sleeve, Sunroom (99-02)
15261

24.5^L x 20^W x 14^H

$1500 show level

	Org$	AVG	HIGH
B	210	195	231
C^P	255	213	298

Umbrella (98-04)
11282^C/18822^{WB}

10RD x 17.5^H

Classic or Warm Brown

	Org$	AVG	HIGH
B	100	128	148
C^P	119	145	154

Soup Tureen (01-04)
36765^B/ 36773^G/ 36781^R/ 36790^I

8.5RD x 7^H

Blue, green, red and ivory. Introduced as Hostess line then moved to Regular line.

Org$	AVG	HIGH
149	--	--

Wash Day (00-04)
Med: 19372^C/18938^{WB}

18.75^L x 18.25^W x 9.5^H

Small: 15695^C/18842^{WB}

16.25^L x 15.75^W x 8.5^H

	Org$	AVG	HIGH
med	159	169	176
C$^{P/L}$	217	--	--
small	139	149	150
C$^{P/L}$	189	--	--

Step It Up (04-06)
10690

18.75^L 9^W 12.75^{FH} 5.25^{BH}

The revamped Odds & Ends basket.

Photo Not Available Coming Soon!

	Org$	AVG	HIGH
B	170	--	--

Weekender (01-04)
10362^C/18857^{WB}

10.5^L x 9^W x 8^H

Classic or Warm Brown. Moved to Regular Line in Mar2004

	Org$	AVG	HIGH
B	139	139	157
C$^{P/L}$	193	--	--

Table Lamp (02-03)
77287

6.5RD x 31^H

Shade features a faint leaf design

	Org$	AVG	HIGH
B	329	310	329

Wildflower (92-98)
10111

13.5RD x 8.5^H

$250 show level

	Org$	AVG	HIGH
B	64.95	70	99
C$^{P/L}$	95.85	103	175

Work-A-Round (03-04)
10228
19.75RD x 12.5^H
Moved to Regular Line in Mar2004

	Org$	AVG	HIGH
B	199	--	--

Woven Panel Chest(03-04)
50793
29.25^L x 13.75^W x 14.5^H
Features one sliding self

Org$	AVG	HIGH
400	370	400

NATIONWIDE PHOTO WINNER

Susan Peck
Republic, MO

Proud to be an American, proud to be Longaberger!

This photo entry inspired us to remember those who fight for our freedom so that we can enjoy the things that mean the most in our lives ... including Baskets!!

Hostess Collection
76

Hostess Appreciation

1994
Hostess Appreciation
8^L x 4^W x 2^H
Given to Hostesses with shows in both Oct 1993 and Jan 1994

	Org$	AVG	HIGH
B		26	43

2002 Lucky Charm
11482
5.25^L 4.25^W 1.75^{FH} 3^{BH}
Shows in both Oct 2001 and Jan 2002. Accessories sold separately.

	Org$	AVG	HIGH
B	39	39	55
C$^{P/L}$	55	55	70
FS$^{C/Ld}$	70	79	95

1996
Hostess Appreciation
5.5^L x 5.5^W x 2.5^H
QTY: 181,337 – given to Hostesses with shows in both Oct 1995 and Jan 1996. Liner sold separately.

	Org$	AVG	HIGH
B		27	44

2003
Hostess Appreciation
10162
4RD x 3.25^H
Shows in Jan 2003 and Apr 2003. Accessories sold separately.

	Org$	AVG	HIGH
B	39	48	70
C$^{P/L}$	55	55	95
FS$^{C/Ld}$	70	70	123

1998
Hostess Appreciation
5.75^L x 3.75^W x 3^H
Given to Hostesses with shows in both Oct 1997 and Jan 1998. Liner sold separately.

	Org$	AVG	HIGH
B	29.95	27	50

2004
Hostess Appreciation
10541 | TO 28003
6.25^L x 3^W x 4^H
Note cards sold for $6

	Org$	AVG	HIGH
B	39	45	62
C$^{P/L}$	57	64	81
FS$^{C/Ld}$	75	75	95
TO	8	9	11

1999 Little Joy
19445
5^L x 3.75^W x 4.5^H
Given to Hostesses with shows in both Oct 1998 and Jan 1999. Accessories sold separately.

	Org$	AVG	HIGH
B	38	38	50
C$^{P/L}$	53	59	69

2005
Hostess Appreciation
10704
5RD x 3.25^H
Collector Club Members could earn free lid

	Org$	AVG	HIGH
B	39	40	50
C$^{P/L}$	58	58	69
FS$^{C/Ld}$	74	74	85

2000 Celebration
13498 | TO 36196
7.5^L x 4.5^W x 3.5^H
Shown with the Classic version that was available to everyone (see Feature)

	Org$	AVG	HIGH
B	44	44	68
C$^{P/L}$	63	63	85
FS$^{C/Ld}$	80	80	105
TO	8	12	16

2006
Hostess Appreciation
10390
7^L x 4^W x 3.5^{FH} x 5^{BH}
Shows in Oct 2005 and Jan 2006. Accessories sold separately.

	Org$	AVG	HIGH
B	39	39	51
C$^{P/L}$	63	65	75

2001
Hostess Appreciation
15873
5.5^L x 4^W x 4^H
Same as 2001 Inaugural, without stain

	Org$	AVG	HIGH
B	39	40	60
C$^{P/L}$	56	63	85
FS$^{C/Ld}$	70	72	90

Incentive & Award Baskets

These baskets were given to Consultants as Incentives or Awards, no original prices

COLLECTION INDEX
BEE AWARDS
Bee Speaker 78
VIP 79
National Sponsoring 82
National Sales 83
Branch Sponsored 85
Region Sponsored 86
Director Sponsored 87

Consultant Level Baskets 90
Trip Awards 91
Misc Recruit/Sponsor 92
Misc Sales 94

BEE: Bee Speaker (year)

1988 Bee Speaker Medium Market
15^L x 10^W x 7.5^H
QTY: 15
Blue shoestring weave, brass tag

	AVG	HIGH
B	85	100

1989 Bee Speaker Keepsake
5.75^L x 3.75^W x 3^H

	AVG	HIGH
B	118	125

1990 Bee Speaker Harvest
16^L x 9^W x 6^H
No color, brass tag

	AVG	HIGH
B	120	130

1991 Bee Speaker Spring
11^L x 8^W x 5.5^H
Dark blue trim and weave

	AVG	HIGH
B	--	200

1992 Bee Speaker Spring
11^L x 8^W x 5.5^H
Green trim and weave

	AVG	HIGH
B	189	203

1993 Bee Speaker Spring
11^L x 8^W x 5.5^H
Teal and pink accent weave, teal trim

	AVG	HIGH
B	235	260

1994 Bee Speaker Spring
11^L x 8^W x 5.5^H
Pink and purple trim and weave

	AVG	HIGH
B	230	250

1995 Bee Speaker Spring
11^L x 8^W x 5.5^H
Purple and green trim and weave

	AVG	HIGH
B	--	270

1996 Bee Speaker Spring
11^L x 8^W x 5.5^H
Blue, gold and red weave and trim

	AVG	HIGH
B	100	200

1997 Bee Speaker Spring
11^L x 8^W x 5.5^H
Green, red and blue weave and trim

	AVG	HIGH
B	130	175

Incentive & Award

Incentive & Award Baskets

BEE: Bee Speaker (con't)

1998 Bee Speaker Spring
11^L x 8^W x 5.5^H
Green, yellow, blue and red accents, red trim. Accessories sold separately.

	AVG	HIGH
B	--	--

1999 Bee Speaker Spring
11^L x 8^W x 5.5^H
Green, rose, blue and purple accents, rose trim. Accessories sold separately.

	AVG	HIGH
B	--	--

2000 Bee Speaker Spring
11^L x 8^W x 5.5^H
Blue trim and weave. Accessories sold separately.

	AVG	HIGH
B	230	245

2001 Bee Speaker Spring
11^L x 8^W x 5.5^H
Sage, brown and blue trim and weave. Accessories sold separately.

	AVG	HIGH
B	--	--

2002 Bee Speaker Spring
11^L x 8^W x 5.5^H
Blue and red trim and weave, featuring star tacks

	AVG	HIGH
B	305	320

2003 Bee Facilitator Large Berry
8.5^L x 8.5^W x 5^H
Blue and red trim and weave, featuring star tacks. Accessories sold separately.

	AVG	HIGH
B	--	--

2005 Bee Facilitator Wall Pocket
11^L x 6^W x 8.75^{FH} x 11^{BH}
Navy, natural & sage trim and accents, pewter tag, leather loop

	AVG	HIGH
B	--	--

BEE: VIP Honorable Mention/Achiever

1995 VIP Honorable Mention
3RD x 2.5^H
Given to consultants who attained $20,000 - $34,999 in sales.

	AVG	HIGH
	--	--

1996 VIP Honorable Mention
3RD x 2.5^H
Given to consultants who attained $20,000 - $34,999 in sales

	AVG	HIGH
	--	--

1997 VIP Honorable Mention
3RD x 2.5^H
Given to consultants who attained $20,000 - $34,999 in sales

	AVG	HIGH
	--	33

1998 VIP Honorable Mention
3RD x 2.5^H
QTY: ≈2800, given to consultants who attained $20,000 - $34,999 in sales.

	AVG	HIGH
	--	--

1999 VIP Honorable Mention
3RD x 2.5^H
First year for personalization, printed on both sides. Last year for tie-on award.

	AVG	HIGH
	--	--

2000 VIP Honorable Mention
7^W x 13^H

First time for personalized plaque

AVG	HIGH
--	--

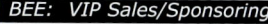
BEE: VIP Sales/Sponsoring

1986 VIP Sales
12^L x 7^W x 10^H
QTY: 69
Dark blue accents, velcro dots on basket are not original

	AVG	HIGH
B	375	400

2001 VIP Sponsor & Sales Achiever
10^L x 7.5^W

Plaque given to both Sponsor (3-5 recruits) & Sales achievers ($20-$35k). Engraving is specific to award.

AVG	HIGH
--	--

1987 VIP Sales
12^L x 7^W x 10^H
Red or Green$^{(pictured)}$ accents given for different award time periods

	AVG	HIGH
B	363	400

2002 VIP Sponsor & Sales Achiever
7.75^L x 5.5^W

Plaque/lid given to both Sponsor (3-5 recruits) & Sales achievers ($20-$35k), fits Bee Basket, engraving is specific to award.

AVG	HIGH
40	45

1988 VIP Sales
12^L x 7^W x 10^H
Dark blue trim and weave

	AVG	HIGH
B	310	400

2003 VIP Sponsor & Sales Achiever
9.25^L x 5^W
QTY: Sales 2149/Sponsor 651

Plaque/lid given to both Sponsor (3-5 recruits) & Sales achievers ($20-$35k), fits Bee Basket, engraving is specific to award.

AVG	HIGH
--	--

1989 VIP Sales
12^L x 7^W x 10^H
QTY: 163
Red and blue accent, red trim

	AVG	HIGH
B	86	119

2004 VIP Sponsor & Sales Achiever
10.25^L x 8^W

Plaque/lid given to both Sponsor (3-4 recruits) & Sales achievers ($20-$35k), fits Bee Basket, engraving is specific to award.

AVG	HIGH
--	--

1990 VIP Sales
12^L x 7^W x 10^H
QTY: 359
Natural, pink and blue accents, pink trim

	AVG	HIGH
B	120	155

2005 VIP Sponsor & Sales Achiever
7.5RD

Plaque/lid given to both Sponsor (3-4 recruits) & Sales achievers ($20-$35k), fits Bee Basket, engraving is specific to award.

AVG	HIGH
--	--

1991 VIP Sales
12^L x 7^W x 10^H
Blue accents and trim

	AVG	HIGH
B	118	121

Incentive & Award
80

Incentive & Award Baskets

BEE: VIP Sales/Sponsoring (con't)

1992 VIP Sales
12^L x 7^W x 10^H
Green accents and trim, exclusive liner was included

	AVG	HIGH
B^L	100	173

1998 VIP Sales
12^L x 7^W x 10^H
QTY: 1800
Green, yellow, blue, red accents and trim. Liner, protector and handle-tie included

	AVG	HIGH
B$^{P/L/HT}$	95	152

1993 VIP Sales
12^L x 7^W x 10^H
Teal and pink accents and trim, liner and protector included

	AVG	HIGH
B$^{P/L}$	111	179

1999 VIP Sales
12^L x 7^W x 10^H
QTY: 2079
Green, rose, blue, purple accents and trim. Liner, protector and handle-tie included

	AVG	HIGH
B$^{P/L/HT}$	200	300

1994 VIP Sales
12^L x 7^W x 10^H
Rose pink and purple accents and trim, liner, protector and handle-tie included

	AVG	HIGH
B$^{P/L/HT}$	216	220

2000 VIP Sales
12^L x 7^W x 10^H
Blue accents and trim. Liner, protector and handle-tie included

	AVG	HIGH
B$^{P/L/HT}$	132	200

1995 VIP Sales
12^L x 7^W x 10^H
Purple and green accents and trim, liner, protector and handle-tie included

	AVG	HIGH
B$^{P/L/HT}$	113	130

2001 VIP Sales
12^L x 7^W x 10^H
Sage, brown, blue accents and trim. Liner, protector and handle-tie included

	AVG	HIGH
B$^{P/L/HT}$	125	188

1996 VIP Sales
12^L x 7^W x 10^H
QTY: 1356
Red, blue, gold accents and trim. Liner, protector and handle-tie included

	AVG	HIGH
B$^{P/L/HT}$	93	110

2002 VIP Sales
12^L x 7^W x 10^H
Warm Brown, red and blue accents and trim, star tacks. Liner, protector and handle-tie included

	AVG	HIGH
B$^{P/L/HT}$	178	180

1997 VIP Sales
12^L x 7^W x 10^H
Red, blue, green accents and trim. Liner, protector and handle-tie included

	AVG	HIGH
B$^{P/L/HT}$	111	156

2003 VIP Sales & Sponsoring
12^L x 7^W x 10^H
QTY: Sales 661/Sponsor 203
First year for Sponsoring VIP (natural). Brown and leather accents. Leather handle gripper included.

	AVG	HIGH
sales^{HT}	145	160
sponsor^{HT}	344	552

Incentive & Award

2004 VIP Sales & Sponsoring
12ᴸ x 7ᵂ x 10ᴴ
Sponsoring (Natural), Sale (Warm Brown). Brown and leather accents with leather covered handles.

	AVG	HIGH
sales	--	216
sponsor	--	103

2005 VIP Sales & Sponsoring
12ᴸ x 7ᵂ x 10ᴴ
Sponsoring (Natural), Sale (Warm Brown). Black and leather accents with leather covered handles.

	AVG	HIGH
sales	--	350
sponsor	--	--

BEE: National Sponsoring Awards (year)

1992
19.75ᴸ x 12ᵂ x 3.5ᴴ
Blue-ish green accents, made by Larry Longaberger

	AVG	HIGH
B	1184	1700

1992 Mini Discovery
4.5ᴿᴰ x 2.5ᴴ
No color accents, woven by Larry, inverted bottom. Given to top Sponsoring winners, starting with second level.

	AVG	HIGH
	--	1276

1993 Gathering
Small/Med/Lg/XLg
Red accents, made by Larry, open-weave bottom, **personalized** brass tag, engraved lid included

	AVG	HIGH
small⁽⁵⁻⁹ ʳᵉᶜʳᵘⁱᵗˢ⁾	--	250
medium⁽¹⁰⁻¹⁴⁾	--	415
large⁽¹⁵⁻¹⁹⁾	--	--
xlarge⁽²⁰⁺⁾	--	596

1993 Mini Cake
4.75ᴸ x 4.75ᵂ x 2.5ᴴ
Red accents, woven by Larry, open-weave bottom, included mini divider shelf. Given to top Sponsoring winners, starting with second level.

	AVG	HIGH
B	--	860

1994 Gathering
Small/Med/Lg/XLg
Pink & purple accents, engraved lid included

	AVG	HIGH
small⁽⁵⁻⁹ ʳᵉᶜʳᵘⁱᵗˢ⁾	200	220
medium⁽¹⁰⁻¹⁴⁾	--	415
large⁽¹⁵⁻¹⁹⁾	--	--
xlarge⁽²⁰⁺⁾	--	596
mini	--	--

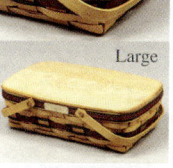

1995 Gathering
Small/Med/Lg/XLg
Green/purple accents, engraved lid included

	AVG	HIGH
small⁽⁵⁻⁹ ʳᵉᶜʳᵘⁱᵗˢ⁾	110	180
medium⁽¹⁰⁻¹⁴⁾	--	--
large⁽¹⁵⁻¹⁹⁾	--	--
xlarge⁽²⁰⁺⁾	--	--

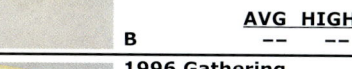

1995 Mini Gathering
7ᴸ x 4.5ᵂ x 2.5ᴴ
3 different Minis offered, each an exact ratio replica of basket given to the top Sponsoring winners, starting with second level

	AVG	HIGH
B	--	--

1996 Gathering
Small/Med/Lg/XLg
Red/blue/gold accents, engraved lid included

	AVG	HIGH
small⁽⁵⁻⁹ ʳᵉᶜʳᵘⁱᵗˢ⁾	108	120
medium⁽¹⁰⁻¹⁴⁾	--	--
large⁽¹⁵⁻¹⁹⁾	--	--
xlarge⁽²⁰⁺⁾	--	--

1996 Mini Gathering
7ᴸ x 4.5ᵂ x 2.5ᴴ
3 different Minis offered, each an exact ratio replica of basket given to the top Sponsoring winners, starting with second level

	AVG	HIGH
B	--	--

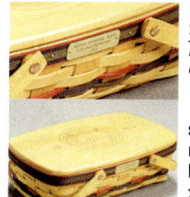

1997 Gathering
Small/Med/Lg/XLg
Red/blue/green accents, engraved lid included

	AVG	HIGH
small⁽⁵⁻⁹ ʳᵉᶜʳᵘⁱᵗˢ⁾	--	--
medium⁽¹⁰⁻¹⁴⁾	--	--
large⁽¹⁵⁻¹⁹⁾	--	--
xlarge⁽²⁰⁺⁾	--	--
mini	--	--

Incentive & Award

Incentive & Award Baskets

BEE: National Sponsoring Awards (con't)

Large

1998 Gathering
Small/Med/Lg/XLg
Red/blue/gold accents, engraved lid included

	AVG	HIGH
small(6-10 recruits)	--	80
medium(11-15)		
large(16-20)	--	117
xlarge(21+)	--	--

1998 Mini Gathering
7^L x 4.5^W x 2.5^H
3 different Minis offered, each an exact ratio replica of basket given to the top Sponsoring winners, starting with second level

	AVG	HIGH
B	248	475

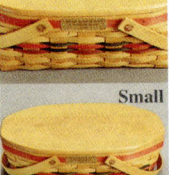
Small

1999 Octagonal
Small/Med/Lg/XLg
Green/rose/blue/purple accents, engraved lid included

	AVG	HIGH
small(6-10 recruits)	80	160
medium(11-15)	--	--
large(16-20)	--	300
xlarge(21+)	--	--

1999 Mini Octagonal
7^L x 4.5^W x 2.5^H
3 different Minis offered, each an exact ratio replica of basket given to the top Sponsoring winners, starting with second level

	Org$	AVG	HIGH
B		--	1500

XLarge

2000 Octagonal
Small/Med/Lg/XLg
Dark blue accents, engraved lid included

	AVG	HIGH
small(6-10 recruits)	--	--
medium(11-15)		
large(16-20)		
xlarge(21+)	--	--
mini	1085	1600

2001 Octagonal
Small/Med/Lg/XLg
Sage/brown/blue accents, engraved lid included

	AVG	HIGH
small(6-8 recruits)	--	--
medium(9-12)	--	--
large(13-16)	--	--
xlarge(17-21)	--	--
mini	--	394

2002 Octagonal
Small/Med/Lg/XLg
Warm Brown/Blue/Red accents, engraved lid included

	AVG	HIGH
small(6-8 recruits)	--	80
medium(9-12)	--	--
large(13-16)	--	--
xlarge(17-21)	--	--
mini	--	--

L1: 8.25RD
L2: 9.5RD

2003-04 Ware
6 sizes
Natural with brown & leather accents, engraved lid included

	AVG	HIGH
level1(7-8 recruits)	--	--
level2(9-10)	--	--
level3(11-15)	--	--
level4(16-20)	--	--
level5(21-24)	--	--
level6(25+)	--	--

2005-P Ware
6 sizes
Natural with black & leather accents, engraved lid included

	AVG	HIGH
level1(7-8 recruits)	--	325
level2(9-10)	--	--
level3(11-15)	--	--
level4(16-20)	--	--
level5(21-24)	--	--
level6(25+)	--	--

BEE: National Sales Awards (year)

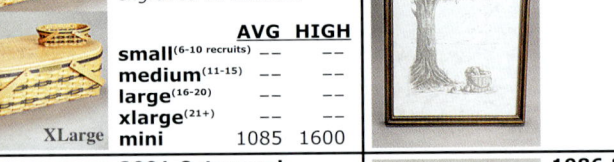

1983 Punched Tin Plaque
8^W x 10^H
QTY: 35
Given to Top Sellers

	AVG	HIGH
	400	500

1984 High Sales
11^W x 13^H
Given to Top Sellers

	AVG	HIGH
	275	350

1986 Red

1986 & 1988 Coverlet
16^L x 16^W x 8^H
1986 version is Red and 1988 is Navy blue. Given to Top Sellers.

	AVG	HIGH
B	1000	1200

1989 Flag
10.75^L x 5.75^W x 7.5^H
QTY: 20
Given to top sellers

	AVG	HIGH
B	1767	3083

1993 Sales Fruit
6.5RD | 8RD | 13RD
Red accents, three sales levels offered, engraved lid included

	AVG	HIGH
small	73	190
medium	--	135
large	--	--

1994 Sales Measuring
5RD | 7RD | 9RD | 11RD
Pink/purple accents, four sales levels offered, engraved lid included

	AVG	HIGH
5"	--	150
7"	168	185
9"	--	--
11"	--	400

1994 Mini Measuring
5.25RD x 4.25^H
Pink/purple accents, given to top Sales winners, starting with second level

	AVG	HIGH
B	--	--

1995 Sales Measuring
5RD | 7RD | 9RD | 11RD
Purple/green accents, four sales levels offered, engraved lid included

	AVG	HIGH
5"	60	125
7"	150	175
9"	--	280
11"	--	--

1995 Mini Measuring
5.25RD x 4.25^H
Purple/green accents, given to top Sales winners, starting with second level

	AVG	HIGH
B	--	--

1996 Sales Measuring
5RD | 7RD | 9RD | 11RD
Blue/gold/red accents, four sales levels offered, engraved lid included

	AVG	HIGH
5"	188	200
7"	--	82
9"	--	76
11"	--	300

1996 Mini Measuring
5.25RD x 4.25^H
Blue/gold/red accents, given to top Sales winners, starting with second level

	AVG	HIGH
B	--	--

1997 Sales Measuring
5RD | 7RD | 9RD | 11RD
Green/red/blue accents, four sales levels offered, engraved lid included

	AVG	HIGH
5"	--	51
7"	--	--
9"	--	100
11"	--	--
mini	--	--

1998 Sales Measuring
5RD | 7RD | 9RD | 11RD | 13RD
Green/yellow/blue/red accents, engraved lid included

	AVG	HIGH
5"	50	83
7"	--	48
9"	--	100
11"	--	90
13"	--	--
mini	--	--

1999 6-side Measuring
5RD | 7RD | 9RD | 11RD
Green/rose/blue/purple accents, engraved lid included

	AVG	HIGH
level 1	--	70
level 2	--	--
level 3	--	75
level 4	--	--
mini	--	--

2000 6-side Measuring
5RD | 7RD | 9RD | 11RD
Dark blue accents, engraved lid included

	AVG	HIGH
level 1	--	--
level 2	--	75
level 3	--	--
level 4	--	--
mini	--	--

Inventory & Award

Incentive & Award Baskets

BEE: National Sales Awards (con't)

2001 6-side Measuring
Sage/brown/blue accents, engraved lid included

	AVG	HIGH
level 1	--	75
level 2	--	--
level 3	--	--
level 4	--	--
level 5	--	--
level 6	--	--

7in

1997 Branch Bouquet
10.5^L x 6^W x 4^H
First year for Branch Advisor to sponsor own award. Only Branch Award without red accents

	AVG	HIGH
B	29	60

2001 Mini Measuring
5.5^L x 5^H
Different Minis offered, each an exact ratio replica of basket given to the top Sales winners, starting with second level

	Org$	AVG	HIGH
B		591	788

1998 Branch Excellence & Sponsoring Charm
6.5^L x 6.5^W x 3^H
Basket given for 50+ shows, charm for 1+ recruit

	AVG	HIGH
B	31	50
charm	--	73

2002 Sales Ware
Warm Brown with red/blue accents, star tacks, lid included

	AVG	HIGH
level 1	--	--
level 2	222	314
level 3	--	--
level 4	--	--
level 5	--	--
level 6	--	--
mini	--	--

1999 Branch Excellence
sales: 9.5^L x 6^W x 6^H
sponsor: 7^L x 5^W x 3.5^H
Sales given for 50+ shows or $12k sales, Sponsor for 2+ recruits

	AVG	HIGH
sales	37	70
sponsor	30	47

Level 4: 16RD
mini

2003-04 Sales Ware
Warm Brown with brown & brown leather accents, lid included

	AVG	HIGH
level 1	--	--
level 2	222	314
level 3	--	--
level 4	--	--
level 5	--	--
level 6	--	--
mini	--	--

2000 Branch
sales: 7.75^L x 3.75^W x 4.5^H
sponsor: 5.75^L x 3.75^W x 3^H
Sales given for 50+ shows or $12k sales, Sponsor for 2+ recruits

	AVG	HIGH
sales	36	45
sponsor	41	53

Level2: 9.5RD

2005-P Sales Ware
Warm Brown with black & black leather accents, lid included

	AVG	HIGH
level 1	--	--
level 2	--	--
level 3	--	--
level 4	--	--
level 5	--	--
level 6	--	--
mini	--	--

2001 Branch
sales: 8^L x 7.75^W x 3.5^H
sponsor: 7^L x 6.75^W x 3^H
Sales given for $12k sales, Sponsor for 2+ recruits

	AVG	HIGH
sales	31	40
sponsor	33	40

BEE: Branch Sponsored Awards

Branch Sponsored Awards are given by Branch Advisors within their own branch. Most baskets will feature the color RED, which the company uses to represent the Branch level, and often are a smaller version of the similar basket given at the Regional, Director, or National Sales Leader level. Accessories are not included.

2002 Branch
sales: 5.75^L x 5.25^W x 6.25^H
sponsor: 5.25^L x 5.25^W x 4.5^H
Sales given for $12k sales, Sponsor for 2+ recruits

	AVG	HIGH
sales	48	51
sponsor	47	59

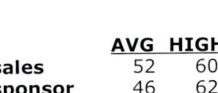

2003 Branch
sales: 7.5^L x 4.75^W x 2.5^H
sponsor: 4.75^L 3.75^L 2.25^H
Sales given for $12k sales, Sponsor for 2+ recruits

	AVG	HIGH
sales	52	60
sponsor	46	62

1992 Small Oval
8.5^L x 5^W x 3.5^H
Green, blue and red shoestring weave

	AVG	HIGH
B	41	76

2004 Branch
5.75RD x 4.25^H
Given for $12k+ sales, no sponsoring level given

	AVG	HIGH
B	77	138

1993 Potpourri
5^L x 5^W x 2.5^H
Blue weave and trim

	AVG	HIGH
B	64	100

2005 Branch Sales
7.5^L x 5.75^W x 2.75^H
Oval basket, stained with red accents. Given for $15k+ sales.

	AVG	HIGH
B	--	41

1994 Small Purse
9.5^L x 6^W x 6^H
Blue trim and shoestring accents, two braided ears

	AVG	HIGH
B	40	50

2005 Branch Top Achiever
7.75^L x 6.25^W x 2.75^H
Oval basket, whitewash or Stained with red accents. Given to Top Achievers within the Branch.

	AVG	HIGH
B	34	53

1995 Medium Berry
7.5^L x 7.5^W x 3.5^H
Blue trim and accents

	AVG	HIGH
B	39	71

BEE: Region Sponsored Awards

Region Sponsored Awards were given by Regional Advisors within their own Region. Most baskets will feature the color BLUE, which the company uses to represent the Regional level, and often are a medium-size version of the other baskets given at the Branch or Director level. Accessories were not included.

1996 Darning
10RD x 4^H
All Branch, Region and Director baskets this year were round and featured red accents

	AVG	HIGH
B	190	210

1991 Region
10^L x 6^W x 4^H
Blue accents, given for high sales

	AVG	HIGH
B	100	225

1997 Rose Garden
12^L x 7^W x 4.5^H
All Branch, Region and Director baskets this year were oval, stationary handle and and featured green accents

	AVG	HIGH
B	69	90

Incentive & Award
86

Incentive & Award Baskets

BEE: Region Sponsored Awards (con't)

1998 Region Excellence
sales: 8.5^L x 8.5^W x 5^H
sponsor: 4.25^L x 4.25^W x 3^H
Blue trim, Green/red/blue accents. Sales given Top Performers, Sponsor for 4+ recruits

	AVG	HIGH
sales	150	170
sponsor	--	127

2004 Region
7.25RD x 5.25^H
Stained or Whitewash, dark blue upsplints

	Org$	AVG	HIGH
B		77	103

1999 Region Excellence
15^L x 9.5^W x 5.5^H
Blue trim, Green/red/blue accents. Stained version given for Top Sales, Natural to Top Sponsors

	AVG	HIGH
sales	40	85
sponsor	49	59

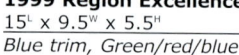

BEE: Director Sponsored Awards

Director Sponsored Awards were given by Directors within their own directorship. Most baskets will feature the color GREEN, which the company used to represent the Director level, and often are a larger version of the similar basket given at the Branch and Regional level. Accessories were not included.

2000 Region
9.25^L x 5^W x 6.5^H
Blue trim, Green/red/blue accents. Stained version given for Top Sales, Natural to Top Sponsors

	AVG	HIGH
sales	37	41
sponsor	30	44

1988 Top Performer
10.5^L x 9^W x 8^H
Red weave and trim in both Classic and Natural

	AVG	HIGH
B	160	250

2001 Region
10^L x 9.25^W x 4^H
Blue trim, Green/red/blue accents, either stained or natural

	AVG	HIGH
B	31	51

1989 Top Performer
10.5^L x 9^W x 8^H
Dark blue weave and trim in both Classic and Natural

	AVG	HIGH
B	--	--

2002 Region
6.5^L x 6.5^W x 6.5^H
Blue trim and accents, either stained or whitewashed

	AVG	HIGH
B	54	100

1990 Top Performer
10.5^L x 9^W x 8^H
Red weave and trim in both Classic and Natural

	AVG	HIGH
B	--	153

2003 Region
10^L x 6^W x 4^H
Double trim with blue accents, either stained or natural

	Org$	AVG	HIGH
B		56	90

1991 Top Performer
10.5^L x 9^W x 8^H
Purple weave and trim in both Classic and Natural

	AVG	HIGH
B	300	334

Incentive & Award

1991 Pom Pom Peggy
12^H
Could be earned for 50+ shows. The basket charm attached at her neck could be earned with 1 recruit.

	AVG	HIGH
	62	90

1994 Top Performer
10.5^L x 9^W x 8^H
Teal trim and weave, stained only, given to Top 10 in each Directorship

	AVG	HIGH
B	103	128

1992 Treasure Chest
5.75^L x 3.75^W x 3^H
Earned with 50+ shows

	AVG	HIGH
B	80	150

Reach for the Stars Collection

1995 Star Bound
4.75^L x 3.75^W x 2.25^H
Blue weave and trim, earned with 4+ recruits

	AVG	HIGH
B	92	175

1992 Top Performer
10.5^L x 9^W x 8^H
Green, blue and red weave, stained only. Given to Top 10 in each Directorship

	AVG	HIGH
B	154	255

1995 Shining Star
5.75^L x 3.75^W x 3^H
Blue weave and trim, earned with 50+ shows

	AVG	HIGH
B	30	76

1993 Paint The Town
5.75^L x 3.75^W x 3^H
Green, blue and red weave, earned at 50+ shows

	AVG	HIGH
B	55	80

1995 Star Team
7^L x 5^W x 3.5^H
Blue weave and trim, given to Branch Advisors when 30% of their Branch earned the Shining Star basket.

	AVG	HIGH
B	95	197

1993 Top Performer
10.5^L x 9^W x 8^H
Green, blue and red weave, stained only. Given to Top 10 in each Directorship.

	AVG	HIGH
B	63	76

1995 High Achiever
12RD x 5.75^H
Blue weave and trim, given to Top 10 in each Directorship

	AVG	HIGH
B	125	200

1994 Over the Rainbow
4.5RD | 5.5RD | 6.5RD
Gold/green/blue/red accents. Gold Nugget $^{(4+ recruits)}$, Pot of Gold $^{(50+ shows)}$, Gold Rush $^{($40k sales)}$

	AVG	HIGH
gold nugget	178	235
pot of gold	40	55
gold rush	178	270

(continued next page)

Incentive & Award

Incentive & Award Baskets

BEE: Director Sponsored Awards (con't)
Our Business is Show Business

1996 Associate Producer
5.5RD x 2.5^H
Red weave and trim, earned with 4+ recruits

	AVG	HIGH
B	128	130

1996 Show Star
7RD x 3^H
Red weave and trim, earned with 50+ shows

	AVG	HIGH
B	34	52

1996 Best Supporting Role
8.5RD x 4^H
Red weave and trim, given to Branch Advisors when 30% of their Branch earned the 50+ show basket

	AVG	HIGH
B	105	150

1996 High Achiever
12RD x 5.75^H
Red weave and trim, given to Top 10 in each Directorship

	AVG	HIGH
B	177	210

Everything's Coming Up Roses

1997 Rose Bud
8^L x 4^W x 2^H
Green weave and trim, earned with 4+ recruits

	AVG	HIGH
B	72	150

1997 Rose Petal
8.5^L x 5^W x 3.5^H
Green weave and trim, earned with 50+ shows

	AVG	HIGH
B	45	85

1997 Mini Rose Bud Flower Pots
2.5RD x 2.5^H
Set of 2, given to Branch Advisors when 30% of their Branch earned the 50+ show basket

	AVG	HIGH
pots²	62	155

1997 American Beauty
13.5^L x 8.25^W x 5.25^H
Green weave and trim, given to Top 10 in each Directorship

	AVG	HIGH
B	85	155

1998 Director Excellence
12^L x 12^W x 4^H
Green trim with green/red/blue accents in either Classic (sales) or Natural (sponsor)

	AVG	HIGH
sales	90	125
sponsor	50	65

1998 Team Excellence
8.25^L x 8.25^W x 3.5^H
Green trim with green/red/blue accents in either Classic or Natural

	AVG	HIGH
B	40	55

1999 Director Excellence
16^L x 11^W x 9^H
Green trim with green/red/blue accents in either Classic (sales) or Natural (sponsor)

	AVG	HIGH
sales	71	75
sponsor	68	110

1999 Team Excellence
15^L x 10^W x 7.5^H
Green trim with green/red/blue accents in either Classic or Natural

	AVG	HIGH
B	87	127

2000 Director
14.5ᴸ x 5.5ᵂ x 9.5ᴴ
Classic or *Natural*,
green trim with green/
red/blue accents

	AVG	HIGH
B	68	100

2004 Director
team: 9.25ᴿᴰ x 7.25ᴴ
leader: 11.25ᴿᴰ x 9ᴴ
Both available either
Warm Brown or *White-
wash*, pale green
accents

	AVG	HIGH
team	95	132
leadership	--	--

BEE: National Sales Leader Awards

2000 Team Excellence
9.5ᴸ x 4.5ᵂ x 5ᴴ
Classic or *Natural*,
green trim with green/
red/blue accents

	AVG	HIGH
B	34	54

In 2004, the leadership was reorganized and the Regional and Director levels were combined to create National Sales Leaders (NSL). These sponsored Awards are given within their group. Most baskets will feature the color PURPLE, which the company used to represent the NSL level. Accessories were not included.

2001 Director
team: 12ᴸ x 11ᵂ x 4.5ᴴ
leader: 14ᴸ 12.75ᵂ 5ᴴ
Both available either
Classic or *Natural*

	AVG	HIGH
team	53	69
leadership	43	90

2005 NSL Award
10.75ᴸ x 9.75ᵂ x 4.5ᴴ
Available either *Warm Brown* or *Whitewash*
with purple trim and accents

	AVG	HIGH
B	78	92

Consultant Advancement Baskets

2002 Director
team: 6.5ᴸ x 6.5ᵂ x 8.5ᴴ
leader: 8ᴸ x7.5ᵂ x 10.5ᴴ
Both available either
Classic or *Whitewash*

	AVG	HIGH
team	68	129
leadership	80	125

MBA Basket ⁽⁸⁸⁻⁰³⁾
1000-FO
9.5ᴸ x 5ᵂ x 9.5ᴴ
No color accents, no tag

	AVG	HIGH
B	55	85

2003 Director
15ᴸ x 9.5ᵂ x 5.5ᴴ
Available both *Warm
Brown* and *Whitewash*

	AVG	HIGH
B	140	150

MBA Basket ⁽⁰³⁻⁰⁴⁾
12.5ᴸ x 6.75ᴴ x 8.5ᴴ
Three colors represent
the succession of management: Red (Branch),
Blue (Region), Green
(Director)

	Org$	AVG	HIGH
B	99	214	272

2003 Team
12ᴸ x 8ᵂ x 4.25ᴴ
Available both *Warm
Brown* and *Whitewash*

	AVG	HIGH
B	85	152

Branch Advisor ⁽⁸⁸⁻⁰²⁾
15.75ᴸ x 6.5ᵂ x 11ᴴ
Red trim and weave, no tag

	AVG	HIGH
B	100	170

Incentive & Award

Incentive & Award Baskets

Consultant Advancement Baskets (con't)

Branch Advisor(02-04)
17.75^L x 10.5^W x 12^H
Red/blue shoestring weave. Qty: unknown

	AVG	HIGH
B	128	253

Branch Leader(04-P)
17.75^L x 10.5^W x 12^H
Same as one shown, except in <u>Warm Brown</u> stain, not Classic

	AVG	HIGH
B	--	300

Regional Advisor(88-02)
15.75^L x 6.5^W x 11^H
Blue trim and weave, no tag

	AVG	HIGH
B	250	279

Regional Advisor(02-04)
17.75^L x 10.5^W x 12^H
Same as one shown, except with <u>BLUE</u> accents

	AVG	HIGH
B	290	310

Director Basket(88-02)
15.75^L x 6.5^W x 11^H
Green trim and weave, no tag

	AVG	HIGH
B	107	146

Director Basket(02-04)
17.75^L x 10.5^W x 12^H
Same as one shown, except with <u>GREEN</u> accents

	AVG	HIGH
B	488	636

National Sales Leader(04-P)
17.75^L x 10.5^W x 12^H
Purple accent weave

	AVG	HIGH
B	252	285

Trip Awards

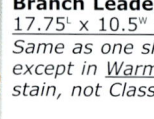

1992 Fantasy in Paradise
5^L x 5^W x 2.5^H
Red accents, very small number given to Top Achievers during an incentive trip to Bahamas

	AVG	HIGH
B	--	--

1993 Fiesta del Sol
5^L x 5^W x 2.5^H
QTY: 140
Teal accents, given to Top Achievers during an incentive trip to Cancun

	AVG	HIGH
B	--	--

1994 Hawaiian Holiday
unknown
QTY: 331
Features 3 colors, given to Top Achievers during a Hawaiian incentive trip.

	AVG	HIGH
B	--	--

1995 Ports of Paradise
5.5^RD x 3.75^H
QTY: 20
Blue trim, blue/yellow/red shoestring, given to Top Achievers during a Caribbean Cruise incentive trip

	AVG	HIGH
B	--	--

1995 Ports of Paradise Captain's Clock
Cherry case, also given during the 1994 Caribben Cruise, but unconfirmed in what capacity

	AVG	HIGH
B	--	--

Incentive & Award

1996 Sunsational Celebration
6.5^L x 6.5^W x 3^H

QTY: 24 Burgundy/red accents, this trip was to the Bahamas, but the top 12 were treated to a trip to NY City to launch the festivities

	AVG	HIGH
B	--	--

2003 Hawaii Medium Boardwalk
12.5^L x 6.75^W x 8.5^H

Whitewash, included exclusive drawstring liner and protector

	AVG	HIGH
B	266	335

1997 Magical Journey
4RD x 4.25^H

Same form as the Pencil basket, given to Top Achievers during a trip and company celebration at Disney

	AVG	HIGH
B	--	--

2003 Leadership Excellence
Sm: 10^L x 7.5^W x 4.25^H
Lg:13.75^L 10.75^W 5.75^H

QTY: <250 each. Given to Advisors attending an incentive trip to Arizona. Protector/liners included.

	AVG	HIGH
small$^{P/L}$	154	200
large$^{P/L}$	313	585

Misc Recruit/Sponsor Awards

2001 Cancun Large Boardwalk
17.75^L x 10.5^W x 12^H

Whitewash featuring brass tacks and symmetrical weave pattern. Included protector and Cancun tote/liner.

	AVG	HIGH
B	180	205

1988 Recruit Building Branches
6.5RD | 8RD | 13RD

QTY: 65 total. Fruit baskets given for three different award levels

	AVG	HIGH
small	--	140
medium	--	165
large	--	--

2001 Cancun Barbeque Buddy
12.5^L x 6.25^W x 7^H

Orange, yellow, red accents, also given to Top Achievers during the 2001 incentive trip to Cancun

	AVG	HIGH
B	154	204

1988,89 Recruit Share the Tradition
13000-BBRS
5^L x 5^W x 2.5^H
No tag on basket

	AVG	HIGH
B	63	83

2002 Pineapple
6.5RD x 9^H

Given to Top Achievers during the an incentive trip to Hawaii. No accessories.

	AVG	HIGH
B	178	193

1988,89 Sponsor Share the Tradition
1500-BBRS
8.5^L x 8.5^W x 5^H
No tag on basket

	AVG	HIGH
B	70	104

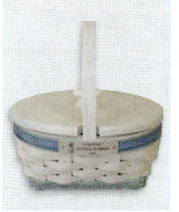

2002 Aloha Hawaii
6.25^L x 5.25^W x 3^H

Whitewashed. Pastel blue/pastel green trim, pastel green shoestring at bottom.

	AVG	HIGH
B	--	--

1990 Recruit Together We're Growing
45000-ABRST
5.75^L x 3.75^W x 3^H

Tag reads "Together – 1990 Recruit"

	AVG	HIGH
B	169	180

Incentive & Award

Incentive & Award Baskets

Misc Recruit/Sponsor Awards (con't)

1990 Sponsor
Together We're Growing
1100-ABRST
9^L x 5^W x 5^H
Tag reads: "Together – 1990 Sponsor"

	AVG	HIGH
	175	200

1993 Sponsor
All-Star Recruiting
13323
8.5^L x 5^W x 3.5^H
Red/blue weave, blue trim. Tag denotes award.

	AVG	HIGH
sponsor	130	175

1990-91 Recruit & Superstar Sponsor
Longaberger Rising Star
1700-DST
12^L x 12.25^W x 16.25^H
Tag denotes award

	AVG	HIGH
recruit	185	195
superstar	155	200

1996 Recruit & Sponsor
Opportunity Reigns
34^H
Incentive for both Recruits & their Sponsors from Jan – March 1996, in the exclusive Father's Day fabric

	AVG	HIGH
	63	75

1990-91 Sponsor
Longaberger Rising Star
1600-DST
16.5^L x 16.5^W x 21.5^H
Tag denotes award

	AVG	HIGH
sponsor	185	230

1996 Recruit & Sponsor
Pegged for Success
Recruit: 5^L x 5^W x 4.5^H
Sponsor: 6.5^L x 6.5^W x 8^H
Burgundy/Dresden Blue. Accessories could be earned with additional Recruits.

	AVG	HIGH
recruit	46	90
sponsor	193	225
C$^{P/L}$	--	--

1992 Recruit & Superstar – *Flying High with Longaberger*
10154
5RD x 4.5^H
Dresden blue shoestring weave, tag denotes award

	AVG	HIGH
recruit	119	125
superstar	118	175

1992 Sponsor – *Flying High with Longaberger*
10162
7RD x 6.5^H
Dresden blue shoestring weave, tag denotes award

	AVG	HIGH
sponsor	125	175

1997 Recruit & Sponsor
Watch Your Business Bloom
5RD x 4.5^H
Red/Navy accents. Given to both Recruit & Sponsor, tag is specific to award.

	AVG	HIGH
	90	125

1997 Snowflake Sponsor
10^L x 9.25^W x 6.5^H
Red/green accents. Only Sponsor basket given, nothing for Recruit. Accessories sold separately.

	AVG	HIGH
	123	250

1993 Recruit & Superstar – *All-Star*
16101
8^L x 4^W x 2^H
Red/blue weave, blue trim. Tag denotes award.

	AVG	HIGH
recruit	138	200
superstar	113	160

1998 Flag Recruit & Sponsor
7^L x 3.5^W x 4.75^H
Given to both Recruit and Sponsor, tag is specific to award

	AVG	HIGH
recruit	192	200
sponsor	73	147

1999 Make Your Dreams Come True
5RD x 4.5^H

Given to both Recruit and Sponsor. A tie-on was available at higher incentive level.

	AVG	HIGH
recruit	49	70
TO	--	--

1985 Grouping D
Oval bowl, Pie plate with lattice cover, Hurricane Lamp with globe

	AVG	HIGH
oval bowl	108	125
pie plate	150	175
lamp	82	175

2002 Sponsor Red, White & You
5.5^L x 6^W x 2.25^H

Basket given to Sponsor for 1 Recruit, Ramekin (with candle) for 2+ recruits. No item for actual Recruit. Ramekin only in ivory.

	AVG	HIGH
basket	159	174
ramekin	218	255

1985 Grouping E
14RD x 3^H

Pasta bowl, Meat platter (not shown, measuring 16^L x 11^W)

	AVG	HIGH
pasta bowl	99	165
platter	70	78

Misc Sales Awards
Meadow Blossoms Pottery

"Longaberger Pottery by Hartstone" logo | Peach, navy, green floral design

1986 December Recognition
4700-AO

14.5^L x 7.5^W x 3.75^H

Given for sales of $500 or more in Dec 1986. Some were signed by Dave.

	AVG	HIGH
B	145	175

1985 Grouping A
11RD | 3.75^H | 2.5^H

4 dinner plates, 4 mugs, 4 napkin rings

	AVG	HIGH
dinner plate	30	35
mug	25	30
napkin ring	20	55

1986 Advisor Recognition
2300-

14^L x 9^W x 4.5^H

Dark blue trim and weave. Given to all Advisors during an 1986 Meeting.

	AVG	HIGH
B	164	178

1985 Grouping B
4 salad plates, 1 sugar & creamer, 1 pitcher, 1 honey pot

	AVG	HIGH
salad plate	--	20
sugar bowl	50	75
creamer	33	45
pitcher	75	125
honey pot	150	175

1987 10th Anniversary
500-A

15^L x 10^W x 7.5^H

Blue shoestring weave

	AVG	HIGH
B	173	180

1985 Grouping C
Soup Tureen, 1 soup bowl, 1 buffet tray

	AVG	HIGH
soup tureen	108	125
soup bowl	40	45
buffet tray	35	35

1987 10th Anniversary Plate & Candleabra
QTY: 660

Given for three $1000 sales months, stand for photo only

	AVG	HIGH
plate	76	108
candelabra	--	--

Incentive & Award

Incentive & Award Baskets

Misc Sales Awards (con't)

1987, 88 Herb May Incentive
4500-
11.5^L x 5^W x 3^H
No color, no tag.

	AVG	HIGH
B	80	80

1994-P Spirit of Longaberger
9^L x 6^W x 6.75^H
Very limited award, only one given at each Bee session, each year, totaling three a year.

	AVG	HIGH
B	--	300

1988 Garden May Incentive
4700-
15^L x 8^W x 2.25^H
No color, no tag

	AVG	HIGH
B	80	80
w/Herb	142	175

1996-97 Growing Strong Together
9.5^L x 5^W x 9.5^H
QTY: 50   Yellow/green trim, green weave. Given to Advisors who help facilitate Branch Advisor training

	AVG	HIGH
B	112	128

1991 Planter Sleeve High Road to Success
31.5RD x 18^H
QTY: 190

	AVG	HIGH
B	605	652

1997 $500 Million
10^L x 6^W x 4^H
QTY: 1225
Given to all Advisors at JAM to celebrate achieving $500 Million in Sales in Nov 1996

	AVG	HIGH
B	175	190

1992-98 Success Start Pencil, Paper, Pen
pencil: 4RD x 4.25^H
paper: 7.5^L 5.5^W 2^{FH} 3.5^{BH}
Each item earned at different qualification levels as new Consultant

	AVG	HIGH
pencil	36	40
paper	38	70
set:	123	138

1997 Christmas Votive
34932
3RD x 2.5^H
Given to all consultants who hosted a Christmas Open House by 9/12/97

	AVG	HIGH
	--	--

1993 Holiday Basket of Thanks
7^L x 5^H x 3.5^H
Red and green trim, given for meeting December incentives

	AVG	HIGH
B	35	40

1998-02 Growing Strong Together
9.5^L x 5^W x 9.5^H
Red trim and weave, given to Advisors who help facilitate Branch Advisor training

	AVG	HIGH
B	242	272

1993-96 Management Excellence
19.5RD x 10^H
All Advisors given the chance to earn this basket based on specific criteria. Each year featured a different color.
1995: Red

	AVG	HIGH
B	--	500

1998 25th Anniversary Basket Sleeve
31.5RD x 18^H
QTY: 26
Given as a surprise thank you to Sales Directors at Bee 1998

	AVG	HIGH
B	914	1304

1998 JAM Recognition
15^L x 10^W x 7.5^H
QTY: 35
Medium Market with navy/red trim and weave, took the place of the Management Excellence Award

	AVG	HIGH
B	96	100

2000 Horizon of Hope Frame & Flower Pot
7^L x 5^H | 3.5^H
Frame given at $700-$1599 sales, Flower Pot and pebbles given when selling 30+ HOH baskets

	AVG	HIGH
frame	--	--
flower pot	91	130

1999 Thanks-A-Million
5.5^L x 4^W x 4^H
Given to all Advisors who attended JAM 99, it is a retagged 97 Horizon of Hope Basket

	AVG	HIGH
B	53	110

2000-P Success Start
Address:
  8.25^L x 6.25^W x 3.75^H
Business Card: 17361
  4.75^L x 3.75^W x 2.25^H
Diskette: 16276
  6^L x 6^W x 4.25^{FH} x 5.25^{BH}
Catalog Caddy
  12^L x 6^W x 4.5^{FH} x 11.5^{BH}

1999-00 Success Start
Pencil: 15000
  4RD x 4.25^H
Note Paper: 16000
  7.5^L x 5.5^W x 2^{FH} x 3.5^{BH}
Business Card: 17361
  4.75^L x 3.75^W x 2.25^H
Mini Waste: 11258
  7.5^L x 7.5^W x 10^H
Tapered Tray: 19062
  12^L x 14.5^W x 3^{FH} x 5.5^{BH}

	AVG	HIGH
pencil	23	30
note paper	30	38
business card	45	75
mini waste	68	85
tapered tray	39	57

Each tag says Success Start, lids included

	AVG	HIGH
address	75	100
business card	45	75
diskette	54	57
catalog caddy	122	210

2000 JAM Recognition
5.5RD x 3.75^H
Given to all Advisors attending JAM 2000, liner, protector and tie-on included

	AVG	HIGH
B	51	80

2001 Discover the Gift
10RD x 8^H
Given as a surprise to Directors to celebrate the 20th Bee in 2001

	AVG	HIGH
B	--	466

2000 Associate Homestead Tour
10RD x 6.25^H
Dresden blue shoestring, accessories sold separately

	AVG	HIGH
B	63	89
C^{P/L}	89	125
FS^{C/Ld}	126	175

2001 Bee Attendance
9^L x 5.5^W x 6.5^H
Red/green trim, given to Branch Advisors with the highest Bee attendance

	AVG	HIGH
B	40	46

2001 Growing Great People
11.5^L x 9.25^W x 10.5^H
Sage/burgundy accents, give to Regionals with the most Branch breakoffs. Liner, protector and handle grip included

	AVG	HIGH
B	--	--

Incentive & Award

Incentive & Award Baskets

Misc Sales Awards (con't)

2002 JAM Facilitator
Given to Associates who presented at Jam 2002, accessories included

	AVG	HIGH
B	--	318

2003 Little Membership
10577
7.5^L x 4^W x 3.5^H
Collectors Club green and blue accents, incentive for Consultants to sign 3 new Club Members

	AVG	HIGH
B	116	175

2002 JAM Recognition
11^L x 9.75^W x 4.75^H
Red/blue shoestring weave, 2 sw/h. Given to all Advisors attending JAM 2002

	AVG	HIGH
B	--	--

2003 Discover the Gift
15RD x 7^H
Given to Directors only, third and final year for this gift

	AVG	HIGH
B	--	510

2002 Branch Mini Bee
5.75^L x 3.75^W x 3^H
Red/blue accents with star tacks. Given to all Branch Advisors who attended Bee 2002

	AVG	HIGH
B	186	199

2004 JAM Recognition
6^L x 5.5^W x 7^H
Red/blue upsplints, given to all Advisors attending JAM 2004

	AVG	HIGH
B	530	540

2002 Little Membership
16187
6^L x 3.5^W x 5.75^H
Collectors Club green and blue accents, given to Consultants who signed 3 new Club Members between Jun-Aug 2002

	AVG	HIGH
B	176	200

2004 JAM Easter
10627^{WB}/10628^W
7RD x 3^H
Warm Brown/Whitewash, Easter prototypes that were available for purchase to Advisors attending JAM 2004 and then through Longaberger Attic. Sold only as set.

	Org$	AVG	HIGH
C$^{P/L}$	45	99	145

2002 Discover the Gift
8.5RD x 10.25^H
Given to Directors only, second year for this gift

	AVG	HIGH
B	438	595

2004 Autumn
4.75^L x 4.75^W x 2^H
QTY: 100
Also known as the **Canadian Referral Basket**. Available only to Consultants through Longaberger Attic. Only sold as a Combo, not separately.

	Org$	AVG	HIGH
B		95	150
C$^{P/L}$	39	131	200

2002 Leading Strong Together
6.5^L x 6.5^W x 8^H
This is a Heartland Basket, made in 2002 specifically for this award. Replaced the Growing Strong Together basket.

	AVG	HIGH
B	--	--

2004 Leadership Vase
6.75RD x 6^H
Given to all National Sales Leaders during Bee 2004, announcing the new leadership changes.

	AVG	HIGH
B	68	100

Incentive & Award

2004-P Signature Med Shoulder Bag
11^L x 5.5^W x 9^H

Given to all National Sales Leaders during Bee 2004 and 2005. Shown here with the Hostess Small Bag for size comparison.

B	AVG	HIGH
	250	331

2005 Horizon of Hope Tote
23163
7.25^L x 4^W x 9^H

Incentive for Consultants who sold 6+ HOH baskets

B	AVG	HIGH
	18	20

2005 Berry Serving Plate
31114
11RD

Sales incentive for Consultants during May 2005

B	AVG	HIGH
	45	85

2005-P Tour with Me Street Basket
26RD x 17.5^H

Given free to Associates who organize Homestead Tours of 15+ people, features 26 horizontal splints and 20 upsplints

B	Org$	AVG	HIGH
	200	215	375

NATIONWIDE PHOTO WINNER

Audrey Mesaros
Cardington, OH

We love a Collector with pride and a goal! That's what Audrey's entry said to us!

What a fun glimpse into her J.W. Collection, many of which were located at yard sales. Much history here, as is evident in the gorgeous shades of stain. We are so excited for her as she continues her hunt for the perfect Market and Waste to finish this precious collection!

You go, girl!

Incentive & Award

J.W. Collection®

1983 Medium Market
500-AT
15^L x 10^W x 7.5^H
QTY: 6,300
Liner added in 1993

	Org$	AVG	HIGH
B	32.95	910	1257

1989 Banker's Waste
1900-BBST
12.5RD x 13.5^H
QTY: 53,328
Included the first box the company ever offered for a product.

	Org$	AVG	HIGH
B	59.95	155	385

1984 Waste
1800-OT
9.5^L x 9.5^W x 12^H
QTY: 3,544

	Org$	AVG	HIGH
B	34.95	1047	1450

1990 Large Berry
1500-BBSt
8.5^L x 8.5^W x 5^H
QTY: 37,009
Liner added in 1993, Box

	Org$	AVG	HIGH
B	48.95	81	125
C^P	53.90	85	150
FS$^{C/L}$	71.85	115	210

1985 Apple
3200-BT
13RD x 8.5^H
QTY: 10,467
Also referred to as a Large Fruit

	Org$	AVG	HIGH
B	45.95	379	700

1991 Corn
4400-JBST
17RD x 11.5^H
QTY: 48,332
Included box, no liner offered

	Org$	AVG	HIGH
B	89.95	200	273
C^P	103.90	232	365

1986 Two-Pie
4800-BT
12^L x 12^W x 10^H
QTY: 44,363

	Org$	AVG	HIGH
B	34.95	201	425

1992 Cake
100-CBST
12^L x 12^W x 6^H
QTY: 98,557
Included riser and box

	Org$	AVG	HIGH
B	55.95	85	125
C$^{P/L}$	69.95	115	200

1987 Bread & Milk
2100-ABT
16^L x 8^W x 11^H
QTY: 17,818
Liner added in 1993, Magazine protector used from Regular Line

	Org$	AVG	HIGH
B	43.95	300	375
C$^{P/L}$	82.95	348	525

1993 Original Easter
13722
16^L x 9^W x 6^H
QTY: 77,000
Included box

	Org$	AVG	HIGH
B	65.95	93	139
C$^{P/L}$	82.95	120	199

1988 Gathering
2400-ABT
18^L x 11^H x 4.5^H
QTY: 49,495
Liner available added in 1983

	Org$	AVG	HIGH
B	36.95	157	300
C$^{P/L}$		310	450

1994 Umbrella
11215 | BK 72214
10RD x 17.5^H
QTY: 95,000 Included box, no liner offered book sold separately

	Org$	AVG	HIGH
B	74.95	116	195
C^P	79.95	133	240
Bk	24.95	28	39

J.W. Collection

J.W. Originals

Identifying Features

Braided Trim
A wider, heavier material was also often used

Continuous Weave
This technique is evident by a split upsplint

Open-weave bottom
Common among J.W.'s baskets, he also closed the bottoms with filler splints.

Stamp
Made in Dresden, Ohio. It is unknown when or for how long J.W. used this stamp on his baskets.

Tacks vs. Staples
J.W. used both tacks and staples on his baskets

Upside down "V"
Almost all of J.W.'s baskets with stationary handles have this trademark tacking for added strength.

Other features

Color: Sometimes used red, green or blue

Handle: very smooth, hand-carved

Signatures: Since only family members can authenticate these baskets, many have family signatures on the bottom

Weave: very tight with square corners, sometimes used double weaving technique

Cake Baskets
12^L x 12^W x 6^H
These blonde baskets were most likely never stained, and would be considered natural.

	Org$	AVG	HIGH
B		700	1500

Corn
19RD x 14^H
This Corn Basket is much larger than what was once offered in the Regular Line. J.W. also made Corn Baskets with leather handles. The nail in the center of the reinforced bottom is another J.W. trademark.

	Org$	AVG	HIGH
B		775	1200

Gathering
19^L x 12^W x 6^H

	Org$	AVG	HIGH
B		799	1000

Hamper
15^L x 15^W x 21^H
Notice the metal hinges on the back and the glass knob – two unique features.

	Org$	AVG	HIGH
B		800	1400

Laundry
28^L x 16.5^W x 10.75^H
Features cutout handles and metal reinforcements, common for a basket this large.

	Org$	AVG	HIGH
B		900	1300

Market, Medium
16.5^L x 11^W x 8.75^H
If you look closely, you can see this Market had red accents. The inset shows the original price written in pencil on the handle.

	Org$	AVG	HIGH
B		1255	1575

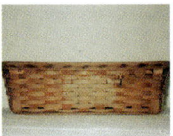
Pool Basket
22^L x 14.5^W x 6.25^H
J.W. made these for the Dresden Pool to hold clothes. Some still have the metal rings used to hold the basket in place.

	Org$	AVG	HIGH
B		500	1100

Other common J.W. Original baskets

	AVG	HIGH
Apple	700	950
Berry Baskets	350	500
Bread & Milk (Auto)	750	1200
Key Baskets	300	400
Market, Large	1255	1575
Picnic, Large	800	1400
Pottery Ware Basket	900	1500
Purse	300	500
Waste, Banker's	700	950
Waste, Square	700	900
Umbrella	900	1000

May Series™

1990 Violet
14000-BVS

5ᴸ x 5ᵂ x 4.5ᴴ

QTY: 49,591. There were 28,791 Combos sold this year.

	Org$	AVG	HIGH
B	24.95	251	360
Cᴾ/ᴸ	34.95	300	400

1996 Sweet Pea
14915 | TO 32883

8.25ᴿᴰ x 7ᴴ

QTY: 156,288

	Org$	AVG	HIGH
B	45.95	50	100
Cᴾ/ᴸ	59.95	70	115
TO	6.95	30	35

1991 Rose
4700-CSS

14.5ᴸ x 7.5ᵂ x 3.75ᴴ

	Org$	AVG	HIGH
B	29.95	208	285
Cᴾ/ᴸ	39.95	230	355

1997 Petunia
12947 | TO 34461

9.5ᴿᴰ x 5ᴴ

	Org$	AVG	HIGH
B	45.95	80	90
Cᴾ/ᴸ	59.95	85	100
Fᶜ/ᴸᵈ	88.90	93	110
TO	6.95	17	26

1992 Pansy
10006

7ᴿᴰ x 4.5ᴴ

	Org$	AVG	HIGH
B	29.95	123	150
Cᴾ/ᴸ	39.95	157	199

1998 Snapdragon
10863 | TO 31658

7.5ᴸ x 9.25ᴴ

Protector included a bundler lid for flowers

	Org$	AVG	HIGH
B	47	50	62
Cᴾ/ᴸ	59	65	100
TO	8	18	21

1993 Lily of the Valley
15717

5.5ᴿᴰ x 3.75ᴴ

3/8" weave. No color. Bottom is flat, not inverted.

	Org$	AVG	HIGH
B	28.95	62	115
Cᴾ/ᴸ	39.95	83	128

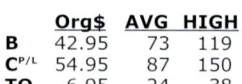

1998 Grandma Bonnie's Favorites Print
84999

20ᵂ x 24ᴴ

Frame not included

	Org$	AVG	HIGH
B	48	48	80

1994 Lilac
16209 | 31291

6.5ᴿᴰ x 6.5ᴴ

	Org$	AVG	HIGH
B	34.95	73	120
Cᴾ/ᴸ	42.95	84	145
TO	5.95	32	44

1999 Daisy
13056 | 36544

6.75ᴿᴰ x 6ᴴ

Note cards available free with Combo.

	Org$	AVG	HIGH
B	39	49	93
Cᴾ/ᴸ	49	70	103
TO	8	26	35

1995 Tulip
14648 | TO 31542

14.25ᴸ x 6.25ᵂ x 3.25ᴴ

	Org$	AVG	HIGH
B	42.95	73	119
Cᴾ/ᴸ	54.95	87	150
TO	6.95	24	38

2000 Morning Glory
18899 | TO 36226

7.5ᴸ x 7.5ᵂ x 4.75ᴴ

Grandma Bonnie's book, "Reflections on the Simple Life" included with every Combo.

	Org$	AVG	HIGH
B	43	66	79
Cᴾ/ᴸ	59	70	103
TO	8	15	20

2001 Peony
10184 | TO 39535
12.75^L x 6.25^W x 2.75^H
QTY: 108,820

	Org$	AVG	HIGH
B	39	65	85
C$^{P/L}$	49	75	99
TO	8	13	18

2002 Geranium
12373 | TO 30012
10.25^L x 6.25^W x 7.5^H
QTY: 181,223

	Org$	AVG	HIGH
B	49	67	88
C$^{P/L}$	59	70	119
TO	8	18	22

BEST SEAT IN THE HOUSE!

Deanna Jones
Greenwood, DE

Deanna's pup, *Panda-Bear Bentley* sure knows how to live high on life! He reminds us that there's nothing quite like snuggling up to a Collectors Club basket – no matter how far you have to climb!

Did we choose him just because he was named after our Guide? While it certainly didn't hurt, everyone knows that no one can resist a Bentley!

May Series

Mother's Day

1987 Large Peg
11000-BPS

6.5^L x 6.5^W x 8^H

No accessories originally offered

	Org$	AVG	HIGH
B	26.95	85	165

1992 Mother's Day
110-CPS

10.5^L x 10.5^W x 4.5^H

	Org$	AVG	HIGH
B	34.95	45	82
C$^{P/L}$	49.95	51	95

1988 Spring
900-APS

11^L x 8^W x 5.5^H

Protector not originally offered

	Org$	AVG	HIGH
B	28.95	74	130
C^L	39.90	92	150

1993 Mother's Day
12904

8.5^L x 8^W x 6^H

3/8" weave. No color.

	Org$	AVG	HIGH
B	44.95	52	69
C$^{P/L}$	57.95	60	75

1989 Mini Chore
700-APS

7^L x 5^W x 3.5^H

Protector not originally offered, note cards included

	Org$	AVG	HIGH
B	21.95	93	100
C^L	29.95	99	125

1994 Mother's Day
16004 | Bk 72087

6.75^L x 9.25^W x 3.75^H

Journal sold separately

	Org$	AVG	HIGH
B	37.95	41	60
C$^{P/L}$	49.95	54	85
Bk	5.95	10	21

1990 Small Oval
33000-JPS

8.5^L x 5^W x 3.5^H

Protector not originally offered

	Org$	AVG	HIGH
B	28.95	51	86
C^L	36.95	60	95

1995 Basket of Love
18805 | TO 31470

8.5RD x 4^H

TO QTY: 90,515

	Org$	AVG	HIGH
B	37.95	45	65
C$^{P/L}$	49.95	54	70
TO	6.95	18	25

1991 Purse
800-EPS

9.5^L x 6^W x 6^H

	Org$	AVG	HIGH
B	34.95	55	80
C$^{P/L}$	54.85	92	128

1996 Vanity
14753 | TO 32328

14.5^L 7.5^W 4.5^{FH} 6.5^{BH}

QTY: 224,278

	Org$	AVG	HIGH
B	44.95	61	89
C$^{P/L}$	59.95	70	99
FS$^{C/Ld}$	82.90	76	110
TO	6.95	14	23

1992 Potpourri
13000-APS

5^L x 5^W x 2.5^H

Hostess only. Sold as the Touch of Pink Potpourri.

	Org$	AVG	HIGH
B	21.95	60	100
C^L	30.90	75	125

1997 Timeless Memory
13030 | TO 33995

11.25^L x 9.25^W x 5.75^H

	Org$	AVG	HIGH
B	49.95	60	79
C$^{P/L}$	69.95	93	99
FS$^{C/Ld}$	92.90	100	140
TO	6.95	12	18

1998 Rings & Things
10383 | TO 34002
7ᴿᴰ x 3ᴴ

QTY: 180,000. Combo included jewelry pouch (not pictured)

	Org$	AVG	HIGH
B	34	40	65
Cᴾ/ᴸ	48	65	95
FSᶜ/ᴸᵈ	54	73	115
TO	8	20	30

2004 Weekend Tote
10701 | TO 28155
16ᴸ x 6.5ᵂ x 11ᴴ
Tote has metal feet

	Org$	AVG	HIGH
B	152	175	179
Cᴾ/ᴸ	218	218	250
TO	10	14	15

1999 Tea for Two
14931 | TO 36251
7.75ᴸ x 5.75ᵂ x 3.25ᴴ
2 fabrics offered

	Org$	AVG	HIGH
B	39	55	70
Cᴾ/ᴸ	49	61	75
FSᶜ/ᴸᵈ	68	82	87
TO	8	13	16

2004 Mom's Essentials
10668
6ᴿᴰ x 4ᴴ
Both leather or wood lid offered

	Org$	AVG	HIGH
B	49	73	83
Cᴾ/ᴸ	69	79	86
FSᶜ/ᴸᵈ	83	83	119

2000 Early Blossoms
19682 | TO 37133
11ᴸ x 7.25ᵂ x 2.75ᴴ
First ever 3-D tie-on. Pottery sold separately (see pg114).

	Org$	AVG	HIGH
B	45	45	59
Cᴾ/ᴸ	56	56	100
TO	8	16	21

2004 Cosmetic Bag
28609130
5ᴿᴰ x 3.5ᴴ
Designed to fit inside the Mom's Essentials. Only offered in this fabric

	Org$	AVG	HIGH
B	18	--	--

2001 Vintage Blossoms
10222 | TO 39527
7.5ᴸ x 5.75ᵂ x 6.5ᴴ
QTY: 118,837. Soap Dish/soap sold separately (see pg117).

	Org$	AVG	HIGH
B	49	58	79
Cᴾ/ᴸ	59	66	99
FSᶜ/ᴸᵈ	81	83	115
TO	8	12	15

2005 Mother's Day Tie-On
23100
1.75ᴸ x 1.25ᴴ
Only a tie-on was offered this year, no basket. Designed to coordinate with the At Home Garden items.

	Org$	AVG	HIGH
B	8	--	--

2002 Mom's Memories
12136 | Frame/TO 30806
9.5ᴸ x 7.75ᵂ x 6ᴴ
QTY: 95,610

	Org$	AVG	HIGH
B	55	59	83
Cᴾ/ᴸ	69	74	83
FSᶜ/ᴸᵈ	93	109	118
TO	10	11	18

2006 Mother's Day Tie-On
23288
1.5ᴸ x 1ᴴ
Only a tie-on was offered this year, no basket. Designed to coordinate with the Dogwood items.

	Org$	AVG	HIGH
B	8	--	--

2003 Special Things
10021 | Pin/TO 20533
8.5ᴸ x 4.5ᵂ x 2ᴴ
Both a fabric and wood lid offered. Pin is also a tie-on.

	Org$	AVG	HIGH
B	39	39	55
Cᴾ/ᴸ	55	57	75
FSᶜ/ᴸᵈ	73	73	79
TO	12	14	17

Mother's Day

Ornaments

1993 Santa Collection
Set: 70661

FatherChristmas	70653
Kriss Kringle	70637
Santa Claus	70629
St. Nick	70645

	Org$	AVG	HIGH
Set	29.95	33	50

1999 Angel Collection
Set: 71072
Sold only as a set of 4:
Faith, Friendship,
Gratitude, Kindness

	Org$	AVG	HIGH
Set	30	25	35

1994 Basket Collection
Set: 72311

Candle	72273
Sleigh	77281
Bell	72290
Holly	72303

	Org$	AVG	HIGH
Set	29.95	28	55

1999 Snow Friends
Set: 72800
Sold only as a set of 2:
Flurry and Snowball

	Org$	AVG	HIGH
Set	15	13	20

1995 Basket Collection
Set: 71803

Cookie	72141
Candy Cane	71838
Mistletoe	71943
Poinsettia	72460

	Org$	AVG	HIGH
Set	29.95	22	45

2000 Roger & Ginger
73369
Sold only as a set of 2:
Roger & Ginger

	Org$	AVG	HIGH
Set	19	20	24

1996 Basket Collection
Set: 71901

Memory	71951
Gingerbread	72028
Yuletide Traditions	72001
Season's Greetings	71935

	Org$	AVG	HIGH
Set	29.95	25	40

2000 Snowflake Set
73431
Sold only as a set of 2

	Org$	AVG	HIGH
Set	19	20	48

1997 Basket Collection
Set: 71927

Bayberry	71897
Jingle Bell	71960
Cranberry	71978
Holiday Cheer	71986

	Org$	AVG	HIGH
Set	29.95	24	40

2000 12 Gifts of Christmas
72931
Sold only as a set of 12

	Org$	AVG	HIGH
Set	59	60	65

1998 Angel Collection
Set: 71757

Peace	71765
Hope	71773
Love	71781
Joy	71790

	Org$	AVG	HIGH
Set	30	23	30

2001 Baby's First Christmas
30444
3^L x 4^W
Hand-painted porcelain.
Two-sided design.

	Org$	AVG	HIGH
	24	--	--

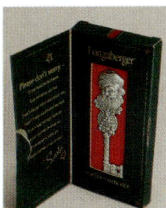

2001 Santa's Key
77721
1.5ᴸ x 4.25ʷ

Pewter. Two-sided design Features Christmas tree and toys.

Org$	AVG	HIGH
16	21	26

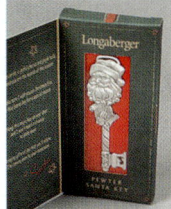

2003 Santa's Key
28085
1ᴸ x 4ʷ

Pewter. Third and final key in the series. Two-sided design features Santa's face with shette music and violin.

Org$	AVG	HIGH
16	16	18

2001 Star Ornaments
77623
Lg: 3ʷ | Sm: 2.25ʷ

Pewter. Only sold as a set of 3

Org$	AVG	HIGH
34	34	37

2005 Bluster Set of 4
Set: 60029

Handpainted ceramic featuring 4 scenes:
  Bluster Sledding
  Bluster Skating
  Bluster Trimming
  Bluster Giving

	Org$	AVG	HIGH
Set	40	--	--

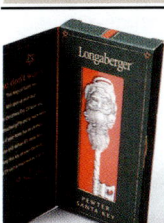

2002 Santa's Key
77382
1ᴸ x 4ʷ

Pewter. Two-sided design features a stocking filled with candy and toys.

Org$	AVG	HIGH
16	21	30

2005 Basket Collection
23170
2ᴸ x 2.5ʷ

Pewter only sold as a set of 4

Org$	AVG	HIGH
39	--	--

2002 Basket Set
77455
2ᴴ

Pewter. Only sold as a set of 4

Org$	AVG	HIGH
34	34	40

2005 Pewter Frame
23172
3ᴸ x 3.25ʷ

Celebrating 25th year of the Christmas Baskets Collection

Org$	AVG	HIGH
15	--	--

2002 Patchwork Frame
77436
2.75ᴸ x 3.5ᴴ

Can be used as a frame, ornament or tie-on

Org$	AVG	HIGH
15	--	--

2003 Sounds of the Season Ornaments
28084
2.75ᴸ x 1.25ᴴ

Sold on as a set of 4 in this decorative tin

Org$	AVG	HIGH
34	--	--

Fun Fact

Did you know?

J.W. used to cut down the trees himself that were used to make his baskets. He drove 80 miles to drop them at a mill and then when the splints were ready, he would bring them home and dry them on his yard.

Ornaments

Pottery & Glass

Roseville Pottery

Roseville Embossing
Roseville was produced by Friendship Pottery from 1990-1991. See page 165 for more info.

Bowl, Batter
7.75RD x 5.5^H

Patterns: WTR: 31992
WTB: 31968 WTI: 31984
WTG: 31976

	Org$	AVG	HIGH
WT⁰⁰⁻⁰⁴	56	56	69

Bowls, Roseville
Large: 30023 | 10RD
Medium: 30091 | 8RD
Small: 30058 | 6RD

	Org$	AVG	HIGH
Lg	29.95	43	65
Md	22.95	37	55
Sm	17.95	34	55

Bowl, Dessert
6^{oz}
Cereal Bowl still available, shown for size comparison only

Patterns: WTR: 30236
WTB: 30147 WTI: 33278
WTG: 30350

	Org$	AVG	HIGH
WT⁹¹⁻⁹⁸	12.95	25	40

Pie Plate, Roseville
30015
9RD
Came boxed and included a recipe for Grandma Bonnie's famous apple pie

	Org$	AVG	HIGH
	23.95	35	51

Bowls, Mixing
6RD | 8RD | 10RD | 12RD
Small: S,WT
Medium: S,WT
Large: AA,S WT
XLarge: WT

	Org$	AVG	HIGH
Small			
S⁰²⁻⁰⁴	24	30	55
WT⁹¹⁻⁰⁴	18	30	55
Med			
S⁰²⁻⁰⁴	32	42	45
WT⁹¹⁻⁰⁴	23	35	45
Lg			
AA⁹⁹⁻⁰¹	39	54	70
S⁰²⁻⁰⁴	42	43	60
WT⁹¹⁻⁰⁴	30	43	55
XLg			
WT⁹⁶⁻⁰²	40	75	100

Pitchers, Roseville
Large: 30031 | 7.5^H
Small: 30082 | 5.75^H

	Org$	AVG	HIGH
Lg	27.95	46	60
Sm	21.95	42	50

Regular Pottery

Baking, 8x8
8^L x 8^W x 2^H
Patterns: AA: 39306

	Org$	AVG	HIGH
AA⁰¹	39	45	65

Bowl, Pasta Small
10.75RD | 20^{OZ}
Large Pasta Bowl still available
Patterns: WTR: 38423
WTB: 38415 WTI: 38431
WTG: 38407

	Org$	AVG	HIGH
WT⁰⁰⁻⁰⁴	25	27	45

---

*Pattern Key:

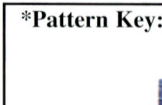  
^(AA)All-American   ^(CC)Candy Corn   ^(TH)Traditional Holly

^(S)Solid:  ^(SC)Cornflower  ^(SE)Eggplant 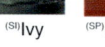 ^(SI)Ivy   ^(SP)Paprika   ^(SB)Butternut   ^(SS)Sage   ^(SSP)Spice

^(WT)Woven Traditions: ^(WTB)Blue  ^(WTG)Green   ^(WTR)Red   ^(WTB)Ivory

Bowl, Salad
8RD | 10^{OZ}
Small, Med & Large still
available only as a set
Patterns: TH: 34894

	Org$	AVG	HIGH
TH$^{93-03}$	22	25	38

Candle Holder$^{(05-06)}$
31454^P/31452^I
4.25RD
Only offered in Paprika
and Ivory

	Org$	AVG	HIGH
	15	18	23

Bowl, Serving $^{(97-01)}$
11.25^L x 8.25^W
Patterns: WTG: 30589
TH: 34916   WTR: 30902
WTB: 30741   WTI: 33774

	Org$	AVG	HIGH
TH$^{97-01}$	41.95	68	79
WT$^{92-03}$	39.95	44	75

Candlesticks
3.25RD x 5^H
Patterns: WTG: 32531
TH: 32395   WTR: 32514
WTB: 32522   WTI: 34037

	Org$	AVG	HIGH
TH$^{96-01}$	39.95	40	79
WT$^{96-99}$	39.95	40	79

Bowl, Serving $^{(04)}$
Get Together
13^L x 9^W x 2.5^H
Patterns: SC: 30083
WTB: 30181   SP: 30084
WTG: 30089   SB: 30086
WTR: 30087   SS: 30085
WTI: 30090

	Org$	AVG	HIGH
	49	49	60

Casserole, 1Qt$^{(98-04)}$
8RD
Shown with 2Qt for size
comparison
Patterns: WTR: 33936
WTB: 33910   WTI: 33944
WTG: 33928

	Org$	AVG	HIGH
WT$^{98-04}$	45	45	60

Bowl, Stackable
5.5RD x 2.25^H
Patterns: WTG: 33120
TH: 37583   WTR: 33103
WTB: 33111   WTI: 33332

	Org$	AVG	HIGH
TH$^{99-03}$	20	20	28
WT$^{96-02}$	19	20	25

Casserole, 2Qt
10.5RD
Patterns: WTG: 32719
TH: 33162   WTR: 32727
WTB: 32701   WTI: 33812

1 Qt

2 Qt

	Org$	AVG	HIGH
TH$^{96-98}$	60	80	94
WT$^{96-04}$	60	60	80

Butter Dish$^{(97-01)}$
8.25^L x 5^W x 2^H
Patterns: WTR: 33367
WTB: 33375   WTI: 33391
WTG: 33383

1997-01

	Org$	AVG	HIGH
WT$^{97-01}$	40	40	43

Casserole, 2^1/$_2$Qt
11^L x 9^W x 6.5^H
30607xxx
WTB: -100   SC   -30
WTG: -110   SP   -40
WTR: -120   SB   -50
WTI: -90   SS   -60

	Org$	AVG	HIGH
S$^{04-06}$	69	55	69
WT$^{04-06}$	69	55	69

Butter Dish$^{(01-06)}$
8.75^L x 4.25^W x 3.5^H
Patterns: SC: 30276
WTB: 30336   SI: 30278
WTG: 30338   SP: 30280
WTR: 30340   SB: 30282
WTI: 30342   SS: 30284

2001-06

	Org$	AVG	HIGH
WT$^{01-06}$	45	45	68
S$^{01-06}$	45	45	45

Casserole, 4Qt
12^L x 10^W x 7^H
30629xxx
WTB: -100   SC: -30
WTG: -110   SP: -40
WTR: -120   SB: -50
WTI: -90   SS: -60

	Org$	AVG	HIGH
S$^{04-06}$	89	69	89
WT$^{04-06}$	89	69	89

Pottery & Glass

Pottery & Glass

Cookie Jar(94-02)
8ᴴ 96ᴼᶻ
Patterns:
WTB: 31348   WTI: 34509
WTG: 31330
WTR: 32409

	Org$	AVG	HIGH
	59.95	69	86

Crock, 1Quart
5.25ᴴ
Patterns: SC: 30266
WTB: 31411 SI: 30268
WTG: 31429 SP: 30270
WTR: 31712 SB: 30272
WTI: 34452 SS: 30274

	Org$	AVG	HIGH
S⁰²⁻⁰⁴	25	37	45
WT⁹⁴⁻⁰⁴	25	28	38

Covered Dish, Small
5.5ᴿᴰ
Patterns:
TH: 31631 WTI: 34801
WTB: 31160
WTG: 31178
WTR: 32425

	Org$	AVG	HIGH
TH⁹⁵⁻⁹⁸	30	43	61
WT⁹⁴⁻⁰⁴	30	30	52

Crock, 2Quart
6.75ᴴ
Patterns: SC: 30184
WTB: 35866 SI: 30186
WTG: 35874 SP: 30188
WTR: 35882 SB: 30190
WTI: 35891 SS: 30192

	Org$	AVG	HIGH
WT⁹⁸⁻⁰⁴	34	37	46
S⁰²⁻⁰⁴	34	40	65

Crescent Dish
14ᴼᶻ
Patterns: SC: 30331
WTB: 30221 SI: 30335
WTG: 30323 SP: 30337
WTR: 30327 SB: 30339
WTI: 30329 SS: 30343

	Org$	AVG	HIGH
S⁰³⁻⁰⁵	22	22	25
WT⁰³⁻⁰⁵	22	22	25

Crock, Condiment
2.75ᴴ
Patterns: WTR: 38784
WTB: 38768 WTI: 38792
WTG: 38776

	Org$	AVG	HIGH
WT⁰⁰⁻⁰²	13	29	45
Set 2	39	40	70

Crock, 1Pint
3.5ᴴ
Traditional Holly included a bayberry green candle
Patterns: TH: 30393
AA: 39314
CC: 37516

	Org$	AVG	HIGH
AA⁰¹	24	34	49
CC⁹⁹⁻⁰⁰	17	27	55
TH⁰¹⁻⁰³	15	24	37

Crock, Woven Drum(03)
7ᴿᴰ 44ᴼᶻ
Promoted during the Christmas 2003 season
Patterns: SI: 30349
WTI: 30487 SP: 30485

	Org$	AVG	HIGH
	34	39	53

Crock, 1Pint SET
3.5ᴴ
Set of 2, with lids. Only available in WTradition colors
Patterns:
WTB: 38890 WTI: 38920
WTG: 38903
WTR: 38911

	Org$	AVG	HIGH
WT⁰⁰⁻⁰²	44	50	55

Cup, Traditional
7.5ᴼᶻ
Still available in
W.Traditions colors
Patterns: TH   34878

	Org$	AVG	HIGH
TH⁹³⁻⁰³	11.95	--	--

---

*Pattern Key:

(AA)All-American   (CC)Candy Corn   (TH)Traditional Holly

(S)Solid (SC)Cornflower (SE)Eggplant (SI)Ivy (SP)Paprika (SB)Butternut (SS)Sage (SSP)Spice

(WT)Woven Traditions: (WTB)Blue (WTG)Green (WTB)Red (WTB)Ivory

Pottery & Glass

Custard Cups
3RD 6^{OZ}
Promoted as Set of 4, values are for single pc
Patterns: WTG: 35050
TH: 36081   WTR: 35068
WTB: 35041   WTI: 35076

	Org$	AVG	HIGH
TH$^{98-03}$	10	15	19
WT$^{98-02}$	10	16	42

Loaf Dishes
Lg: 8.5^L x 4.5^W x 2.5^H
Sm: 8^L x 4^W x 2.25^H
Both available in WTradition colors only. Plastic lids were available, sold separately.

	Org$	AVG	HIGH
Lg$^{98-03}$	39	51	61
Sm$^{99-02}$	29	29	46

Divided Dish
15.5^L x 7^W x 1.5^H
Patterns: SC: 31206
WTB: 31198   SI: 31212
WTG: 31200   SP: 31210
WTR: 31202   SB: 31214
WTI: 31204   SS: 31218

	Org$	AVG	HIGH
S$^{02-04}$	49	49	60
WT$^{02-04}$	49	49	69

Mug - Set of 2
4.25^H 12^{OZ}
Still available in all Woven Tradition and Solid colors
Patterns: TH: 31402

	Org$	AVG	HIGH
TH$^{94-03}$	26.95	27	59

Divided Relish Plate
13.25RD
Patterns: WTR: 36323
WTB: 36307   WTI: 36331
WTG: 36315

	Org$	AVG	HIGH
WT$^{99-04}$	59	59	79

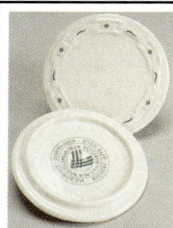
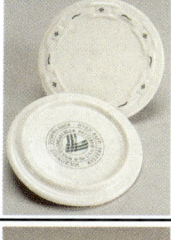

Mug Cover
3.5RD
Also fits Custard or Tea Cups
Patterns: WTR: 35840
TH: 33502   WTI: 35858
WTB: 35823
WTG: 35831

	Org$	AVG	HIGH
TH$^{98-01}$	9	10	12
WT$^{98-02}$	9	9	17

Divided Serving Bowl
13.5^L x 9.5^W/ 36^R
Patterns: WTR: 36161
WTB: 36145   WTI: 36170
WTG: 36153

	Org$	AVG	HIGH
WT$^{98-04}$	49	49	66

Napkin Rings (99-00)
2RD
Sold only as a set of 2
Patterns:
WTB: 37257   WTR: 37273
WTG: 37265   WTI: 37281

	Org$	AVG	HIGH
	19	25	49

Flower Pots
6.5^H | 4.5^H | 3.5^H
Various form numbers, sold individually in WTraditions colors only, included box.

	Org$	AVG	HIGH
Lg$^{97-98}$	30	41	73
Md$^{95-02}$	18	18	49
Sm$^{96-01}$	14	18	35

Pie Plate
Grandma Bonnie's
9RD x 2^D
Still available in all Woven Traditions and Solid colors
Patterns:
AA: 35801/35807
TH: 31381

	Org$	AVG	HIGH
AA$^{98-01}$	30	37	71
TH$^{94-03}$	28	28	55

Lamp w/shade (97-02)
14.5^H
Shades avail in many Regular Line fabrics
Patterns:
WTB: 34266   WTI: 34291
WTG: 34274
WTR: 34282

	Org$	AVG	HIGH
	74.95	77	85

Pillar Candle Holder
7.25RD
Patterns: WTG: 37681
CC: 36391   WTR: 37699
TH: 38032   WTI: 37702
WTB: 37672

	Org$	AVG	HIGH
CC^{00}	23	28	38
TH$^{00-03}$	20	25	31
WT$^{99-02}$	20	20	35

Pottery & Glass

Pottery & Glass

Pitcher, Milk
7.5ʰ   2Qt
Offered in All-American, Solid and Woven Tradition colors
Patterns: S: various
AA: 35491   WT: various

	Org$	AVG	HIGH
AA⁰⁰⁻⁰¹	42	61	76
S⁰¹⁻⁰⁵	44	44	45
WT⁹¹⁻⁰⁵	32	50	59

Platter, Serving
12.75ᴸ x 10.5ᵂ
Patterns:
TH: 34908   WTR: 30856
WTB: 30694   WTI: 33766
WTG: 30538

	Org$	AVG	HIGH
TH⁹⁷⁻⁰¹	52	62	75
WT⁹²⁻⁰³	50	62	84

Pitcher, Juice
5.75ʰ   1Qt
Shown here with the Milk Pitcher for size comparison
Patterns:
WTB: 30082   WTR: 30317
WTG: 30431   WTI: 33791

	Org$	AVG	HIGH
WT⁹¹⁻⁰²	25	37	55

Turkey

Serving

Platter, Turkey
19ᴸ x 15.25ᵂ
Shown with Serving Platter for size comparison
Patterns:
WTB: 35505   WTR: 35521
WTG: 35513   WTI: 35530

	Org$	AVG	HIGH
WT⁹⁸⁻⁰²	89	89	119

Dinner

Luncheon

Bread

Plates Bread, Dinner, & Luncheon
7ᴿᴰ | 9ᴿᴰ | 10ᴿᴰ
Only Traditional Holly pattern has been retired. Still available in all Woven Tradition and Solid colors

	Org$	AVG	HIGH
breadᵀᴴ	12	26	36
dinnerᵀᴴ	30	30	40
lunchᵀᴴ	19	24	29

Quiche Dish
11ᴸ x 9.25ᵂ x 1.5ᴴ
Originally promoted with the 2000 Easter Basket
Patterns:
WTB: 36889   WTR: 36901
WTG: 36897   WTI: 36919

	Org$	AVG	HIGH
WT⁰⁰⁻⁰²	39	48	56

Plate, Cake
14.5ᴿᴰ
Patterns:
TH: 37125   WTR: 36595
WTB: 36579   WTI: 36609
WTG: 36587

	Org$	AVG	HIGH
TH⁰⁰⁻⁰³	45	55	70
WT⁰⁰⁻⁰⁴	45	63	99

Ramekin, Shamrock⁽⁰²⁾
30540
5.5ᴸ x 5.25ᵂ x 1.75ᴴ
Available only in Ivory, with or without a candle

	Org$	AVG	HIGH
	19	24	33

Plate, Leaf ⁽⁰²⁻⁰³⁾
Set: 31158
6.75ᴿᴰ
Sold as a set of 4. Only the paprika plates were available individually.

	Org$	AVG	HIGH
set⁴	79	79	90

Relish Tray⁽⁰⁵⁾
31487ᴾ/31489ᴵ
12.25ᴸ x 10.75ᵂ x 2ᴴ
Available only in Paprika and Ivory

	Org$	AVG	HIGH
	49	--	--

---

*Pattern Key:

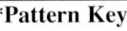   

⁽ᴬᴬ⁾All-American   ⁽ᶜᶜ⁾Candy Corn   ⁽ᵀᴴ⁾Traditional Holly

⁽ˢ⁾Solid   ⁽ˢᶜ⁾Cornflower   ⁽ˢᴱ⁾Eggplant   ⁽ˢᴵ⁾Ivy   ⁽ˢᴾ⁾Paprika   ⁽ˢᴮ⁾Butternut   ⁽ˢˢ⁾Sage   ⁽ˢˢᴾ⁾Spice

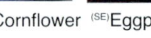

⁽ᵂᵀ⁾Woven Traditions: ⁽ᵂᵀᴮ⁾Blue   ⁽ᵂᵀᴳ⁾Green   ⁽ᵂᵀᴿ⁾Red   ⁽ᵂᵀᴵ⁾Ivory

Roaster, 3Qt
14^L x 9.5^W x 6.25^H
Fits the 2002 Large Easter
Patterns:
WTB: 37095 WTR: 37940
WTG: 37915 WTI: 37982

	Org$	AVG	HIGH
WT^{02}	89	97	125

Soup Tureen$^{(01-04)}$
8.5RD x 7^H
4 piece set. Originally a Hostess item then moved to Regular Line.
Patterns:
WTB: 36765 WTR: 36781
WTG: 36773 WTI: 36790

	Org$	AVG	HIGH
WT$^{01-04}$	149	149	169

Salt & Pepper Shakers
3.25^H
Set of 2. Redesigned in 2001
Patterns: WTG: 30465
TH: 32549   WTR: 30783
WTB: 30627   WTI: 33863

	Org$	AVG	HIGH
TH$^{98-01}$	28	48	75
WT$^{92-01}$	27	37	60

Spice Jars $^{(96-98)}$
4^H
Available in Woven Tradition colors only. Form numbers vary based on the color and the type of spice.

	Org$	AVG	HIGH
WT$^{96-98}$	20	51	72

Salt & Pepper II
3.75^H
Patterns: SC: 30306
WTB: 30544   SI: 30308
WTG: 30548   SP: 30310
WTR: 30550   SB: 30312
WTI: 30552   SS: 30314

	Org$	AVG	HIGH
S$^{01-06}$	34	36	40
WT$^{01-06}$	34	36	36

Spoon Rest, Double$^{(00-03)}$
6.5^L x 4.5^W x 1.25^H
See Booking/Promo for the single spoon rest
Patterns:
WTB: 36722 WTR: 36749
WTG: 36731 WTI: 36757

	Org$	AVG	HIGH
WT$^{00-03}$	26	27	30

Sauce Boat
12^{OZ}
Patterns: WTG: 30601
TH: 31569   WTR: 30929
WTB: 30767   WTI: 34797

	Org$	AVG	HIGH
TH$^{95-98}$	25	74	100
WT$^{93-99}$	25	53	69

Star Dish
9.5^L x 9.5^W x 3^H
Fits the Shining Star Basket, QTY: (WT) 176,000
Patterns: WTR: 30588
TH: 30592   WTI: 30600
WTB: 30598
WTG: 30586

	Org$	AVG	HIGH
TH^{01}	39	49	60
WT^{01}	39	47	62

Soap Dish & Tumbler$^{(99-01)}$
dish: 5.5^L x 3.75^W x 1.5^H
tumbler: 3RD x 4^H
Only offered in WTraditions
Pattern:
  dish: various
  tumbler: various

	Org$	AVG	HIGH
dish	19	30	51
tumbler	15	30	42

Sugar & Creamer
Patterns:
TH: 31593   SC: 30386
WTB: 31119   SI: 30388
WTG: 31127   SP: 30390
WTR: 31801   SB: 30394
WTI: 33839   SS: 30396

	Org$	AVG	HIGH
S$^{01-04}$	44	46	55
TH$^{95-03}$	40	42	69
WT$^{93-04}$	40	42	55

Soap Dispensers
99-02: 3.75RD x 7^H
02-05: 3.25^W x 7.25^H
99-02 version was on avail in WTraditions, while the 02-05 version was avail in both Solid and WTraditions

	Org$	AVG	HIGH
99-02	26	26	40
02-05	26	31	35

Teapots
36^{OZ} | 40^{OZ}
The Large in WTraditions was only offered to hostesses
Patterns: Small: S, WT
                      Large: TH
                Large(Hostess): WT

	Org$	AVG	HIGH
Small	69	69	85
LargeTH	63	91	105
Large^{WT}	60	68	70

Pottery & Glass

Pottery & Glass

Toothpick & Sweetner
4.5^L x 2.5^W | 2RD
Patterns:
TH: 37354 WTR: 37079
WTB: 37052 WTI: 37087
WTG: 37061

	Org$	AVG	HIGH
TH⁰⁰⁻⁰³	29	29	37
WT⁰⁰⁻⁰³	29	32	46

Cookie Jar (04-05)
30689^P/30691^I/30693^C
4QT
Available in Light Paprika, Light Ivy and Light Cornflower

Org$	AVG	HIGH
69	72	96

Trivet
8.5RD
Stand not included
Patterns:
TH   31941 WTR: 32298
WTB: 31364 WTI: 33642
WTG: 31372

	Org$	AVG	HIGH
TH⁹⁶⁻⁰¹	20	31	34
WT⁹⁴⁻⁰³	20	23	40

Covered Casserole (03-05)
30423^P/30525^I/30523^C
10.5^L x 7.5^W x 3.5^H
Available in Light Paprika, Light Ivy^(shown) and Light Cornflower

Org$	AVG	HIGH
69	69	119

Votives
3RD x 2^H
Traditional Holly votive was a Booking item only
Patterns: SC: 30968
WTB: 35904 SI: 30970
WTG: 35912 SP: 30972
WTR: 35921 SB: 30974
WTI: 35939 SS: 30976

	Org$	AVG	HIGH
S⁰²⁻⁰⁵	19	19	27
WT⁹⁸⁻⁰⁵	19	30	45

Pitcher (03-05)
30433^P/30559^I/30557^C
7.5RD x 8^H
Available in Light Paprika^(shown), Light Ivy and Light Cornflower

Org$	AVG	HIGH
49	49	90

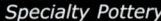

Specialty Pottery
ACO Pottery (See Collectors Club for addl pcs)

Baking Dish (03-05)
30427^P/30551^I/30549^C
13^L x 8.5^W x 2.75^H
Available in Light Paprika, Light Ivy and Light Cornflower ^(shown)

Org$	AVG	HIGH
49	49	75

Platter (04-05)
30699^P/30697^I/30695^C
13.75RD x 1.75^H
Available in Light Paprika, Light Ivy and Light Cornflower

Org$	AVG	HIGH
59	69	138

Bowls, 8" 10" 11" (03-05)
4.75^L | 5.5^H | 6^H
Available in Light Paprika, Light Ivy and Light Cornflower

	Org$	AVG	HIGH
8in	34	34	46
10in	44	53	81
11in	54	54	76
set	120	125	150

Spoon Rest (03-05)
Coasters (04-05)
30425^P/30547^I/30545^C
coasters⁴: 30818
8.25^L x 4.25^W | 4.25RD
Spoon Rest available in all 3 colors, Coasters only sold as shown, set of 4

	Org$	AVG	HIGH
spoon	24	27	31
coasters⁴	26	26	34

Pattern Key:

 ^(AA)All-American
 ^(CC)Candy Corn
 ^(TH)Traditional Holly

 ^(S)Solid: ^(SC)Cornflower ^(SE)Eggplant ^(SI)Ivy ^(SP)Paprika ^(SB)Butternut ^(SS)Sage ^(SSP)Spice

^(WT)Woven Traditions: ^(WTB)Blue ^(WTG)Green ^(WTR)Red ^(WTI)Ivory

Trivet(03-05)
30429ᵖ/30555ⁱ/30553ᶜ
8ᴿᴰ
Available in Light Paprika, Light Ivy(shown) and Light Cornflower

Org$	AVG	HIGH
28	28	36

Soap Dispenser & Tumbler(06-07)
90131
6.5ᴴ | 4.75ᴴ
Set included what is pictured here

Org$	AVG	HIGH
39	--	--

American Holly

American Holly (01-03)
Bowl: 30448 Rings:75736(np)
Mug: 30452 Vase: 30446
Plate: 30492

	Org$	AVG	HIGH
bowl	69	69	75
mug¹	19	21	27
plate	24	24	27
rings	29	29	32
vase	59	59	69

Early Blossom

Flower Pots & Tray(00)
38679
Pots: 4ᴿᴰ x 3.5ᴴ
Tray: 8.75ᴸ x 5ᵂ x 1.75ᴴ
Sold only as set. Featured during 2000 Mother's Day campaign

Org$	AVG	HIGH
39	39	58

At Home Garden

Vase, set of 2 (05)
31309
4ᴿᴰ x 5ᴴ
Sold only as a set of 2

Org$	AVG	HIGH
24	24	26

Easter

Bunny Teapot(06)
31537
8.5ᴸ x 5ᵂ x 10.75ᴴ / 24ᴼᶻ
Hand-painted stoneware

Org$	AVG	HIGH
39	49	55

Berry Design

Bowl, Plate & Mug(05)
31325|31319|31321
5.75ᴿᴰ | 8.25ᴿᴰ | 4.25ᴴ
Sold both as a set of 2 and set of 4

	Org$	AVG	HIGH
bowl²	29	29	32
plate²	29	--	--
mug²	29	29	32

Crocus Teacup & Saucer Set(06)
31541
3.5H | 5.75ᴿᴰ
Sold as a set of 2

Org$	AVG	HIGH
39	49	55

Crock & Pie Plate(05)
31329|31323
3.5ᴴ | 10.25ᴿᴰ

	Org$	AVG	HIGH
crock	15	19	20
plate	24	24	46

Egg Plates(05)
31085
7ᴸ x 5ᵂ
Sold only as a set of 4

Org$	AVG	HIGH
39	40	45

Dogwood

Candle, Flower Pot(06-07)
90121
4.25ᴿᴰ x 4ᴴ
Stoneware. Dogwood lattice design

Org$	AVG	HIGH
24	--	--

Falling Leaves

Vase(01)
30106
6.5ᴿᴰ x 8.5ᴴ
Sold only as a part of a set with the Large Daily Blessings Basket

Org$	AVG	HIGH
46	41	65

Pottery & Glass

Pottery & Glass

Fruit Medley

Fruit Medley (00)
Pasta Bowl & Ramekin
37346 | 38521
13.5RD | 4.75^H
QTY Ramekin: 47,521

	Org$	AVG	HIGH
bowl	69	77	90
ram	15	33	39

Bluster(04)
Crock w/lid
3000xxx
3.5RD | 1 pint
Included pint size candle, 5 scent/color choices

Org$	AVG	HIGH
29	29	30

Fruit Medley (00)
Mug² & Pitcher
37320 | 37338
4.25^H | 8.5^H
QTY Mugs: 34,546. Mugs only sold as a set of 2

	Org$	AVG	HIGH
mug²	36	49	60
pitcher	49	69	113

Nature's Garland
Mugs (4)(05-06)
31462
4.25RD x 4.25^H
Sold only in a set of 4

	Org$	AVG	HIGH
mugs⁴	49	49	52

Halloween

Bowl(04-05)
30963
12.5RD x 2.25^H / 40^{OZ}

Org$	AVG	HIGH
39	39	45

Nature's Garland
Soup Bowls & Plates(05-06)
31460 | 31463
9RD | 9RD
Sold individually only in sets of 4

	Org$	AVG	HIGH
bowl⁴	49	49	57
plate⁴	49	49	52

Pumpkin Dish(05)
31409
5.5RD x 5.5^H
Vitrified china: oven, freezer, microwave and dishwasher safe

Org$	AVG	HIGH
20	20	37

Nature's Garland
Square Bowls(05-06)
Sm: 31459 | Lg: 31490
5^L x 5^W | 9.5^L x 9.5^W
Sold individually

	Org$	AVG	HIGH
small	19	24	32
large	39	43	58

Holiday

Bluster(04)
Bowl & Spreader
30021 | 90013
4.25RD | 5.5^L
Could save buying together, but also sold separately

	Org$	AVG	HIGH
bowl	14	14	26
spread	8	8	10

Roger & Ginger
Plate & Mug(00)
36528 | 36854
9RD | 12^{OZ}
Sold both as a set and separately

	Org$	AVG	HIGH
plate	29	29	36
mug	19	19	25

Bluster(04)
Plates⁴, Platter, Mug¹
30967 | 30019 | 30971
8.5RD | 12.5RD | 4.25^H

	Org$	AVG	HIGH
plate²	39	40	53
platter	39	39	48
mug¹	17	17	36

Santa Gift Bag Bowl & Spreader(05)
31455
4.75^W x 4.75^H | 5.25^L
Sold only as a set

Org$	AVG	HIGH
24	24	29

Santa Plate & Mug[05]
31467 | 31465
7.5^L x 6.75^W | 3.75^H
Sold individually, in sets of 2

	Org$	AVG	HIGH
plate[2]	24	--	--
mug[2]	24	--	--

Snow Friends Cookies for Santa[98]
36021
9RD | 8^{OZ}
Sold as a set only

Org$	AVG	HIGH
40	46	55

Snow Friends Flurry & Snowball[99]
36927
9RD
Final year for Snow Friends plate. No cup sold this year.

Org$	AVG	HIGH
29	39	50

Homestead

Homestead Crock[99]
37352
2QT
Features a sealable lid that was sold separately

	Org$	AVG	HIGH
	45	73	125
w/lid	66	95	144

Lucky Twist

Lucky Twist[05]
31550
5^L x 5^W x 2^H / 14^{OZ}

Org$	AVG	HIGH
19	21	26

Majolica Garden

Flower Pots, Pitcher & Luncheon Plates[06]
31540 | 31553 | 31558
5.75^H | 8^H | 9RD
Peony & Dogwood embossed stoneware

	Org$	AVG	HIGH
pots	30	--	--
pitcher	50	--	--
plate	25	--	--

Matzah

Matzah Tray[01-02]
35611
9.5^L x 9.5^W x 1.25^H

Org$	AVG	HIGH
49	52	61

Modular

Rectangular & Square[05]
5.5^L x 4^W | 4^L x 4^W

Rectangular:		Square:	
SE:	31388	SE:	31387
SS:	31405	SS:	31404
SSP:	31398	SSP:	31397

	Org$	AVG	HIGH
rect	18	18	21
sq	14	24	32
set	49	49	72

Mulligan Pottery

Pet Pottery[00-02]
Canister, Sm & Med Dog Bowls introduced in 2000

	Org$	AVG	HIGH
cat	15	27	41
dog^{Sm}	19	27	40
dog^{Md}	25	39	51
dog^{Lg}	29	59	63
canister	45	52	65

Peony

Flower Pots (2)[01]
30028
3.75RD x 4^H
Promoted along with the May Peony Basket.

Org$	AVG	HIGH
39	43	60

Proudly American

Casserole Dish, Eagle[02-05]
30812
9.25RD x 5.25^H
Introduced in A.American collection. Moved to Regular Line in 2003, retired in 2005.

Org$	AVG	HIGH
59	59	135

Crock, Half-Pint[04-05]
30687
4.5RD x 2^H

Org$	AVG	HIGH
12	13	26

Pottery & Glass
116

Pottery & Glass

Proudly American (con't)

Plate, Candle(04-05) **& Votives(2)** (03-05)
30685 | 30017
7.5RD | 2^H

	Org$	AVG	HIGH
plate	19	19	23
votive²	19	19	22

Heart Plate (01)
30506 | candle 62693
7^L x 7.5^W
Candle sold separately or in a set with plate.

	Org$	AVG	HIGH
plate	19	29	39
w/candle	29	30	40

Platter (03-05)
30003
16^L x 8.75^W x 1.5^H
Designed to fit inside a Med Gathering Basket

Org$	AVG	HIGH
49	49	61

Heart Dish(05)
dish: 31081^I / 31165^P
plate: 31083^I / 31167^P
8.5^L x 8.25^W x 2.5^H | 5.5RD
Available in Ivory/Red ribbon, or Pink/Ivory ribbon. Candle sold separately.

	Org$	AVG	HIGH
dish	35	35	50
plate	15	16	24

Spring Floral

Bowl & Platter (02-03)
30092 | 31106
11.5RD x 3.75^H | 13^L x 11^H

	Org$	AVG	HIGH
bowl	59	60	80
platter	49	49	53

Ruffled Bowl(05)
Be My Valentine
31527
7^W x 4^H
Coordinates with the Be My Valentine products

Org$	AVG	HIGH
34	--	--

Stars & Stripes (Melamine)

Bowls, Lunch Plates & Dinner Plates (04)
40833 | 40864 | 40911
7.5RD | 9RD | 11RD
Tumblers now shown

	Org$	AVG	HIGH
bowls⁴	24	27	32
lunch⁴	24	24	35
dinner⁴	29	29	42
tumbler⁴	19	32	43

Scented Pottery(05)
Be My Valentine
71262
3^L x 3^W
Bisque pottery enfused with exclusive Sweetheart Garden scent

Org$	AVG	HIGH
20	--	--

Sunny Days (Melamine)

Salad Bowls, Snack Bowls, 9" Plates, 11" Plates & Tumblers(05)

	Org$	AVG	HIGH
salad⁴	24	31	35
snack⁴	19	19	46
9in⁴	24	24	32
11in⁴	29	34	45
tumbler⁴	29	29	46

Vintage Blossoms

Soap Dish(01)
36706
5.25^L x 4^H
Promoted with Mother's Day Vintage Blossoms. Box.

	Org$	AVG	HIGH
	24	24	28
w/soap	29	--	--

Sweetheart

Heart Dish(00)
5^L x 4^W x 2^H
Promoted with Sweetheart Little Love, Box.

Patterns: WTR: 39748
WTB: 37192   WTI: 39756
WTG: 39730

Org$	AVG	HIGH
19	35	47

Vase(02)
30808
5.25RD x 3^H
Design coordinates with the Vintage Blossoms fabrics

Org$	AVG	HIGH
26	29	48

Bricks

Bread (90-02)
30074
11^L x 4.25^H
Clay brown pottery

Org$	AVG	HIGH
12.95	14	28

Buffet (90-01)
34568
7.25^L x 7.25^W
Clay brown pottery

Org$	AVG	HIGH
14.95	15	20

Button (91-01)
30198
7RD
Clay brown pottery

Org$	AVG	HIGH
9.95	11	15

Cracker (91-98)
30201
9^L x 2.25^W
Clay brown pottery

Org$	AVG	HIGH
9.95	12	24

Glass

Cake Stand & Candle Pedestal (02-03)
31196 | 90103
10RD | 5RD

	Org$	AVG	HIGH
cake	39	39	65
candle	25	25	34

Crystal Champaigne Flutes (06)
90096
2.75^W x 9.5^H
Set of 2. Initially given free with purchase of CClub Celebration basket.

Org$	AVG	HIGH
32	32	43

Halloween Luminary (04)
96132
3.75RD x 5.5^H
Features a glowing ghost effect created by embossing on the inside of the glass

Org$	AVG	HIGH
29	39	55

Pumpkin (03)
96102
5.75RD x 6.5^H
Milk glass dish made of hand pressed glass. Fits the 7" bowl.

Org$	AVG	HIGH
39	39	40

Knobs

Apple Knob (05)
50292 | 1.5^H
Sold with Bushel Baskets

Org$	AVG	HIGH
8	--	--

Bluster Knob (04)
50112 | 2.25^H
Sold with Christmas 2004

Org$	AVG	HIGH
8	--	--

Bunny Knob (06)
23283 | 2.25^H
Sold with Easter 2006

Org$	AVG	HIGH
8	--	--

Ghost Knob (04)
2.25^H
Only sold with Halloween Basket

Org$	AVG	HIGH
8	--	--

Pumpkin Knob (06)
50293 | 1.5^H
Available Aug 2004 only

Org$	AVG	HIGH
8	--	--

Shamrock (06)
23282 | 1.25^W
Sold for Lucky Twist Basket

Org$	AVG	HIGH
8	--	--

Strawberry Knob (05)
50249 | 1.5^H
Sold with Strawberry Baskets

Org$	AVG	HIGH
8	--	--

Tree, Christmas (05)
50323 | 2^H
Sold with Christmas 2005

Org$	AVG	HIGH
8	--	--

Pottery & Glass

Pottery & Glass

Tie-On

Tie-Ons in this section were offered through the WishList, or for an extended period of time. For Tie-Ons offered within a collection, such as Mother's Day, see that collection.

Apple (05)
23126 | 1.5^W x 1.5^H
Sold with Bushel Baskets

Org$	AVG	HIGH
8	--	--

Botanical Fields (00-03)
1.75^L x 1.5^W
All are identical in design, only the name is different

	Org$	AVG	HIGH
bless you	8	8	11
cookbooks	8	8	11
mail	8	8	11
recipes	8	8	11
tissues	8	8	11
utensils	8	8	11

Baby (96)
32310 | 2.5^L x 1.75^W

Org$	AVG	HIGH
6.95	15	28

Chef Hat (06)
23298 | 1.75^W x 1.75^H
Poofed Chef's Hat design

Org$	AVG	HIGH
8	--	--

Baby (97)
30503 | 2.5^L x 1.75^W

Org$	AVG	HIGH
6.95	10	18

Coffee (98-00)
36030 | 2.5^L x 1.75^W

Org$	AVG	HIGH
8	11	15

Baby (98-99)
34151^{98} | 36099^{99}
Same design, different year

Org$	AVG	HIGH
8	13	18

Congratulations (95-98)
31496 | 2.5^L x 1.75^W

Org$	AVG	HIGH
6.95	9	15

Baby (00)
36293 | 2RD
QTY: 80,060

Org$	AVG	HIGH
8	13	19

Congratulations (98-00)
33685 | 2.5RD

Org$	AVG	HIGH
8	8	10

Baby (01)
39594 | 1.25^L x 2^H

Org$	AVG	HIGH
8	8	12

Dog Bone (00-02)
36188^B/36285^G | 4^L x 1.5^W
Blue or green

Org$	AVG	HIGH
10	16	20

Baby (02)
30572 | 2^L x 1.75^H

Org$	AVG	HIGH
8	8	10

Falling Leaves (01)
39411 | 2^L x 2^H

Org$	AVG	HIGH
8	12	15

Baby (03)
20146 | 2.25^L x 2^H

Org$	AVG	HIGH
8	11	18

From Our House (99-01)
35718 | 1.75^L x 2^H

Org$	AVG	HIGH
8	15	20

Baby (04)
28095 | 2^L x 1.25^W

Org$	AVG	HIGH
8	8	11

Fruit Medley (00-03)
1.5^L x 1^H
All are identical in design, only the name is different

	Org$	AVG	HIGH
bless you	8	8	15
cookbooks	8	14	15
mail	8	11	15
recipes	8	14	16
tissues	8	11	15
utensils	8	12	15

Baby (05)
20026 | 2^L x 1.75^H

Org$	AVG	HIGH
8	--	--

Berry (05-06)
23101 | 1.75^L x 1.5^H
Sold with Strawberry Baskets

Org$	AVG	HIGH
8	--	--

Happy Birthday (95-98)
31488 | 2.5^L x 1.75^W

Org$	AVG	HIGH
6.95	8	14

	**Happy Birthday** (98-00) 31747 | 2RD				**Spring Floral** (02-03) 31108 | 2^W		
	Org$	AVG	HIGH		Org$	AVG	HIGH
	6.95	8	10		8	13	15
	**Happy Birthday** (05-06) 23063 | 2^L x 1.75^H				**Sunny Days** (05) 23065 | 1.75^W x 2^H		
	Org$	AVG	HIGH		Org$	AVG	HIGH
	8	--	--		8	8	11
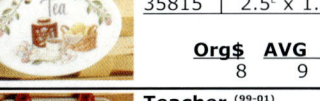	**Happy Halloween** (99-00) 37559 | 2.5^L x 1.75^W				**Tea** (99-03) 35815 | 2.5^L x 1.75^W		
	Org$	AVG	HIGH		Org$	AVG	HIGH
	8	11	18		8	9	10
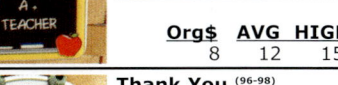	**Happy Halloween Set** (97) 23127 | 1.25^H				**Teacher** (99-01) 36617 | 1.75^L x 1.5^H		
	Org$	AVG	HIGH		Org$	AVG	HIGH
	13	13	16		8	12	15
	Jack-O-Lantern (00) 37800 *Only sold as a 4 piece set*				**Thank You** (96-98) 32336 | 2.5^L x 1.75^W		
	Org$	AVG	HIGH		Org$	AVG	HIGH
	19	23	29		6.95	9	15
	**Old Glory** (02-04) 77277 | 1.5^L x 1.25^W *Solid pewter*				**Thank You** (05-06) 23066 | 2^L x 1.75^H		
	Org$	AVG	HIGH		Org$	AVG	HIGH
	8	8	10		8	--	--
	Postage Stamp (99-01) 36978 | 1.75^L x 1.5^W *Reversible*				**Thinking of You** (97-00) 33464 | 2.5^L x 1.75^W		
	Org$	AVG	HIGH		Org$	AVG	HIGH
	12	17	21		6.95	8	9
	**Provincial Cottage** (00-02) 2.5^L x 1.25^H *All are identical in design, only the name is different*				**Welcome** (97-01) 34096 | 2.5^L x 1.75^W		
		Org$	AVG	HIGH	Org$	AVG	HIGH
	bless you	8	14	15	6.95	12	16
	cookbooks	8	8	15			
	mail	8	14	15			
	recipes	8	14	15			
	tissues	8	8	15			
	utensils	8	8	15			
	**Pumpkin Face** (01) 30096 *Only sold as a 4 piece set*						
	Org$	AVG	HIGH				
	19	23	35				
	**Recipes** (98-03) 31739 | 2.5^L x 1.75^W						
	Org$	AVG	HIGH				
	8	8	20				
	**Shield** (02-05) *All-American* 30816 | 2^L x 2^H						
	Org$	AVG	HIGH				
	10	10	17				

Pottery & Glass

Proudly American

If you are looking for a different Proudly American piece, check the Pottery, Booking or Collectors Club sections, all of which have coordinating Proudly American pieces

Little Star (03)
10617
7.5^L x 8^W x 3^H
Special logo on bottom commemorating Longaberger's 30th Anniversary

	Org$	AVG	HIGH
B	59	77	87
C$^{P/L}$	69	79	95
FS$^{C/Ld}$	88	88	99

Berry, Medium (04-05)
10682
7.5^L x 7.5^W x 3.5^H

	Org$	AVG	HIGH
B	42	42	50
C$^{P/L}$	61	61	65
FS$^{C/Ld}$	82	--	--

Picnic, Small (03-04)
10069
12^L x 12^W x 6^H

	Org$	AVG	HIGH
B	99	99	110
C$^{P/L}$	154	154	160

Button (03-05)
Darning (03-04)
10047 | 10207
7RD x 3^H | 10RD x 4^H

	Org$	AVG	HIGH
button	39	44	55
C$^{P/L}$	60	--	--
darning	59	62	75
C$^{P/L}$	86	86	104

Spring (03-05)
10057
11^L x 8^W x 5.5^H

	Org$	AVG	HIGH
B	59	59	63
C$^{P/L}$	88	--	--

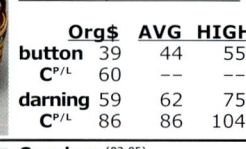

Cracker (03-05)
10039
11.5^L x 5^W x 3^H

	Org$	AVG	HIGH
B	39	39	48
C$^{P/L}$	59	62	72

Tea (04)
10732
7^L x 5^W x 3.5^H
Available Jun 2004 only

	Org$	AVG	HIGH
B	42	42	64
C$^{P/L}$	52	64	75

Gathering, Medium (03-05)
11061
18^L x 11^W x 4.5^H

	Org$	AVG	HIGH
B	89	93	137
C$^{P/L}$	133	--	--

Wash Day, Small (03-05)
10073
16.25^L x 15.75^W x 8.5^H

	Org$	AVG	HIGH
B	169	169	186
C$^{P/L}$	222	--	--

Ice Bucket (04)
10638
9.25RD x 8.5^H
Available Jun 2004 only

	Org$	AVG	HIGH
B	100	114	131
C$^{P/L}$	150	158	180
FS$^{C/Ld}$	174	--	--

Pumpkin Series

These baskets were not declared a series until 1997 when the last items were introduced. Since then, pumpkin-style baskets have been considered Feature items, but not added to this collection.

Liners were available in either Pumpkin fabric (shown on baskets) or Fall Foliage, shown left

1997 Large Pumpkin Hostess
16039
11.25RD x 9^H
Hostess only, only sold as a Combo

	Org$	AVG	HIGH
C$^{P/L}$	117.95	118	203

1995 Pumpkin
19402 | TO 31763
9.25RD x 7.25^H

	Org$	AVG	HIGH
B	47.95	93	129
C$^{P/L}$	59.95	110	149
FS$^{C/Ld}$	84.90	123	168
TO	6.95	14	28

1997 Little Pumpkin
16021 | TO 34517
5.75RD x 4.25^H
QTY (basket): 177,000
Tie-On sold seperately

	Org$	AVG	HIGH
	34.95	42	79
C$^{P/L}$	46.95	53	110
FS$^{C/Ld}$	64.90	65	119
TO	6.95	16	24

1996 Small Pumpkin
16012
7.25RD x 5.25^H
QTY: 134,914

	Org$	AVG	HIGH
B	40.95	56	95
C$^{P/L}$	52.95	79	107
FS$^{C/Ld}$	72.90	87	139

Fun Fact

Solid board bottoms are becoming more common place in the basket designs. What used to be saved for purses and planters is now often found on baskets intended for both serving as well as gifts. What determines if a basket is designed with a board bottom or a woven bottom?

The Company reports two main reasons for choosing a board bottom for a design: to provide a level surface for a function like serving food; or to aid the weaver in the creation of the design.

For example, in the case of the check-weave baskets, the square-edge design was critical to the look of the basket and using solid wood bottom aided in achieving the look.

For baskets intended to be used as a vase, it is imperative that it sits easily without any chance of rocking or tipping over, thus making the board bottom the best choice.

Retired Baskets

Address(98-04)
18546ᶜ/17020ᵂᴮ/10983ᵂᵂ
8.25ᴸ x 6.25ᵂ x 3.75ᴴ
Classic(98-02), *Warm Brown*(02-04) *and Whitewash*(01-02)

	Org$	AVG	HIGH
stain	34	35	60
wwash	35	38	45

Berry, 1sw/h(79-04)
small: 6.5ᴸ x 6.5ᵂ x 3ᴴ
med: 7.5ᴸ x 7.5ᵂ x 3.5ᴴ
large: 8.5ᴸ x 8.5ᵂ x 5ᴴ
Dark(79-85), *Classic*(85-02), *Warm Brown*(02-04). Medium size still available.

	Org$	AVG	HIGH
small	8.95	29	39
large	10.95	38	76

All-In-One Game(05-06)
10395
20.5ᴸ x 15.75ᵂ x 4.5ᴴ
Warm Brown only, accessories sold separately, including reversible game lid & pieces

	Org$	AVG	HIGH
B	110	--	--

Boardwalk, Little(03-04) **Medium**(03-06) **& Small**(03-06)
10578 | 10261 | 10255
little: 6.75ᴸ x 3.75ᵂ x 4.5ᴴ
med: 12.5ᴸ x 6.75ᵂ x 8.5ᴴ
small: 9.25ᴸ x 5ᵂ x 6.25ᴴ
Large still available

	Org$	AVG	HIGH
little	49	49	63
med	89	89	107
small	69	59	68

Bagel(02-06)
10064
16ᴸ x 7.5ᵂ x 3.25ᴴ
Warm Brown

	Org$	AVG	HIGH
B	49	49	52

Book Keeper(00-02)
10516
15ᴸ x 16ᵂ x 3.5ᶠᴴ x 10.25ᴮᴴ
Classic and Warm Brown

	Org$	AVG	HIGH
B	109	110	130

Barbeque Buddy(01-02)
small: 7.5ᴸ x 3.75ᵂ x 2.75ᴴ
med: 12ᴸ x 5.25ᵂ x 3ᴴ
large: 12.5ᴸ x 6.25ᵂ x 7ᴴ
Classic only

	Org$	AVG	HIGH
small	39	39	48
med	49	49	72
large	69	70	85

Bouquet(03-06)
10642
6.75ᴿᴰ x 6ᴴ
Warm Brown

	Org$	AVG	HIGH
B	35	39	46

Basket Bin(99-03)
small: 12ᴸ 11.75ᵂ 3ᶠᴴ 5.5ᴮᴴ
med: 12ᴸ 14.5ᵂ 3ᶠᴴ 5.5ᴮᴴ
large: 16.5ᴸ 12.5ᵂ 5ᶠᴴ 7.75ᴮᴴ
Classic(99-02) *and Warm Brown*(02-03), *Medium is also the Tapered Tray*

	Org$	AVG	HIGH
small	54	54	56
med	55	78	115
large	79	79	99

Bread, New(88-P)
14974ᴺ/10370ᵂᵂ
14.5ᴸ x 7.5ᵂ x 3.75ᴴ
Natural(99-01), *Whitewash*(01-02) *Classic*(88-02), still available in *Warm Brown*

	Org$	AVG	HIGH
natural	34	43	50
wwash	36	41	67

Berry, No Handle(79-99)
small: 6.5ᴸ x 6.5ᵂ x 3ᴴ
med: 7.5ᴸ x 7.5ᵂ x 3.5ᴴ
large: 8.5ᴸ x 8.5ᵂ x 5ᴴ
Dark(79-85) *and Classic*(85-99)

	Org$	AVG	HIGH
small	6.95	29	48
med	7.95	41	70
large	8.95	38	51

Bread, Old (82-88)
4600-OO
15ᴸ x 8ᵂ x 2.25ᴴ
Replaced by a deeper, 'New' Bread in 1988

	Org$	AVG	HIGH
B	11.95	38	53

Brownie(04-06)
10543
11.25ᴸ x 9ᵂ x 2.5ᴴ
Warm Brown

	Org$	AVG	HIGH
B	39	39	50
Cᴾ/ᴸ	68	68	72

Canister Set(79-80)
5ᴿᴰ | 7ᴿᴰ | 9ᴿᴰ
Dark stain. Only sold as a set, no handles, included lids.

	Org$	AVG	HIGH
B	39.95	246	351

Business Card(97-04)
17361ᶜ/17257ᵂᴮ
4.75ᴸ x 3.75ᵂ x 2.25ᴴ
Classic(97-02) & Warm Brown(02-04)

	Org$	AVG	HIGH
B	22.95	36	57

Card File(04-06)
10696ᵂᴮ
7.25ᴸ x 6ᵂ x 4ᴴ
Warm Brown

	Org$	AVG	HIGH
B	39	--	--
Cᴾ/ᴸ	72	72	79

Button(99-P)
19526
7ᴿᴰ x 3ᴴ
Natural(99-01), Classic(99-02), still available in Warm Brown

	Org$	AVG	HIGH
B	27	27	40

Carry Along(05-06)
10042ᵂᴮ
15.5ᴸ x 9ᵂ x 5.5ᴴ
Warm Brown, 1 st/h

	Org$	AVG	HIGH
B	64	64	77

Cake, 1st/h(79-94)
11002
12ᴸ x 12ᵂ x 6ᴴ
Classic only, included riser

	Org$	AVG	HIGH
B	15.95	53	81

Catch-All(00-03)
small: 7.25ᴿᴰ x 2.25ᴴ
med: 9ᴿᴰ x 3ᴴ
large: 12ᴿᴰ x 3.5ᴴ
Classic(00-02), Warm Brown(02-03) Whitewash(01-02)

	Org$	AVG	HIGH
small	32	67	66
smallᵂᵂ	34	44	55
med	37	45	75
large	45	55	70

Cake, 2sw/h(85-P)
16144ᴺ/11011ᶜ
12ᴸ x 12ᵂ x 6ᴴ
Natural(94), Classic(85-02), still available in Warm Brown. Riser included.

	Org$	AVG	HIGH
nat	46.95	62	105
class	26.95	69	112

Chore, Medium(86-02)
13510/3500-C
13ᴸ x 8ᵂ x 5ᴴ
Classic only

	Org$	AVG	HIGH
B	18.95	38	74

Candle(99-02)
19739
9ᴸ x 5ᵂ x 5ᴴ
Classic only

	Org$	AVG	HIGH
B	36	49	80

Clip Keeper(04-06)
10292
3ᴸ x 3ᵂ x 2.5ᴴ
Warm Brown

	Org$	AVG	HIGH
B	24	--	--

Retired Baskets

Retired Baskets

Coaster, ACO (03-05)
10584
5ᴿᴰ x 2.5ᴴ
Warm Brown. Lid available in sage, paprika, cornflower or solid wood

	Org$	AVG	HIGH
B	39	39	42

Cradle, Large (79-86)
2700-M
30ᴸ x 20ᵂ x 10.5ᴴ
Dark(79-85) & Classic(85-86). Was also often customized with red, green, blue, yellow or brown accents

	Org$	AVG	HIGH
B	39.95	323	500

Corn (79-94)
14401
17ᴿᴰ x 11.5ᴴ
Dark or Classic with 2 hand slots. Reintroduced into Hostess Collection with 2 leather ears in 95.

	Org$	AVG	HIGH
B	29.95	78	149
Cᴾ	39.95	82	150

Cradle, Medium (79-83) **& Small** (79-80)
Med: 2700-M | Sm: 2600-M
Med: 28.5ᴸ x 17.75ᵂ x 9.75ᴴ
Sm: 24ᴸ x 17ᵂ x 10ᴴ
Dark stain, also often customized with red, green, blue, yellow or brown accents

	Org$	AVG	HIGH
med	37.95	--	200
small	35.95	--	105

Corner Small (03-05) **& Large** (02-06)
sm 10282 | lg 12470
small: 8ᴸ x 6ᵂ x 5ᴴ
large: 11.25ᴸ x 8.5ᵂ x 5ᴴ
Warm Brown

	Org$	AVG	HIGH
small	39	46	49
large	54	54	57

Cradle, Mini (79-93)
10715/700-K
7ᴸ x 5ᵂ x 3.5ᴴ
Dark(79-85) & Classic(85-93), had two wooden loops prior to 1984

	Org$	AVG	HIGH
B	9.95	45	90

Corner Hamper (04-06)
10333
17.25ᴸ x 17.5ᵂ x 20.75ᴴ
Warm Brown, originally introduced in Hostess Collection and then moved to Regular Line

	Org$	AVG	HIGH
B	299	--	--

Craft Keeper (04-06)
12535ᶜ / 18954ᵂᴮ
18ᴸ x 13.75ᵂ x 9.25ᴴ
Classic(02) & Warm Brown(02-08) Introduced into the Hostess line from 2002-04.

	Org$	AVG	HIGH
B	169	189	204

Cracker (82-P)
17198ᴺ/14508ᶜ
11.5ᴸ x 5ᵂ x 3ᴴ
Natural(94) & Classic(82-02), (Warm Brown still available)

	Org$	AVG	HIGH
natural	21	39	55
classic	10	29	45

Darning (83-06)
500-JOᴰ/15504ᶜ/15521ᴺ/17427ᵂᴮ
10ᴿᴰ x 4ᴴ
Dark(83-85), Classic(85-02) & Natural(94), Warm Brown(02-06)

	Org$	AVG	HIGH
stain	16	39	60
natural	31	64	110

Cradle, Doll (79-86)
2500-LO
19ᴸ x 12ᵂ x 6ᴴ
Dark(79-85) & Classic(85-86), was also often customized with red, green, blue, yellow or brown accents

	Org$	AVG	HIGH
B	25.95	158	255

Desktop, Small (03-04)
10229
6ᴸ x 6ᵂ x 4.25ᶠᴴ x 5.25ᴮᴴ
Warm Brown, the Large Desktop is still available

	Org$	AVG	HIGH
B	39	--	--

Easter, Baby[79-87]
700-BO

7[L] x 5[W] x 3.5[H]
Dark[79-85] & Classic[85-87], featured both 1sw/h and 1st/h (700-AO)

	Org$	AVG	HIGH
st/h	8.95	52	62
sw/h	9.95	56	65

Flower Pot, Small[96-01]
18414

14[L] x 6[W] x 3[H]
Classic only, riser sold separately

	Org$	AVG	HIGH
B	34.95	45	75

Easter, Small[79-87]
3400-AO

10[L] x 6[W] x 4[H]
Dark[79-85] & Classic[85-87], featured both 1st/h and 1sw/h (3400-BO)

	Org$	AVG	HIGH
st/h	9.95	54	70
sw/h	10.95	60	65

Foliage[04-06]
At Home Garden
10667

11.25[RD] x 8[H]
Shown with the Flora basket (still offered) for size comparison only

	Org$	AVG	HIGH
B	66	66	69

Easter, Medium[79-87]
3500-BO

13[L] x 8[W] x 5[H]
Dark[79-85] & Classic[85-87], featured both 1sw/h and 1st/h (3500-AO)

	Org$	AVG	HIGH
st/h	10.95	56	65
sw/h	11.95	50	75

Fruit, 1sw/h[79-05]
small[79-04] 6.5[RD] x 5[H]
med[79-04] 8RD x 6.5[H]
large[79-05] 13RD x 8.5[H]
Dark[79-85], Classic[85-02] & Warm Brown[02-05]

	Org$	AVG	HIGH
small	9.99	34	68
med	12.95	49	70
large	18.95	74	98

Easter, Large[79-87]
3600-AO

14[L] x 7.75[W] x 5.25[H]
Dark[79-85] & Classic[85-87], featured both 1st/h and 1sw/h (3600-BO)

	Org$	AVG	HIGH
st/h	11.95	52	60
sw/h	12.95	58	63

Fruit, Tall[79-95]
3300-BO[D]/13307[C]

8RD x 9[H]
Dark[79-85] & Classic[85-95]

	Org$	AVG	HIGH
B	15.95	43	79

Envelope[99-05]
14311[C]/17443[WB]

12[L] x 5.25[W] x 3.75[FH] x 5[BH]
Classic[99-02] & Warm Brown[02-05]

	Org$	AVG	HIGH
B	43	50	85

Fruit, Hanging[79-80]
sm: 3000-P | med: 3100-P
lrg: 3200-P | tall: 3300-P
Dark stain only, feature wooden splint hangers

	Org$	AVG	HIGH
small	11.95	77	125
med	15.95	50	50
large	21.95	100	140
tall	18.95	--	--

Flower Pot[94-98]
16306

17[L] x 7.5[W] x 4.75[H]
Classic only, riser sold separately

	Org$	AVG	HIGH
B	47.95	52	103

Game Duo[05-06]
10393

7.5[L] x 7.5[W] x 2.75[H]
Warm Brown only, accessories sold separately including reversible game lid & pieces

	Org$	AVG	HIGH
B	39	54	74

Retired Baskets
126

Retired Baskets

Gatehouse (01-06)
xsmall(01-04) 12433^C/17524^WB
small(01-04) 11751^C/17532^WB
large(01-04) 11763^C/17541^WB
3.75^RD | 4.75^RD | 6.5^RD
Classic(01-02) & Warm Brown(02-06)

	Org$	AVG	HIGH
xsmall	29	33	48
small	39	39	51
large	59	69	83

Hamper Small/Med & Large(79-86)
small/med 12^L 12.25^W 16.25^H
large 16.5^L 16.5^W 21.5^H
Dark(79-85) & Classic(85-86).
Attached lid, knob at front of lid, no hand slots

	Org$	AVG	HIGH
sm/med	32	149	175
large	60	158	275

Hanging Measuring(80-86)
5RD | 7RD | 9RD | 11RD | 13RD
Dark(80-85) & Classic(86-86), included rawhide strings for hanging

	Org$	AVG	HIGH
5"	14.95	37	70
7"	15.95	67	75
9"	22.95	40	40
11"	29.95	45	75
13"	35.95	40	90

Gathering, Small(79-06)
1st/h(86-93) 2300-AO^D/12301^C
2sw/h(79-06) 2300-C^D/12319^C
17559^WB/11052^WW
14^L x 9^W x 4.5^H
Dark(79-85) Classic(85-02) Warm Brown(02-06) Whitewash(01-02)

	Org$	AVG	HIGH
st/h	22.95	103	120
sw/h	15.95	57	91
wwash	54	60	70

Hanging Woven Bottom(79-86)
3700-PO
8.25^RD x 7.75^H
Dark(80-85) & Classic(86-86), included rawhide strings for hanging

	Org$	AVG	HIGH
B	14.95	66	89

Gathering, Medium(79-06)
1st/h(80-93) 2400-AO^D/12408^C
2sw/h(79-06) 2400-C^D/12416^C
17567^WB
18^L 11^W x 4.5^H
Dark(79-85) Classic(85-02) Warm Brown(02-06)

	Org$	AVG	HIGH
st/h	41.95	83	120
sw/h	17.95	69	80

Inverted Waste(79-84)
small 12.5^RD x 13.5^H
large 14RD x 16^H
Dark stain only, both sizes offered either 1sw/h or no handle

	Org$	AVG	HIGH
sm^no/h	21.95	90	100
sm^sw/h	23.95	75	125
lg^no/h	26.95	95	130
lg^sw/h	28.95	114	120

Gathering, Large(79-94)
1st/h(83-93) 2500-A^D/12505^C
2sw/h(79-94) 2500-C^D/12513^C
19^L x 12^W x 6^H
Dark(79-85) & Classic(85-02)

	Org$	AVG	HIGH
st/h	26.95	70	105
sw/h	19.95	73	110

Key(79-05)
small(79-04) 10723^C/17640^WB
med(79-04) 11100^C/17656^WB
tall(79-05) 11053^C/17711^WB/14630^N
3.5^L | 5^H | 9.5^H
Dark(79-85) Classic(86-02) Warm Brown(02-06), Tall also Natural(94)

	Org$	AVG	HIGH
small	7.95	32	50
med	9.95	34	65
tall	11.95	44	96
tall^N	31.95	50	60

Generations(98-04)
7RD | 8RD | 10RD | 12RD | 14RD
7", 8", 12" Classic(98-02) only.
10" & 14" both Classic(98-02) & Warm Brown(02-04)

	Org$	AVG	HIGH
7"	29	37	57
8"	35	38	65
10"	39	44	75
12"	54	68	85
14"	58	68	99

Laundry(79-98)
small(79-98) 24^L x 17^W x 10^H
med(79-83) 28.5^L x 17.75^W x 9.75^H
large(79-85) 30^L x 20^W x 10.5^H
Dark & Classic(86-98), also often customized with red, green, blue, yellow or brown accents

	Org$	AVG	HIGH
small	29.95	95	132
med	31.95	93	150
large	34.95	208	300

Little Bin(00-03)
top: 16489^C/17052^{WB}
bottom: 16586^C/17079^{WB}
top 7.25^L x 7.5^W x 2^{FH} x 3^{BH}
bot 7.25^L x 8^W x 2.5^H x 3.75^{BH}
Classic$^{(00-02)}$ & Warm Brown$^{(02-03)}$

	Org$	AVG	HIGH
top	34	45	52
bottom	37	54	65

Loaf, Small(99-02)
12823
7.5^L x 4.75^W x 2.5^H
Classic only, designed to fit the Small Loaf Dish

	Org$	AVG	HIGH
B	32	38	45

Measuring Baskets
1/2" weave(79-98)
Dark & Classic stain

5in:	3800-B^D/13803^C	
7in:	3900-B^D/13901^C	
9in:	4000-B^D/14001^C	
11in:	4100-B^D/14109^C	
13in:	4200-B^D/14206^C	

3/8" weave(00-02)
Classic stain

5in:	11415^C
7in:	19861^C
9in:	19763^C
13in:	19968^C

Magazine(79-06)
2sw/h$^{(79-06)}$ 2100-C^D/12106^C
17753^{WB}
lid/feet$^{(79-98)}$ 2100-W^D/12114^C
feet/nolid$^{(79-95)}$ 2100-U^D/12122^C
16^L x 8^W x 11^H
DarK, Classic, WarmBrown

	Org$	AVG	HIGH
2sw/h	21.95	89	135
lid/ft	25.95	74	88
ft/nolid	21.95	63	116

	Org$	AVG	HIGH
5 in	7.95	37	56
7 in	10.95	59	92
9 in	13.95	56	80
11 in	17.95	60	88
13 in	20.95	72	133

Mail(00-02)
small: 9.75^L x 6.25^W x 8.5^H
med: 10.75^L x 7.75^W x 10.25^H
large: 12^L x 8.75^W x 11^H
Classic only

	Org$	AVG	HIGH
small	79	--	--
med	99	110	135
large	115	115	135

Media(04-06)
10697
11.5^L x 7.5^W x 7^{FH} x 9^{BH}
Warm Brown only

	Org$	AVG	HIGH
B	59	59	99

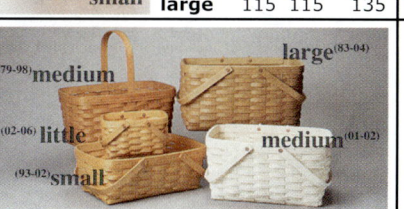

Note Pal(00-06)
11606^C/17958^{WB}/11003 ^{WW}
7.5^L x 5.5^W x 2^{FH} x 3.5^{BH}
Classic$^{(00-02)}$ Warm Brown$^{(02-04)}$ & Whitewash$^{(01-02)}$

	Org$	AVG	HIGH
stain	32	48	61
wwash	34	--	--

Market Baskets
sm: 15^L x 9.5^W x 5.5^H
md: 15^L x 10^W x 7.5^H
lg: 16^L x 11^W x 9^H
little: 7.75^L x 5.5^W x 4.5^H

	Org$	AVG	HIGH
sm$^{st/h}$	15	60	71
sm$^{2sw/h}$	46	48	61
md$^{st/h}$	17	77	89
md^{ww}	69	95	111
lg$^{st/h}$	20	93	119
lg$^{2sw/h}$	30	79	120
little	44	50	69

Pantry(86-02)
12327
14^L x 9^W x 4.5^H
Classic only

	Org$	AVG	HIGH
B	21.95	43	68

Retired Baskets

Retired Baskets

Paper Tray(99-04)
tapered: 19062ᶜ/17133ᵂᴮ
bottom: 18961ᶜ/18008ᵂᴮ
taprd 12ᴸ x 14.5ᵂ x 3ᶠᴴ x 5.5ᴮᴴ
bottom 12ᴸ x 14.5ᵂ x 3ᴴ
Classic(99-02) & Warm Brown(02-04)
(see page 63 for stand)

	Org$	AVG	HIGH
top	55	78	115
bottom	50	58	81

Pie Basket(86-02)
12203
12ᴸ x 12ᵂ x 4ᴴ
Classic only

	Org$	AVG	HIGH
B	22.95	47	80

Peg Baskets(85-99)
small: 5ᴸ x 5ᵂ x 4.5ᴴ
med: 5.5ᴸ x 5.5ᵂ x 6ᴴ
large: 6.5ᴸ x 6.5ᵂ x 8ᴴ
Classic only

	Org$	AVG	HIGH
small	15.95	30	53
med	17.95	38	65
large	19.95	48	57

Planter, Large Fern(79-86)
3200-RO/SO/TO
13ᴿᴰ x 8.5ᴴ
Dark(79-85) & Classic(85-86)
Available with feet(-RO), or
with 13"(-SO) or 20"stand(-TO)

	Org$	AVG	HIGH
feet	27.95	94	130
13in	23.95	121	200
20in	26.95	105	190

Pen Pal (00-P)
11541ᶜ/10931ᵂᵂ
4ᴿᴰ x 4.25ᴴ
Classic(00-02) & Whitewash(01-02)
still available in Warm Brown

	Org$	AVG	HIGH
stain	29	29	32
wwash	29	29	32

Planter, Small Fern(79-86)
2900-RO/SO/TO
8.5ᴿᴰ x 7.5ᴴ
Dark(79-85) & Classic(85-86)
Available with feet(-RO), or
with 13"(-SO) or 20"stand(-TO)

	Org$	AVG	HIGH
feet	21.95	108	175
13in	21.95	102	115
20in	24.95	138	150

Picnic, Family(83-86)
2600-HO
24ᴸ x 17ᵂ x 10ᴴ
Dark(83-85) & Classic(85-86)
Red gingham liner also offered

	Org$	AVG	HIGH
B	98.95	303	345
Cᴸ	135.90	346	390

Purse, Kiddie(79-06)
700-Eᴰ/ 10731ᶜ/17019ᴺ/
11350ᵂᵂ/18211ᵂᴮ
7ᴸ x 5ᵂ x 3.5ᴴ
Dark(79-85), Classic(85-02),
Natural(94), Whitewash(01-02),
WarmBrown(02-06)

	Org$	AVG	HIGH
stain	11	39	90
natural	29	40	60
wwash	39	57	81

Picnic, Medium(79-84)
200-H
15ᴸ x 15ᵂ x 7.5ᴴ
Dark stain only

	Org$	AVG	HIGH
B	26.95	195	240

Purse, Medium(79-97)
900-Eᴰ/10901ᶜ
11ᴸ x 8ᵂ x 5.5ᴴ
Dark(79-85) & Classic(85-97)

	Org$	AVG	HIGH
B	16.95	59	72

Picnic, Small(79-02)
11029
12ᴸ x 12ᵂ x 6ᴴ
Dark(79-85) & Classic(85-02)

	Org$	AVG	HIGH
B	21.95	87	103

Purse, Medium Split Lid(82-86)
900-QO
11ᴸ x 8ᵂ x 5.5ᴴ
Dark(82-85) & Classic(85-86)

	Org$	AVG	HIGH
B	24.95	120	255

Purse, Shoulder(96-99)
18210
9.5^L x 5.75^W x 7^H
Classic only

	Org$	AVG	HIGH
B	84.95	95	120

Saddlebrook(00-02)
Country Estates
Sm 17698 | Lg 19764
small: 5.5^L x 3.5^W x 4.5^H
large: 9.5^L x 5.5^W x 9.25^H
Classic only

	Org$	AVG	HIGH
small	79	85	119
large	139	139	169

Purse, Small(79-99)
800-E^D/10821^C
9.5^L x 6^W x 6^H
Dark(79-85) *& Classic*(85-99)

	Org$	AVG	HIGH
B	14.95	50	75

Salt & Pepper(01-04)
12044^C/18369^{WB}
5.75^L x 3.75^W x 3^H
Classic & Warm Brown

	Org$	AVG	HIGH
B	34	49	52

Purse, Tall(79-89)
1000-EO
9.5^L x 5^W x 9.5^H
Dark(79-85) *& Classic*(85-89)

	Org$	AVG	HIGH
B	27.95	70	95

Serving Solutions(99-02)
8x8:15393 | 9x13:15491
8x8: 9.5^L x 9.5^W x 2.75^H
9x13: 14.5^L x 9.5^W x 2.75^H
Classic only

	Org$	AVG	HIGH
8x8	37	40	68
9x13	49	49	59

Recipe Baskets
Large Recipe(96-P)
17418^C/19542^N/10461^{WW}
8^L x 5.5^W x 4.5^{FH} x 6^{BH}
Classic(96-01) *Natural*(99-01)*&*
Whitewash(01-02)*, still*
available in WarmBrown

	Org$	AVG	HIGH
stain	30	35	79
natural	25	36	45
wwash	35	48	65

Sewing, Rectangular(78-83)
600-F
16^L x 11^W x 9^H
Dark stain only, featured
split attached lid. Metal
hinges were replaced
with leather in 1979.

	Org$	AVG	HIGH
B	26.95	381	400

Small Recipe(01-02)
19469^C/10451^{WW}
7^L x5.25^W x3.75^{FH} x4.5^{BH}
Classic & Whitewash

	Org$	AVG	HIGH
stain	34	49	80
wwash	34	--	--

Sewing, Round(78-86)
3200-NO
13RD x 8.5^H
Dark stain only, attached
split lid. Metal hinges
were replaced with leather
in 1979. Sold with or
without 13" stand.

	Org$	AVG	HIGH
stand	29.95	140	250
no stand		111	187

Row Your Boat(02-05)
12494^C/18326^{WB}
13.5^L x 6.5^W x 4^H
Classic(02)*& WarmBrown*(02-05)

	Org$	AVG	HIGH
B	54	56	69

Sewing Notions
10424^C/18415^{WB}/10435^{WW}
11.25^L x 9.25^W x 5.75^H
Classic(01-02)*, Warm Brown*(02-04)*, Whitewash*(01-02)

	Org$	AVG	HIGH
stain	59	59	79
wwash	59	59	88

Retired Baskets

Retired Baskets

Small Comforts(01-04)
17558^C/18512^{WB}
7.75^L x 5.25^W x 4.25^H
Classic(01-02) & *Warm Brown*(02-04)

	Org$	AVG	HIGH
B	42	42	52

Tiny Tote(02-05)
12512^C/18628^{WB}
6^L x 5.5^W x 7^H
Classic(02) & *Warm Brown*(02-05)

	Org$	AVG	HIGH
B	59	69	95

Spoon Baskets(82-04)
teaspoon: 5^L x 5^W x 4.5^H
small: 5.5^L x 5.5^W x 6^H
med: 6.5^L x 6.5^W x 8^H
large: 7.5^L x 7.5^W x 10^H
Dark(82-85), *Classic*(85-02), *Natural*(00-01) & *Warm Brown*(02-04). Accessories sold separately.

Tissue(97-P)
15831^C/14184^N/10473^{WW}
6.5^L x 6.5^W x 6.25^H
Classic(97-02), *Natural*(99-01), *Whitewash*(01-05), still available in Warm Brown. Accessories sold separately.

	Org$	AVG	HIGH
stain	32	34	72
natural	32	32	35
wwash	34	53	72

	Org$	AVG	HIGH
tea$^{C/WB}$	25	33	45
tea^N	25	--	30
sm$^{C/WB}$	17	32	55
sm^N	26	31	45
med$^{D/C}$	15	40	65
med^N	34	--	--
large$^{D/C}$	17	68	77
large^N	45	45	56

Tissue, Long(00-02)
10412
12^L x 7.25^W x 5.75^H
Classic only

	Org$	AVG	HIGH
B	44	75	80

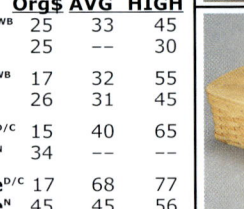

Spring(83-P)
11283^{WW}/10928^C
11^L x 8^W x 5.5^H
Whitewash(01-05) & *Classic*(01-02), still offered in Warm Brown

	Org$	AVG	HIGH
stain	15	46	58
wwash	39	--	--

Umbrella(79-94)
1200-OO/11207
10RD x 17.5^H
Dark(79-85) & *Classic*(85-94). Brought back into the Hostess Collection in 1999.

	Org$	AVG	HIGH
B	18.95	58	99

Stuck on You(01-04)
11865^C/18590^{WB}
4.75^L x 4.75^H x 2^H
Classic(01-02) & *Warm Brown*(02-04)

	Org$	AVG	HIGH
B	29	40	55

Vanity(98-06)
18449^C/18679^{WB}
14.5^L x 7.5^W x 4.5^{FH} x 6.5^{BH}
Classic(98-02) & *Warm Brown*(02-06)

	Org$	AVG	HIGH
B	50	56	75

Tea(79-P)
10740^C/10847^N
7^L x 5^W x 3.5^H
Classic(79-02) & *Natural*(99-01), still offered in Warm Brown

	Org$	AVG	HIGH
stain	7.95	29	65
natural	25	33	40

Vegetable(82-02)
small: 10.5^L 6.5^W 3^{FH} 7^{BH}
med: 13^L x 7.5^W x 3^{FH} x 8^{BH}
large: 16^L 9^W 3.5^{FH} 9^{BH}
Dark(82-85), *Classic*(85-02), *Natural*(Med)(94)

	Org$	AVG	HIGH
small	13	39	55
med	15	37	69
med^N	39	60	75
large	27	67	135

Retired Baskets

Waste[79-00]
Med 11703 | Sm 11801
med: 13.5^L x 13.5^W x 16^H
small: 9.5^L x 9.5^W x 12^H
Dark[79-85] & Classic[85-00]

	Org$	AVG	HIGH
med	21.95	95	113
sm	16.95	63	119

Window Box[05-06]
At Home Garden
10181
21.25^L x 9^W x 5^H
Warm Brown only

	Org$	AVG	HIGH
B	86	--	--

Waste, Oval[00-06]
small: 11.5^L x 9.25^W x 10.5^H
med: 14.25^L x 11.5^W x 12.75^H
large: 16.25^L x 13^W x 16^H
Classic[00-02] & Warm Brown[02-06]

	Org$	AVG	HIGH
small	79	79	97
med	104	104	134
large	149	--	--

Wine, Large[83-86]
5200-CO
16^L x 9^W x 3.5^H x 9^{BH}
Dark[83-85] & Classic[85-86], included dividers (wine rack)

	Org$	AVG	HIGH
B	30	92	145

Weekender[04-05]
18857^{WB}
10.5^L x 9^W x 8^H
Warm Brown only, originally offered in the Hostess Collection only

	Org$	AVG	HIGH
B	139	139	157

Work Load[01-04]
Sm: 12032^C / 18760^{WB}
Lg: 11776^C / 18776^{WB}
small: 19^L x 10.5^W x 8.25^H
large: 24^L x 13.25^W x 8.75^H
Classic[01-02] & Warm Brown[02-04]

	Org$	AVG	HIGH
Small	149	153	173
Large	179	179	222

NATIONWIDE PHOTO WINNER

Peggy Elkins
Toney, AL

How sweet it is ... to be a Longaberger Collector!

Peggy reminds us that collecting is not just about baskets! Here, she displays Longaberger's versatility as she brings together a beautiful grouping of reds from three separate collections: Sweetheart, American Craft Original Pottery and Paprika Regular Line Pottery.

Certainly made our hearts race!

Retired Baskets

Shades of Autumn

1990 Pie
2200-AGUBS
12^L x 12^W x 4^H

	Org$	AVG	HIGH
B	31.95	75	149

1994 Recipe
17400
8^L x 5.5^W x 4.5^{FH} x 6^{BH}
Included set of recipe cards, lid sold separately

	Org$	AVG	HIGH
B	29.95	54	77
C$^{P/Lid}$	44.95	70	90

1990 Small Vegetable
5000-CGUBS
10.5^L x 6.5^W x 3^{FH} x 7^{BH}
Hostess only

	Org$	AVG	HIGH
B	35.95	117	180

1991 Small Gathering
2300-CGUBS
14^L x 9^W x 4.5^H

	Org$	AVG	HIGH
B	36.95	63	85
C$^{P/L}$	48.95	100	115

1995 Basket of Plenty
15563 | TO 31755
12RD x 5.75^H
Fall Foliage Tie-on and other accessories sold separately

	Org$	AVG	HIGH
B	53.95	70	103
C$^{P/L}$	69.95	80	125
FS$^{C/Ld}$	101.85	105	138
TO	6.95	17	23

1996 Maple Leaf
13935 | TO 32999
7RD x 6.5^H
Maple Leaf Tie-on and other accessories sold separately

	Org$	AVG	HIGH
B	40.95	43	59
C$^{P/L}$	54.95	57	65
FS$^{C/Ld}$	74.90	80	125
TO	6.95	11	17

1991 Acorn
700-BGUBS
7^L x 5^W x 3.5^H

	Org$	AVG	HIGH
B	24.95	59	71
C$^{P/L}$	35.95	63	100

1997 Bountiful Harvest
12254
10.25^L x 10.25^W x 4.5^H
Promoted along with the 1Qt Casserole Dish, see Pottery section

	Org$	AVG	HIGH
B	44.95	59	72
C$^{P/L}$	61.95	66	95
FS$^{C/Ld}$	86.90	90	100

1992 Bittersweat
10804
5.5^L x 5.5^W x 6^H

	Org$	AVG	HIGH
B	24.95	54	50
C$^{P/L}$	29.95	46	79

1998 Baker's Bounty
11771 | TO 33669
10^L x 6.25^W x 3.75^H
Promoted along with the Small Loaf Dish, see Pottery section

	Org$	AVG	HIGH
B	39	53	75
C$^{P/L}$	49	63	90
FS$^{C/Ld}$	71	71	109
TO	8	10	17

1993 Harvest
14303 | Runner 20150
7^L x 4.75^W x 7.75^H
Liner shown is Autumn fabric, reversible table runner is showing Sunset fabric

	Org$	AVG	HIGH
B	39.95	44	60
C$^{P/L}$	48.95	55	82
runner	34.95	--	--

Special Events

The items in this collection were created in honor of a Special Event or cause.

COLLECTION INDEX:
Bob & Dolores Hope 134
Homestead Events 134
Heisey Horse 135
Inaugural 135
Made To Order 136
Misc Events 137

Bob & Dolores Hope

1989: First Edition
11^L x 8^W x 5.5^H
QTY: 500
Classic stain, brown trim and center weave, blue shoestring

	AVG	HIGH
B	500	750

1990: Second Edition
11^L x 8^W x 5.5^H
QTY: 500
Classic stain, blue trim and center weave, brown shoestring

	AVG	HIGH
B	500	733

1991: Third Edition
11^L x 8^W x 5.5^H
QTY: 500
Classic stain, blue trim, brown/blue/brown center weave, no shoestring weave

	AVG	HIGH
B	667	750

1992: Fourth Edition
11^L x 8^W x 5.5^H
QTY: 500
Classic stain, brown trim, blue/brown/blue center weave, no shoestring weave

	AVG	HIGH
B	500	753

1993: Fifth Edition
11^L x 8^W x 5.5^H
QTY: 500
Classic stain, blue trim, brown/blue/brown center weave, no shoestring weave

	AVG	HIGH
B	558	750

1994: Sixth Edition
11^L x 8^W x 5.5^H
QTY: 500
Classic stain, blue trim and center weave, brown shoestring weave

	AVG	HIGH
B	500	774

1995: Seventh Edition
11^L x 8^W x 5.5^H
QTY: 250
Classic stain, blue trim and center weave, brown shoestring weave

	AVG	HIGH
B	613	625

1996: Eighth Edition
11^L x 8^W x 5.5^H
QTY: 250
Classic stain, blue trim and center weave, brown shoestring weave.
FINAL YEAR

	AVG	HIGH
B	677	729

Homestead Events

The baskets in this section were offered exclusively during special events held at The Homestead. Each had accessories that were considered to be "official" for the event, but since they were sold at the Homestead, they are often found in the market with alternative accessories that could be purchased from the Homestead at the same time.

1998 Barn Raising
222806 | TO 221833
7RD x 6.5^H
Sold as a Combo, other accessories sold separately

	Org$	AVG	HIGH
B		81	92
C$^{P/L}$	59.95	115	135
FS$^{C/Ld}$	85.95	125	160
TO	5	18	25

2003 Heritage Days
123814
8RD x 6.75^H
Available at Heritage Days or via mail order to Consultants who attended the Bee

	Org$	AVG	HIGH
B		80	99
C$^{P/L}$	79	97	169
FS$^{C/Ld}$	107	125	210
TO		(shown next page)	

Special Events

Homestead Events (con't)

2003 Heritage Days
Heritage Days TO 196628
Garland TO 841792
The pewter version was the 'official' one, but the garland was also offered on order forms

	Org$	AVG	HIGH
TO^{HDays}	8	14	15
TO^{Garland}	10	--	--

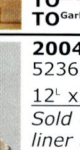

2004 Heritage Days
523670
12^L x 7^W x 4.5^H
Sold only as a set, with liner and protector. Tie-ons/other accessories sold separately

	Org$	AVG	HIGH
C^{P/L}	84	91	96
FS^{C/Ld}	116	--	--

2004 Heritage Days
Heritage Days TO 328102
Garland TO 328101
The pewter version was the 'official' one, but the garland was also offered on order forms

	Org$	AVG	HIGH
TO^{HDays}	8	14	15
TO^{Garland}	10	--	--

2005 Heritage Days
7.5RD x 5^H
Sold only as a set, with liner and protector. Tie-ons/other accessories sold separately

	Org$	AVG	HIGH
C^{P/L}	84	131	175
FS^{C/Ld}	104	--	--
TO	10	--	--

Heisey Horse

1998 Red Horse
6.5^W x 6.75^H
QTY: 900, Introduced at the 1998 Barn Raising Event. First of 3 horses produced exclusively by Heisey Glass for Longaberger.

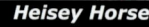

	Org$	AVG	HIGH
horse	95	1400	2125

1999 Cobalt Blue Horse
6.5^W x 6.75^H
QTY Horse: 3000, first year to offer colts

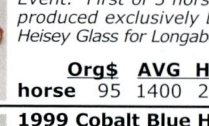

	Org$	AVG	HIGH
horse	98	188	250
balking	50	65	110
kicking	50	65	96
standing	50	55	75

2000 Emerald Horse
6.5^W x 6.75^H
Final horse in the series

	Org$	AVG	HIGH
horse	98	188	250
balking	50	--	--
kicking	50	--	--
standing	50	--	--

2001 Ruby Filly
8.5^H
Limited to one per customer

	Org$	AVG	HIGH
filly	98	138	213

Inaugural Basket

1989 Inaugural
3800-ABRST
5RD x 4.5^H
In honor of President Bush (41) Inauguration

	Org$	AVG	HIGH
B	19.89	175	400

1993 Inaugural
11461
5^L x 5^W x 4.5^H
In honor of President Clinton (42) Inauguration

	Org$	AVG	HIGH
B	24.95	37	65
C^{P/L}	34.95	42	99

1997 Inaugural
15326 | TO 71609
5.5RD x 3.25^H
QTY: 298,318, in honor of President Clinton's 2nd Inauguration

	Org$	AVG	HIGH
B	32.95	47	70
C^{P/L}	42.95	60	90
TO	6.95	15	28

2001 Inaugural
16080 | TO 73903
5.5^L x 4^W x 4^H
QTY: 227,763, in honor of President Bush (43) Inauguration

	Org$	AVG	HIGH
B	39	53	79
C^{P/L}	49	60	105
FS^{C/Ld}	63	75	130
TO	8	15	26

2005 Inaugural
10737 | TO 20040

7.25RD x 2.75^H

Made in 2004 for the 2005 Inaugural in honor of President Bush

	Org$	AVG	HIGH
B	49	58	79
C^{P/L}	59	63	85
FS^{C/Ld}	82	82	128
TO	8	10	12

Made To Order

Design-A-Basket

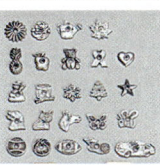

Design-A-Basket
In 2005, the company replaced the Group Sales program with the Design-A-Basket. This program allows customers the opportunity to create a one-of-a-kind basket for their group, company, fundraiser or whatever their needs. This program offers literally over 2 million possible combinations, 10 minimum order required:

- *7 different baskets*:
  Pen Pal, Knick Knack, Card File, Spring, Media Basket, Carry Along, Medium Market
- *2 stain options*:
  Warm Brown, Whitewash
- *Trim strips: 12 colors, 2 sizes*:
  Black, Dark Blue, Gray, Green, Light Blue, Red, Maroon, Orange, Pink, Purple, Sage, Yellow
- *2 types of tags, 6 messages*:
  Brass or Nickel: Celebrate! Congratulations, Happy Anniversary, Happy Holidays, Thank You, Welcome
- *25 different tack covers*:
  Apple, Baseball, Basketball, Bee, Butterfly, Race Car, Cat Head, Dog Head, Drum w/sticks, Flower, Football, Golf green/ball/flag, Heart, Holiday, Horse head, Maple Leaf, Pineapple, Ribbon, Rose, Snowflake, Snowman, Soccer ball, Star, Teddy Bear, Watering Can
- *Accessories*:
  Protectors and engraved Lids could also be added to some baskets

Group Sales

2003-05 Group Sales Custom Program
This program was the first for the company to offer custom-designed baskets to a Group, minimum order of 10.

- *3 different baskets*:
  Pen Pal, Little Market, Cake
- *1 stain*:
  Warm Brown
- *Trim strips: 5 colors*:
  Red, Blue, Green, Purple and Black
- *1 tag, 4 messages*:
  Brass only: Celebrate! Congratulations, Happy Holidays, Thank You

	Org$	AVG	HIGH
penpal	30	30	52
l.mkt	48	48	55
cake	70	70	81

Make-A-Basket

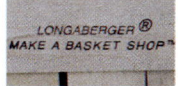

1996-present
Starting in 1996, Longaberger opened the first Make-A-Basket Shop in Dresden giving collectors the once-in-a-lifetime experience of making their very own basket. While the main shop was moved to The Homestead, the experience has also been offered at many company events, such as the Bee, Club Gatherings and different Advisor meetings throughout the year. Each basket has the Make-A-Basket logo on the bottom of the basket.

In 2006, visitors were given the ability to add different color trim strips and specialty tacks, very similar to what is offered in the Design-A-Basket program.

(not all forms listed)

	Org$	AVG	HIGH
spring	55	--	--
berry	55	--	--
m.key	55	--	--
l.peg	55	--	--
m.chore	55	--	--
s.brook	55	--	--

Special Events

Special Events

Misc Special Events

Basket Fest⁽⁰⁵⁾
13ᴸ x 8ᵂ x 5ᴴ
QTY: 1000, event done in co-ordination with Boyds Bears. Natural Medium Chore, 2sw/h with bear tacks. Make-A-Basket logo.

	Org$	AVG	HIGH
B	55	--	226

Fraternal Order of Police⁽⁰⁶⁾
60857
8ᴸ x 5.5ᵂ x 4.5ᶠᴴ x 6ᴮᴴ
Large Recipe Basket, blue trim, star tacks, FOP logo engraved on lid. Sold only as a set.

	Org$	AVG	HIGH
Bᴸᵈ	55	--	--

Basket Fest⁽⁰⁶⁾
13ᴸ x 8ᵂ x 5ᴴ
Also called the John Deere Basket. Natural Medium Chore, yellow/green trim with John Deere tractor tacks. Make-A-Basket logo.

	Org$	AVG	HIGH
B	55	--	--

Nurses Inaugural⁽⁹⁹⁾
15423-ONA
7ᴿᴰ x 3ᴴ
Heartland Button customized with an exclusive liner honoring the Ohio Nurses' Association

	Org$	AVG	HIGH
B	53	--	--

Discovery⁽⁹²⁾
5700-AO
5.5ᴿᴰ x 3.5ᴴ
In honor of the Discovery of America. Only a liner was originally offered

	Org$	AVG	HIGH
B	19.92	35	65
Cᴸ	29.87	41	109

Ohio Statehouse⁽⁹⁶⁾
11ᴸ x 8ᴴ x 5.5ᴴ
QTY: 400, Spring basket with red/blue accent weave. Given to those hosting a table at the Ohio Statehouse re-opening. Came as seen here, full of Ohio-made items.

	AVG	HIGH
B	--	80

Fraternal Order of Police⁽⁰⁵⁾
0440
7.25ᴸ x 6ᵂ x 4ᴴ
Blue trim, star tacks, FOP logo engraved on lid. Sold only as a set with basket and lid

	Org$	AVG	HIGH
Bᴸᵈ	55	110	135

25th Anniversary
17612
8.75ᴸ x 4.75ᵂ x 6.5ᴴ
QTY: 213,000, Available to the public in celebration of the Company's 25th Anniversary

	Org$	AVG	HIGH
B	49.95	63	113
Cᴾ/ᴸ	71.85	86	135

THE FUTURE OF LONGABERGER

Rita Dayton
Allison, 4 | MiKayla, 2
Seaford, DE

We're not sure of which Mom is more proud, the baskets or the girls, but we're glad that she chose to share them with us!

Maybe some day, Allison or MiKayla will have an Inaugural made in their honor!

Sweetheart Baskets

1990 Sweetheart
45000-ARS
5.75^L x 3.75^W x 3^H

	Org$	AVG	HIGH
B	24.95	77	115
C^L	32.95	86	159

1995 Sweet Sentiments
19046 | TO 31780
4.25^L x 4.25^W x 3^H
Accessories sold separately

	Org$	AVG	HIGH
B	28.95	33	49
C$^{P/L}$	33.95	37	80
TO	5.95	14	23

1990 Getaway
300-CRS
17^L x 14^W x 11^H
Hostess only

	Org$	AVG	HIGH
B	79.95	141	195

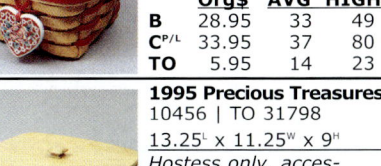

1995 Precious Treasures
10456 | TO 31798
13.25^L x 11.25^W x 9^H
Hostess only, accessories sold separately

	Org$	AVG	HIGH
B	89.95	104	133
C$^{P/L}$	99.95	110	150
FS$^{C/Ld}$	129.95	140	155
TO	6.95	15	20

1993 Sweetheart
11347 | TO 72036
5^L x 5^W x 2.5^H
Accessories sold separately

	Org$	AVG	HIGH
B	25.95	38	52
C$^{P/L}$	29.95	51	60
TO	8.95	21	42

1996 Bouquet
11240 | TO 33596
6.5RD x 6.5^H
Accessories sold separately

	Org$	AVG	HIGH
B	34.95	49	75
C$^{P/L}$	44.95	51	95
TO	6.95	11	17

1993 Gateway
10359
17^L x 14^W x 11^H
Hostess only

	Org$	AVG	HIGH
B	119.95	130	190
C$^{P/L}$	139.95	178	199

1997
Gourmet Gathering
15946^R/16063^G/16055^B/16071^P
18^L x 11^W x 4.5^H
Red, green, blue, purple

	Org$	AVG	HIGH
B	74.95	85	91
C$^{P/L}$	99.95	105	140
FS$^{C/Ld}$	144.90	145	162

Sweet Treats
15938^R/15962^G/15954^B/15971^G | TO 71617
8^L x 5^W x 3^H
Red, green, blue, purple

	Org$	AVG	HIGH
B	32.95	38	50
C$^{P/L}$	42.95	46	78
TO	6.95	12	18

1994 Be Mine
18601
8.5^L x 5^W x 3.5^H

	Org$	AVG	HIGH
B	27.95	66	90
C$^{P/L}$	36.95	67	85

1994 Forever Yours
10367 | TO 22659
20.5^L x 15^W x 10.5^H
Hostess only, accessories sold separately

	Org$	AVG	HIGH
B	109.95	134	65
C$^{P/L}$	139.95	150	199
TO	6.95	14	25

1997 Trivets
2366390^R/2366391^G/2366392^B/2366292^P
14^L x 9^W
Red, green, blue, purple

	Org$	AVG	HIGH
	13.95	21	37

Sweetheart Baskets

1998
Cherished Memories
17531^R/16268^B/16365^G/
16462^P/16560^C
14.25^L x 6.25^W x 9.5^H
*Red, blue, green, purple,
or Classic/no color*

	Org$	AVG	HIGH
B	89	91	115
C$^{P/L}$	119	121	167
FS$^{C/Ld}$	153	153	195

Picture Perfect
17523^R/16250^B/16357^G/
16454^P/16551^C
7.25^L x 4^W x 4.5^H
*Red, blue, green, purple,
or Classic/no color*

	Org$	AVG	HIGH
B	39	52	84
C$^{P/L}$	49	65	90
FS$^{C/Ld}$	55	77	130

1998 Tie-Ons
Frame TO: 72770
Lapel Pin TO: 72761
Sold separately

	Org$	AVG	HIGH
frame	10	14	18
pin	8	12	23

1999
Love Treasures
13064 | TO 37184
13.25^L x 12.5^W x 4.25^H

	Org$	AVG	HIGH
B		68	96	120
C$^{P/L}$	89	103	155
FS$^{C/Ld}$	137	137	170
TO	8	13	17

Love Letters
12963
8.75^L x 7.75^W x 2.75^H
Letters of Love stationary also promoted this year

	Org$	AVG	HIGH
B	44	60	90
C$^{P/L}$	56	65	125
FS$^{C/Ld}$	82	90	135

2000 Little Love
17728^R/10874^B/18062^G/
10850^P/10885^C
6.25^L x 4.75^W x 2.25^H
*Red, blue, green, purple,
or Classic/no color. See
Foundry for stand.*

	Org$	AVG	HIGH
B	34	41	59
C$^{P/L}$	39	53	89
FS$^{C/Ld}$	58	65	100

2001 Love Notes
12055^C/10826^R
TO 78328 | hook 78123
5.75^L x 3.75^W x 5^H
*Classic or red, accessories
sold separately*

	Org$	AVG	HIGH
B	39	53	78
C$^{P/L}$	49	57	90
TO	8	11	14
hook	16	21	27

2002-03 Sweetest Gift
Large
10300 | TO 20265
10.5^L x 10.5^W x 9^H
Accessories sold separately

	Org$	AVG	HIGH
B	79	85	124
C$^{P/L}$	118	129	160
FS$^{C/Ld}$	157	157	165
TO	8	11	15

2002-03 Sweetest Gift
Small
10288
4^L x 4^W x 3.5^H
QTY: 118,855

	Org$	AVG	HIGH
B	39	55	80
C$^{P/L}$	49	64	99
FS$^{C/Ld}$	75	77	100

2004 Let Me Call
You Sweetheart
10644 | TO 28162
6RD x 5.5^H
*Also known as the Rose Bowl
basket, features rose tacks*

	Org$	AVG	HIGH
B	49	53	56
C$^{P/L}$	59	63	79
FS$^{C/Ld}$	80	80	110
TO	8	11	16

2005 Sweetest Heart
10192^{WB}/10240^{WW} | TO 23044
8^L x 8.5^W x 2.5^H
*Warm Brown or Whitewash,
lid available in Warm Brown,
Whitewash or Red. See
Pottery for the dish.*

	Org$	AVG	HIGH
B	59	59	85
C$^{P/L}$	84	85	95
FS$^{C/Ld}$	102	102	110
TO	8	8	12

2006 Be My Valentine
10411^R/10415^{WB}|TO 23044
8RD x 4.25^H
*Red or Warm Brown with
red accents*

	Org$	AVG	HIGH
B	59	--	--
C$^{P/L}$	69	69	81
FS$^{C/Ld}$	91	--	--
TO	8	--	--

Tour Baskets

These baskets are only available on tour in Dresden, at The Homestead or in Hartville. Accessories can vary widely as the stores carry many different options.

COLLECTION INDEX:
- Dresden 140
- Golf 140
- Hartville 141
- Woven Memories 141
- Miscellaneous 142

Dresden Tour Basket

1988-1999
5600-BO/15601
8.75^L x 4.75^W x 6.5^H
Featured same basket each year with only the tag changing to reflect the year

	Org$	AVG	HIGH
88		--	--
89		119	140
90		70	70
91		53	90
92		44	69
93	24.95	53	60
C^P	30.90	63	70
94	29.95	44	65
C^P	35.90	48	80
95-99	34.95	43	60
C^P	40.90	47	60

1999-00 Dresden
7^L x 3.5^W x 4.75^H
Same form as what was considered the TourII Basket

	Org$	AVG	HIGH
B	29.95	59	66

2001-02 Dresden
7^L x 3.5^W x 4.75^H
First year for color

	Org$	AVG	HIGH
B	29.95	50	60

2003 Dresden
4.75^L x 5^W x 3.25^H

	Org$	AVG	HIGH
B	38.95	78	80
C^P	41.90	83	86

2004 Dresden
4.75^L x 5^W x 3.25^H
Same form as the Let It Snow basket, with the Proudly American color design

	Org$	AVG	HIGH
B	38.95	59	99
C^P	41.90	75	110

2005 Dresden
5.5^{RD} x 3.75^H
Same form as the Lily of the Valley, available Warm Brown or Warm Brown with red accents

	Org$	AVG	HIGH
B	34.95	--	--

2006 Dresden
5.25^L x 4^W x 5.5^H
Same form as the 2004 Horizon of Hope, available Warm Brown with choice of Cinnamon, Sage or Purple trim

	Org$	AVG	HIGH
B	39.95	--	--

Dresden II

1996-99 Dresden II
15814
7^L x 3.5^W x 3.75^H
This new form first appeared in Dresden/Hartville in Jan 1996

	Org$	AVG	HIGH
B	29.95	33	66
C$^{P/L}$	33.90	40	75

Golf Baskets

2000 Golf
16098
6.75^{RD} x 6^H
Green accents, logo on bottom, sold at all store locations

	Org$	AVG	HIGH
B	39.95	62	95
C$^{P/L}$	59.90	73	113
FS$^{C/Ld}$	89.90	109	132

2001 Golf
6.75^{RD} x 6^H
Black accents, logo on bottom, sold at all store locations

	Org$	AVG	HIGH
B	44.95	75	80
C$^{P/L}$	65.90	86	95

Tour Baskets

Golf Baskets (con't)

2002 Golf
9RD x 5.5^H
Navy accents, accessories sold separately

	Org$	AVG	HIGH
B	54.95	74	75
C$^{P/L}$	88.90	131	142
FS$^{C/Ld}$	118.90	--	--
TO	8	--	--

2003 Golf
6.5RD x 6.75^H
Navy accents, accessories sold separately

	Org$	AVG	HIGH
B	59.95	74	85
C$^{P/L}$	92.90	90	95
FS$^{C/Ld}$	127.90	--	--

2004 Golf
7.5RD x 5.5^H
Navy accents with navy leather trim, accessories sold separately

	Org$	AVG	HIGH
B	59.95	62	75
C$^{P/L}$	87.90	89	89
FS$^{C/Ld}$	117.90	--	--

2005 Golf
10087 | TO 475156
10RD x 6.25^H
Navy accents, all accessories sold separately

	Org$	AVG	HIGH
B	54.95	--	--
C$^{P/L}$	82.90	--	--
FS$^{C/Ld}$	117.90	--	--
TO	8	8	10

2006 Golf
10483 | TO 622947
10.5^W x 7^H
Heartwood weave, walnut and cherry trim, brass tacks

	Org$	AVG	HIGH
B	59.95	--	--
C$^{P/L}$	91.95	--	--
FS$^{C/Ld}$	126.95	--	--
TO	8	--	--

Hartville Baskets

1995-99 Hartville Tour
15661
8.75^L x 4.75^W x 6.5^H
Same form as Dresden Tour, but with different tag

	Org$	AVG	HIGH
B	34.95	50	60
C^P	40.90	60	70

1996-99 Hartville Tour II
15814
7^L x 3.5^W x 4.75^H
Same form as Tour II with Hartville tag

	Org$	AVG	HIGH
B	29.95	40	45
C^P	33.90	50	57

Woven Memories

1999 Woven Memories Small Chore
10^L x 6^W x 4^H
Classic or Classic with blue shoestring weave, accessories sold separately

	Org$	AVG	HIGH
B	39.95	60	104
C$^{P/L}$	61.90	75	125

2000 Woven Memories Small Chore
10^L x 6^W x 4^H
Classic or Classic with red shoestring weave. Inset shows a special embroidered liner sold separately, along with all accessories.

	Org$	AVG	HIGH
B	39.95	63	69
C$^{P/L}$	61.90	90	104

2001 Woven Memories Small Chore
10^L x 6^W x 4^H
Classic or Classic with green accents, accessories sold separately

	Org$	AVG	HIGH
B	39.95	71	128
C$^{P/L}$	61.90	89	159

2002 Woven Memories Small Apple
7.5RD x 4.5^H
Classic or Classic with red accents, accessories sold separately

	Org$	AVG	HIGH
B	44.95	58	90
C$^{P/L}$	72.90	117	185

2003 Woven Memories
728812^{WB}/914887^R
6.5^L x 5^W x 4^H
Warm Brown or Warm Brown with red accents, new form, accessories sold separately

	Org$	AVG	HIGH
B	48.95	74	81
C$^{P/L}$	72.90	110	164

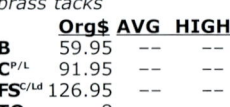

2004 Woven Memories
6.5^L x 7.25^W x 4^H
Warm Brown or Warm Brown with sage accents, new form, accessories sold separately

	Org$	AVG	HIGH
B	48.95	77	84
C$^{P/L}$	70.90	128	148

2005 Woven Memories
7.25^L x 4^W x 6.5^H
Warm Brown or Warm Brown with red accents, new form, accessories sold separately

	Org$	AVG	HIGH
B	44.95	50	55
C$^{P/L}$	67.90	69	100

Colors: Pink, Teal, Red, Navy, Teal with Whitewash overstain, Teal with Warm Brown overstain and Whitewash with Warm Brown overstain

2005 Woven Memories Consumer Testing
For a short period, the 05 Woven Memories took on a different look as the company tested different colors. Quantities were said to be under 250 for each color.

	Org$	AVG	HIGH
B	44.95	90	166
C$^{P/L}$	67.90	--	--

2006 Woven Memories
10.75^L x 7.5^W x 4.25^H
Open weave bottom, offered in 6 solid colors: Warm Brown, Soft White, Soft Pink, Blue, Red and Medium Green

	Org$	AVG	HIGH
B	49.95	--	--
C$^{P/L}$	67.90	--	--

Misc Tour Baskets

Homestead Tie-On$^{(00)}$
Postcards were sent to Collectors Club Members & Consultants inviting them to visit the Homestead. They could redeem the postcard for this free Tie-On.

	Org$	AVG	HIGH
B		10	10

20th Century$^{(97-99)}$
17575
8.75^L x 4.75^W x 6.5^H
Tag on the 1997 Basket says FIRST EDITION

	Org$	AVG	HIGH
B	49.95	70	93
C$^{P/L}$	70.90	80	104

Fun Fact

Pottery changes underfoot . . .

Beginning February 1, 2006, Longaberger converted the balance of the pottery pieces from once featuring a glazed foot (bottom of the pottery) to now having what is called a polished dry foot.

The dry foot means that there is no glaze applied to the part of the pottery that comes in contact with the surface of the table or other dishes when stacked. This change makes the firing process a lot easier and faster, helping to increase efficiencies!

Traditions® Collection

This collection was started in 1995 to replace the J.W. Collection. It was developed by Dave Longaberger himself, who determined these qualities to be the most important that a person could possess: Family, Community, Fellowship, Hospitality & Generosity. The series features Heritage Green weave and trim with all unique forms. Collection completed in 1999, just months after Dave passed away.

1997 Fellowship
15920
12.5^L x 6.5^W x 7.75^H
Handle gripper not shown, all accessories sold separately. Box.

	Org$	AVG	HIGH
B	69.95	70	80
C$^{P/L}$	89.95	108	128
FS$^{C/ld}$	129.95	130	150

1995 Family
19101
15.25^L x 11^W x 7.75^H
3/8" weave, liner not originally offered, added in 1996. Box.

	Org$	AVG	HIGH
B	89.95	95	100
C^P	95.95	110	126
FS$^{P/L}$	125.90	130	189

1998 Hospitality
10669
18.5^L x 13.5^W x 5.25^H
Accessories sold separately, no box.

	Org$	AVG	HIGH
B	89	89	130
C$^{P/L}$	114	115	155

1996 Community
19119
14.75^L x 13.5^W x 6.25^H
QTY: 171,381   Riser and other accessories sold separatley. Box.

	Org$	AVG	HIGH
B	84.95	84	110
C$^{P/L}$	109.95	110	119
FS$^{C/div}$	117.90	125	150

1999 Generosity
13358
19.25^L x 13.5^W x 7.75^H
Accessories sold separately, no box.

	Org$	AVG	HIGH
B	119	119	131
C$^{P/L}$	159	163	180
FS$^{C/Ld}$	218	200	220

NATIONWIDE PHOTO WINNER
GRAND PRIZE

Lisa Ayers   Annville, PA

We love how this display draws out the teal within Lisa's Traditions Collection, giving them a very fresh look! She's been collecting for 14 years and while Traditions are Lisa's favorite baskets, her real passion is Pottery!

Tree-Trimming Collection

1999 Peppermint
19364^R/16837^G
5.5RD x 2.75^H
Red or green, basket included tie-on, other accessories sold separately. Box.

	Org$	AVG	HIGH
B^{TO}	45	48	69
C$^{TO/P/L}$	59	70	99

2003 Melody
10452
5RD x 3^H
Only available with both red and green upsplints. Box.

	Org$	AVG	HIGH
B^{TO}	49	63	75
C$^{TO/P/L}$	67	73	79
FS$^{C/Ld}$	78	78	99

2000 Let It Snow
18147^R/18155^G
4.75^L x 5^W x 3.25^H
QTY: 200,500. Red or green, included tie-on, other accessories sold separately. Box.

	Org$	AVG	HIGH
B^{TO}	45	55	75
C$^{TO/P/L}$	59	63	80
FS$^{C/Ld}$	74	75	89

2004 Gumdrop
10735^R/10736^G
7.5^L x 5.5^W x 3.5^H
Red or green, basket included tie-on, other accessories sold separately. Box.

	Org$	AVG	HIGH
B^{TO}	49	53	75
C$^{TO/P/L}$	67	67	85
FS$^{C/Ld}$	78	--	--

2001 Twinkle Twinkle
10664^R/10672^G
5.5^L x 6^W x 2.25^H
Red or green, basket included tie-on, other accessories sold separately. Box.

	Org$	AVG	HIGH
B^{TO}	49	55	75
C$^{TO/P/L}$	65	77	82
FS$^{C/Ld}$	82	82	97

2005 Tinsel
10331^R/10334^G/10372^{WB}
6.5^L x 6.5^W x 2.75^H
Red, green or Warm Brown with no color. Box.

	Org$	AVG	HIGH
B^{TO}	49	49	53
C$^{TO/P/L}$	67	67	79
FS$^{C/Ld}$	78	--	--

2002 Treats
10438^R/10448^G
6.25^L x 4^W x 3^H
Red or green, basket included tie-on, other accessories sold separately. Box.

	Org$	AVG	HIGH
B^{TO}	49	57	75
C$^{TO/P/L}$	65	68	86
FS$^{C/Ld}$	78	78	100

Fun Fact

What's all the buzz about a new logo on the bottom of the baskets? Actually it's more like a hum ... a hum of a laser, that is.

You may have noticed the burned-in logo on the bottom side of many baskets looks a little different ... more crisp, more defined. Actually, the change started in 2002 when the burned-in logo was replaced with a laser process. Techonology has allowed the company to make this change on larger baskets, however, at the request of the family, certain collections will always feature the burned-in process – Collectors Club being one.

Wood Products

Wood Products have been an important part of the Longaberger product line from the very beginning. Most of the early items were produced in Dresden by a family-owned cabinet company, Mock Woodworking. Later, all of the wood items were brought in-house and changed to be called WoodCrafts®.

COLLECTION INDEX:
- Cupboards 145
- Dividers .145
- Paddles .145
- Wall Hangings 146
- Misc Wood Products 147

Original logo, started in 1985. Unknown when logo changed.

Current logo

Cupboards

1980 Cupboard
Pine
15.5^W x 32.75^H x 5^D
2 woven doors

Org$	AVG	HIGH
426	500	

1984-85 Cupboard
Maple
8101-OO
13^W x 27.5^H x 5.35^D
1 woven door

Org$	AVG	HIGH
119.95	434	500

1984-85 Cupboard
Oak
8100-O
22.5^W x 17.5^H x 6.25^D
2 woven doors

Org$	AVG	HIGH
189.95	500	550

1985-86 Cupboard
8100-OO
27.25^L x 15.5^W x 5.25^D
1 woven door

Org$	AVG	HIGH
139.95	378	400

Dividers

4-way Divider[99]
Natural, Fits Spring

4-way Divider[00-01]
Natural, Fits Small Spoon

	Org$	AVG	HIGH
spring	12	--	--
spoon	11	13	21

6-way Divider[92-99]
13^L x 8^W x 5^H
Fits Medium Chore

6-way Divider[92-99]
18^L x 11^W x 4.5^H
Fits Med Gathering

	Org$	AVG	HIGH
chore	18	10	23
gather	20	13	21

8-way Divider[92-99]
14^L x 9^W x 4.5^H
Fits Pantry

8-way Divider[99]
14^L x 9^W x 4.5^H
Natural, Fits Pantry

Org$	AVG	HIGH
19	12	22

Bread Divider[99-01]
59315
Natural

Org$	AVG	HIGH
8	--	--

Paddles

Butter Paddles
28^L x 4.5^W: 8010-O[83-85]
28^L x 6.25^W: 8000-O[85-94]
Both were identical in design, just different sizes

	Org$	AVG	HIGH
4.5^H	14.95	33	55
6.25^H	16.95	38	64

Stencil Paddles[87-88]
goose: 8030-OO
heart: 8020-OO
gingerbread: 8040-OO
12.5^L x 4.5^H

	Org$	AVG	HIGH
goose	14.95	36	65
heart	14.95	50	65
ginger	14.95	53	65

Wall Hangings

Rectangular, with shelf
10^L x 14^H: 7800-OO $^{(79-84)}$
12^L x 24^H: 7801-OO $^{(79-80)}$
Both were identical in design, just different sizes

10x14

	Org$	AVG	HIGH
10	16.95	88	103
12	21.95	160	175

Rectangular, with shelf
12^L x 16^H: 7800-O $^{(85-86)}$
Redesigned with new rounded top

Org$	AVG	HIGH
39.95	80	110

Square, 20" $^{(79-80)}$
7701-O
20^L x 20^H

Org$	AVG	HIGH
26.95	168	180

Square, 10" $^{(79-80)}$
7700-O
10^L x 10^H

Org$	AVG	HIGH
12.95	43	90

Triangular
12^L x 10^H: 7900-OO $^{(79-80)}$
24^L x 21^H: 7901-OO $^{(79-80)}$
Both were identical in design, just different sizes

24x21

	Org$	AVG	HIGH
12	15.95	100	120
24	23.95	95	125

Wall Brackets $^{(79-85)}$
large: 8902-O
4.5^L x 13.5^W x 11.5^{EXT}
small: 8900-O
4.5^L x 8^W x 6.5^{EXT}
The hour glass design in the inset was also done in this time period

	Org$	AVG	HIGH
lg	6.95	39	48
sm	5.95	30	30

Wall Bracket $^{(85-86)}$
8900-OO
2.25^L x 9.25^W x 11^H
Solid wood, looks like an upside down 'L'

Org$	AVG	HIGH
12.95	55	90

Misc Wall Hangings

Cathedral Mirror $^{(80)}$
8060-O
9^W x 25^H

Org$	AVG	HIGH
19.95	390	450

Framed Clock, Mirror or Picture Frame $^{(80)}$
7701-X^{CL}/7701-Y^{MIR}/7701-Z^{FR}
20^L x 20^W
Same design, 8x10 face is different: clock, mirror or empty to frame picture

frame

clock

	Org$	AVG	HIGH
clock	39.95	353	455
mirror	32.95	383	400
frame	29.95	375	500

Fruit Medley™ Prints $^{(99-02)}$
72877/72869/72855/72851
12.5^L x 12.5^W
Blueberry, Blackberry, Grape, Cherry. Sold individually, or as a set of 4

	Org$	AVG	HIGH
single	59	101	109

Nail Board
approx 16^L - 18^L
Dates for this piece have not been confirmed

Org$	AVG	HIGH
	578	800

Peg Board $^{(85-94)}$
7900-OO
23^L x 5^W x 5^H
Often promoted with the Peg Baskets

Org$	AVG	HIGH
21.95	40	47

Wood Products
146

Wood Products

Peg Board (94-99)
51101
23.5ᴸ x 5ᵂ x 3.5ᴴ
Made of hardwood poplar

Org$	AVG	HIGH
39.95	48	55

Mug Tree (94-97)
51306
14.75ᴴ

Org$	AVG	HIGH
34.95	35	42

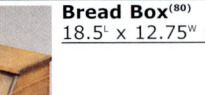

Wood Shelf (94-97)
50601
32ᴸ x 5.75ᵂ x 5ᴴ

Org$	AVG	HIGH
89.95	108	110

Not-So-Lazy Susan (03-05)
50282
14ᴿᴰ x 1.75ᴴ

Org$	AVG	HIGH
69	69*	110

Misc WoodCrafts

Bread Box (80)
18.5ᴸ x 12.75ᵂ x 13.5ᴴ

Org$	AVG	HIGH
	464	510

Pillar Candle Holder (04-06)
50097
6.5ᴿᴰ x 0.75ᴴ
Classic stain, solid maple. First featured with the Basket Splint Candle.

Org$	AVG	HIGH
15	--	--

Carpenter Box (80)
8ᴸ x 6ᵂ x 10ᴴ
Came with divider

Org$	AVG	HIGH
	203	380

Toilet Paper Holder (79-82)
8800-O
8ᴸ x 3.5ᵂ

Org$	AVG	HIGH
6.95	48	50

Cheese Board (80)
15ᴸ x 10ᵂ

Org$	AVG	HIGH
--	260	

Towel Holder (79-80)
12"   15.5ᴸ x 3.5ᵂ: 8801-O
18"   19.5ᴸ x 3.5ᵂ: 8802-O
21"   22.5ᴸ x 3.5ᵂ: 8803-O
24"   25.5ᴸ x 3.5ᵂ: 8004-O

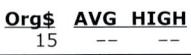
12 inch

	Org$	AVG	HIGH
12	8.95	48	62
18	10.95	35	35
21	11.95	73	110
24	12.95	--	--

Cookbook Nook (80)
13ᵂ x 17ᴴ

Org$	AVG	HIGH
	245	310

Wood Scoop (81)
approx 14ᴸ

Org$	AVG	HIGH
	1000	1195

Woven Traditions®

Berry, Large(92-97)
11533
8.5^L x 8.5^W x 5^H
One of the original three pieces

	Org$	AVG	HIGH
B	30.95	37	55

Peg, Large(95-99)
11142
6.5^L x 6.5^W x 8^H

	Org$	AVG	HIGH
B	39.95	47	69

Bread(92-01)
14737
14.5^L x 7.5^W x 3.75^H
One of the original three pieces

	Org$	AVG	HIGH
B	36.95	43	50
C$^{P/L}$	51.85	52	70

Pie(94)
12211
12^L x 12^W x 4^H

	Org$	AVG	HIGH
B	37.95	56	86
C$^{P/L}$	79.95	89	100

Button(99-01)
12971
7RD x 3^H

	Org$	AVG	HIGH
B	33	35	50
C$^{P/L}$	53	53	55

Recipe(98-01)
10499
8^L x 5.5^W x 4.5^{FH} x 6^{BH}

	Org$	AVG	HIGH
B	39	42	70

Cake(96-00)
11657
12^L x 12^W x 6^H

	Org$	AVG	HIGH
B	59.95	65	85
C$^{P/L}$	90.85	99	105

Spring(95-97)
19038
11^L x 8^W x 5.5^H

	Org$	AVG	HIGH
B	41.95	51	65

Cracker(92-00)
14532
11.5^L x 5^W x 3^H
One of the original three pieces

	Org$	AVG	HIGH
B	26.95	31	54

Tea(95-99)
10710
7^L x 5^W x 3.5^H

	Org$	AVG	HIGH
B	28.95	36	48
C$^{P/L}$	43.85	51	65

Darning(94-01)
15539
10RD x 4^H

	Org$	AVG	HIGH
B	39.95	40	45
C$^{P/L}$	61.85	65	75

Vegetable, Small(95-99)
15016
10.5^L x 6.5^W x 3^{FH} x 7^{BH}

	Org$	AVG	HIGH
B	35.95	40	65
C$^{P/L}$	56.85	58	70

Pantry(98-00)
13854
14^L x 9^W x 4.5^H

	Org$	AVG	HIGH
B	53	61	75
C$^{P/L}$	81	85	85

Guide Indexes

On the following pages, you will find helpful tools and information that will help you enjoy your Longaberger Collection even more!

SIGNATURES

Generally, a Longaberger family member's signature can increase a basket's value, especially if the signature is either Dave's or Grandma Bonnie's. Baskets signed by Tami or Rachel have also garnered interest in the market because there are not many of them in circulation. A collector can have their basket signed by a family member by taking it to Longaberger Homestead™ or meeting up with the family at a Collectors Club Gathering or other Company sponsored event. On page 150, actual signatures can be viewed to help identify these in the market place.

FABRIC ID

This section features a complete list of fabrics offered by the Longaberger Company since the first fabric was offered in 1985. This will help when trying to identify what fabrics you have and/or need and be able to put an actual name to the fabric pattern. Fabrics are listed in alphabetical order.

FUN FACTS

Over the years, we have created many Fun Facts to share fun and interesting facts with the Longbaberger Collector. In this section, we have collected the Fun Facts that we consider to be essential information to fully understanding the collectible. We will still be adding the fun and interesting tidbits throughout the Guide each year.

QUICK FIND

This alphabetical index is designed to help collectors find information quickly and easily regarding their baskets and help to locate items within the Guide pages.

DIMENSIONAL SEARCH

The Dimensional Search tool is designed to help identify a basket by taking a quick measurement. Items are listed in order, by shape and then dimension.

Family Signatures

 **Bonnie Longaberger**
7/16/1908 – _____
More commonly referred to as "Grandma Bonnie", most of her signatures are in black ink but for a short period she used a silver marker. While all of her signatures are highly valued in the market, the silver marker consistently brings an even higher premium.

 **Judy Kay #8**
9/19/1939 – _____

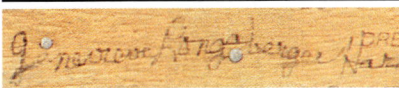
Genevieve #1
3/25/1926 – 7/13/2004
Also known as "Jenny", spouse: Piercy Hard

 **Ginny Lou #9**
10/8/1940 – _____
Spouse: Dick Wilcox

Wendy Jean #2
12/16/1929 – _____
Spouse: Bob Little

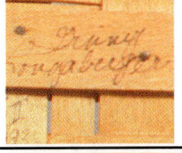 **Gary Conway #10**
1/6/1943 – _____
Gary has also been known to weave Incentive and Award baskets, especially miniatures

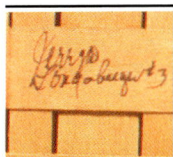 **Jerry Dean #3**
11/23/1931 – _____
Spouse: Donna

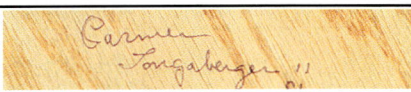
Carmen Lynn #11
11/23/1943 – _____
Spouse: Ronald Fortney

 **Dale "Larry" #4**
6/3/1933 – _____
Known as "Larry", he has woven many award baskets, as well as many of his own 'originals' which he has given to family & friends.

 **Jeff Carl #12**
3/11/1945 – _____
Spouse: Jane, who is also known to sign baskets from time to time

 **Dave Wendell #5**
12/7/1934 – 3/17/1999
The founder and visionary behind the company, Dave's signature is one of the most sought after in the market. The most recognizable feature is that it's not legible.

 **Dave's Children
Tami Lynne #1**
Currently the company's CEO, her signature is most commonly found on Incentive & Award Baskets

 **Richard Lee #6**
12/18/1936 – _____
Know as "Rich", he continues to play very important roles within the company. Spouse: Joanne

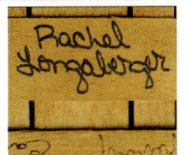 **Dave's Children
Rachel Lynne #2**
Also very active in the Company, Rachel's signatures are also most commonly found on Incentive & Award baskets

 **Maryann #7**
11/29/1937 – _____
Spouse: Wendell McCafferty

See page 12 for more info on Family Signatures and the effect they have on an item's value

Fabric ID Index

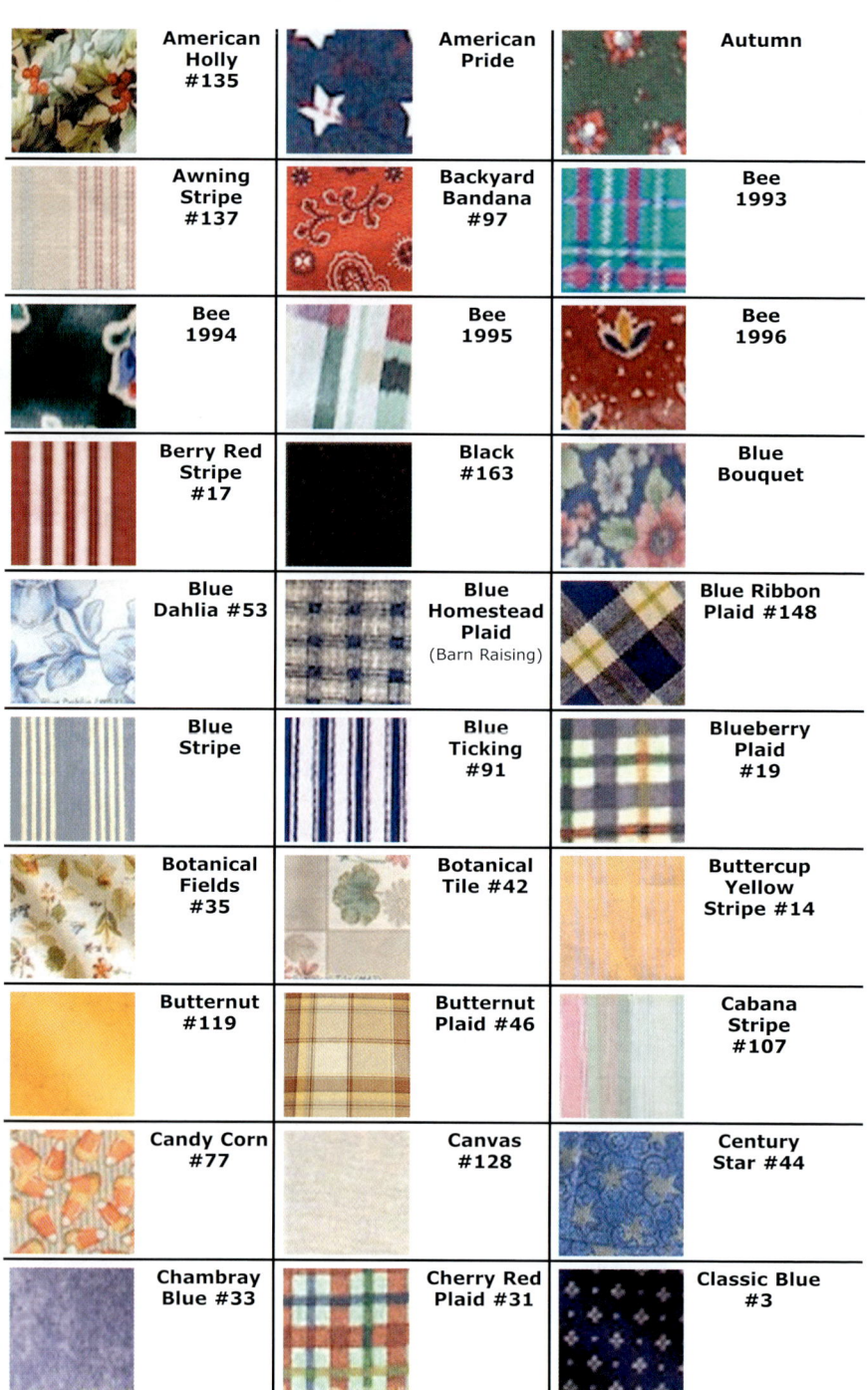

	Collectors Club Stripe #41		Cornflower #88		Cornflower Plaid #123
	Cottage Garden		Cottage Trellis #59		Daisy #68
	Denim #165		Desktop Plaid #61		Discovery
	Dogwood #244		Dusty Rose Stripe #15		Early Blossoms #52
	Easter 1992		Easter 1993		Easter Egg #50
	Easter Egg Hunt #153		Easter Plaid #235		Easter Stripe #234
	Emerald Vine #10		English Garden (1992 MDay)		Evergreen Plaid #82
	Fall Gingham #75		Fall Gingham #75		Falling Leaves #108
	Father's Day (1990-92)		Father's Day Paisley #60 (1995-99)		Festival Stripe #22
	Flax #239		Floral Bouquet #118		Floral Scallop #55 (Mother's Day)

Fabric ID

Fabric ID Index

Fabric ID

JW Plaid	JW Mini Plaid	Jelly Bean #51
Khaki #162	Khaki Canvas #155	Khaki Check #164
Lattice Leaf #37	Letters of Love (Beige) #26	Letters of Love (Blue) #23
Letters of Love (Green) #24	Letters of Love (Purple) #25	Letters of Love (Red) #94
Lilac	Lilac Rose	Lily of the Valley
Longaberger Signature #161	Lots of Luck #49	Majolica Garden #245
Market Day Plaid #2	Market Stripe #130	Mixed Bouquet Large #242
Mixed Bouquet Small #248	Mixed Bouquet Stripe #243	Morning Glory #69
Mother's Day 1993	Muslin	Natural #6
Natural Botanical #36	Natural Sailcloth #29	Oatmeal #89

Fabric ID

Fabric ID Index

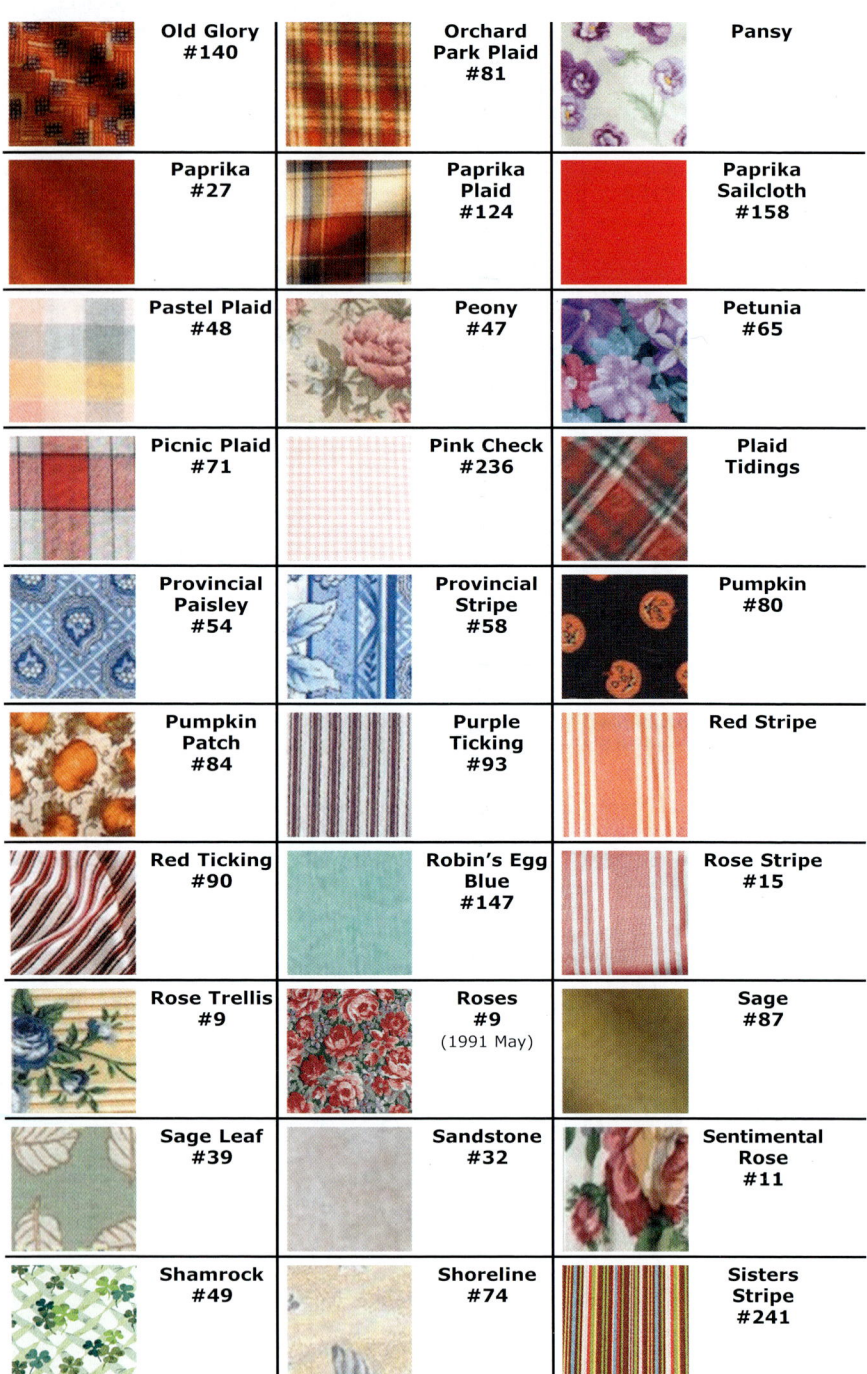

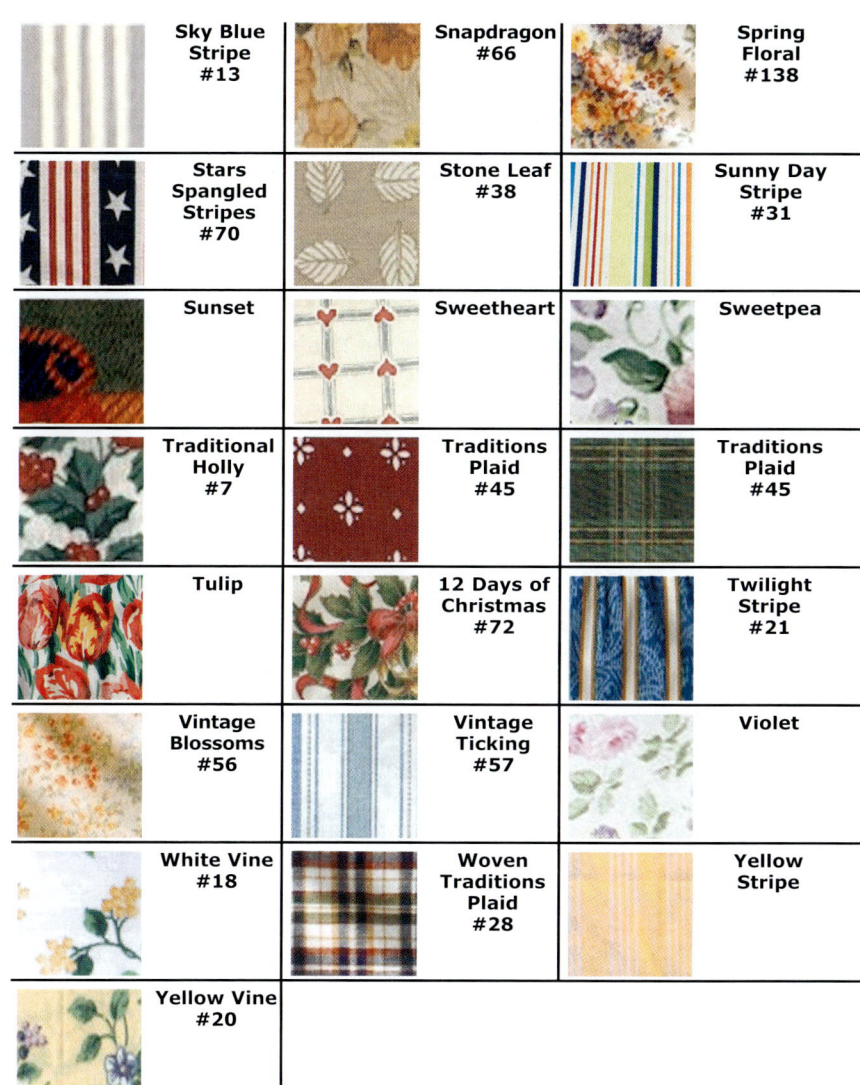

Fabric ID

Fun Facts

Bee Boyds Bears
The Bear Essentials

2000

The Longaberger Company really knows how to throw a party! Ask any home consultant you know and she will probably tell you that The Bee, Longaberger's annual sales convention, is one of the best parties around. With training, shopping, keynote addresses from company leaders and a whole lot of fun, the experience just can't be beat.

2001

At each Bee, a Bee Basket™ is offered and five years ago, a Bee Bear also began to be offered. Boyd's Bears makes these exclusively for the Longaberger Bee and they have become loved by consultants and collectors alike!

Look for these cuties on the secondary market to add to your Longaberger collection!

2000 Bea Berry **2003 Shari Beeberry**
2001 Honey Bea Berry **2004 Starr Beebeary**
2002 Libbee BeeAmerica **2005 Kim Beebeary**

2002   2003   2004   2005

Boyds Bears Treasure Boxes
Tiny Treasures

If you are familiar with Longaberger you may be familiar with Boyd's Bears as well. Longaberger Homestead, which has offered collectibles by other companies in the past, has teamed up with Boyd's on several occasions. One of their latest partnerships produced the extra tiny, extra cute, Boyd's Bear Treasure Boxes.

The resin boxes measure just 2 to 3 inches high and depict a friendly Boyd's Bear with a number of Longaberger products. Examples of these tiny treasures include the *Ho Ho Sparkleberry*, the *Gourdon's Candybear* and the *Sunnie Dae Sanditoes* Treasure Boxes. Open the boxes and you will find a charming bear hiding inside!

Fun Facts

Condition
What is acceptable and what is not

What should you look for when you are evaluating the quality or condition of a Longaberger Basket? It is first helpful to determine what is considered to be "normal" for these handmade baskets. The Company has offered the following to explain what to accept as "normal and acceptable".

- It is normal for there to be some room between splints. This is a natural occurrence as the splints dry and slightly shrink, therefore it is normal to be able to adjust the weaves up and down.

- If your basket has colored accent weaving, there will often be a small amount of dye on the upsplints where they touch. The dye is not completely colorfast, therefore this "bleeding" is very common.

- Small hairline cracks around the tacks are a natural occurrence as the wood dries.

- Some wood has natural swirls or "beauty spots" in the grain that will absorb stain differently. This may cause the stain to appear darker in some areas.

- A trademark of Longaberger Baskets is the wrapping of the trim strip around the band for a cleaner finish. This "turn-under" may fray or crack as the wood dries. Because it is very difficult to bend wood at this angle, this fraying is very common.

Fun Facts

Customized Baskets
What are all those natural baskets with color?

Customized Baskets are from the early Longaberger years, prior to 1990.

Customizing meant baskets could be special ordered with distinct features. Between 1977 and 1978, almost any combination could be ordered – stained, natural, with or without color weaving, lid, no lid, handle, no handle, one handle, two handles, etc. Because they were custom made and the quantity of orders was not as great as they are today, it was not difficult to offer this program.

In 1980, the program was changed to allow customers to choose only between two special order options for an additional $5.00 charge – natural or natural with color accent weave.

The colors available were *blue, green, red and brown*. Prior to 1980, yellow was also an option for a very short time.

Exceptions . . .
Most baskets were included for this option, with the following exceptions:

Natural Only – No Color Weave

Button	Cracker	Medium Vegetable
Bread	Small Vegetable	Wine

Stained Only – No Special Order Options
All promotional baskets

Natural or Natural with Color Only – No Stain
1984 – 1989 : Large (Infant) Cradle, Large Laundry

Discontinued Option . . .
The entire customizing program was discontinued for all Regular Line baskets in 1986. However, the program continued for the Large Cradle and Large Laundry until August 1989.

Market Perception. . .
While there is an interest by some in the market for customized baskets, there are others who do not care for them. Because it is a discontinued feature, it is realistic to expect a premium on the basket's value. Start by determining the value as if it were not customized. It is reasonable to consider the option worth at least $5.00 more because that was the original cost for it. However, the buyer's preference will ultimately determine if more than this can be collected.

Fun Facts

Longaberger Cookbooks
Cooking with Longaberger

You may be surprised to know that The Longaberger Company has produced several cookbooks through the years. We at Bentley are often asked how much these might be worth on the secondary market. While we do not have conclusive data on the cookbooks' market activity, we do know for a fact they are a real treat for cooks and collectors alike!

Take a look at these books filled with not only savory recipes but also with wonderful tips and Longaberger stories.

At Home With the Longabergers, 1990 – 1996
Fresh From the Pantry, 2001 – 2995
Entertaining With Longaberger, 2003 – present
Recipes for Good Cheer, 2004

Director Christmas Baskets

Here is a rare look into the very limited *Director Christmas Basket* collection. From 1993 – 2001, these Sweetheart-inspired baskets were given to each Director as a thank you. While they do resemble members of the Sweetheart Collection®, none of the basket forms in this collection have ever been made available to the public with this red accent weaving.

Quite a special collection indeed!

Fun Facts

Form Number History
What do the letters in older form numbers stand for?

The letters in older form numbers did stand for specific attributes of baskets. They were set up to help customers visualize the baskets without seeing a picture or knowing its name. For example, when a customer saw the letter 'A' in a form number, they could tell that that basket had a stationary handle.

The first letter immediately after the number in each code was used to identify different features of the basket. The remaining letters were specific manufacturing codes pertaining to color or stain. The following are meanings for the letter that appears **immediately after the numeral:**

Letter	=	Meaning	Example
A	=	1 st/h	[Candle: 1100-**A**O]
B	=	1 sw/h	[Poinsettia: 3900-**B**RST]
C	=	2 sw/h	[Yuletide Traditions: 5100-**C**RST]
D	=	Lid	[Large Hamper: 1600-**D**O]
E	=	1 sw/h & Lid	[Tall Purse: 1000-**E**O]
F	=	2 sw/h & Lid	[Rectangular Sewing: 600-**F**]
G	=	1 st/h & Divider	[Cake: 100-**G**BRS]
H	=	2 sw/h, Divider & Lid or, 2 sw/h & Split Lid	[Large Picnic: 300 **H**BRS]
I	=	Loop on Back & Metal Hook	[Small Key: 700-**I**O]
J	=	Ears	[Darning: 500-**J**O]
K	=	Rockers & Ears	[Mini Cradle: 700- **K**O]
L	=	2 sw/h & Rockers	[Doll Cradle: 2500-**L**O]
M	=	Rockers	[Large Cradle: 2800-**M**]
N	=	1 sw/h, Lid & Stand	[Round Sewing: 3200-**N**O]
O	=	Plain Basket	[Bread: 4700-**O**O]
P	=	Large Hanger	[Hanging 13": 4200-**P**O]
Q	=	1 st/h & Divided Lid	[Medium Purse: 900-**Q**O]
R	=	Legs	[Patio Planter: 6000-**R**]
S	=	13-inch Stand	[Small Fern Planter, 13": 2900-**S**O]
T	=	20-inch Stand	[Small Fern Planter, 20": 2900-**T**O]
U	=	1 sw/h (lengthwise) & Legs	[Magazine: 2100-**U**]
V&W	=	1 sw/h (lengthwise), Legs & Lid	[Magazine: 2100-**V**]
X&Y	=	Woven Lid & 2 Swinging Handles	[Weekender: 200-**Y**O]

Baskets with the same first numbers are made from the same form and have the same body dimensions. The differences can only be identified by the letters that follow the form number.

For example, the Mini Cradle and Small Key are both made with the same form (700); however, **KO** follows for the Mini Cradle while **IO** follows for the Small Key to distinguish their features.

Fun Facts

Large Hamper History

The Large Hamper Basket is a favorite among many collectors. Its generous size and sturdy construction make it the perfect place to toss items ready for the laundry. We've also heard the hamper makes a great toy chest, too! Take a look at the history of this unique basket.

Prior to 1979 – July 1986
- Available to all customers through the Regular Line
- Included an attached woven lid with the knob at the front
- Available in the darker stain, natural or natural with color
- No hand slots

May 1986
- Available for the first time as a feature
- No lid included
- Two hand slots added
- Available only in darker stain

Prior to 1979 – 1990
Large Hamper

August 1986 – 1990
- Added to Hostess Collection & available only to hostesses with a pre-determined show total
- Included an attached woven lid with the knob at the front
- Available in the darker stain, natural or natural with color
- No hand slots

1993 – 1994
- Available to all customers through the Regular Line
- Included a detached woven lid with knob in the middle
- Two hand slots
- Classic stain

1986
Feature Hamper

1995 – 2001
- Returned to Hostess Collection & once again available only to hostesses with a pre-determined show total
- Woven with 3/8" weave
- Included a detached woven lid with the knob in the middle
- Two hand slots
- Classic stain

September 2003
- Corner Hamper Basket added to Hostess Collection
- Available only to Hostesses with at least $750 in guest sales
- Included a detached woven lid, knob in the middle
- No hand slots
- Warm brown stain
- Large Hamper Basket also included in Hostess Collection
- Available only to Hostesses with $1000 in guest sales
- Included a detached woven lid with knob in the middle
- Two hand slots
- Warm Brown stain

1991
Shades of Autumn
Hostess Hamper

1993 – 1994 Hamper looks like this with, $1/2$"weave. Returned to $3/8$"weave in 1995 Hostess Collection.

March 2004 – Present
- Large & Corner Hampers are available to all customers through the Regular Line
- Both include a detached woven lid with the knob in the middle
- Large Hamper has hand slots, while the Corner Hamper does not
- Both are available in Warm Brown stain

Fun Facts

Harmony Kingdom

These exclusive edition Harmony Kingdom pieces were available at the Homestead or directly from Harmony Kindgom. Created just for Longaberger, these tiny little boxes are crafted to resemble the May Series baskets complete with the flowers they represent! A special secret is hidden within each one.

Violet
Compote

Basket	Released	No. of Pcs	Orig$
00 Daisy	7/00	3600	$52
00 Morning Glory	10/00	3600	$52
00 Snapdragon	5/01	3600	$52
01 Peony	7/01	3600	$55
01 Petunia	1/02	2500	$54
01 Poinsettia	5/02	2500	$55
02 Geranium	7/02	2500	$55
02 Tulip	1/03	1800	$55
03 Lily of Valley	11/03	1800	$55
04 Lilac	1/05	1500	$52
05 Compote	7/05	1000	$52
05 Violet	1/06	1500	$52

Heisey Plates

1995 Pink

The Heisey Glass Company has become a household name in the homes of many Longaberger Collectors. The special edition Heisey Horse was commissioned by Longaberger in 1998 to celebrate the Crawford Barn™ Raising and has sold in the market for more than <u>any</u> baskets from the J.W. Collection.

1996 Blue

Surprisingly, the successful Heisey Horses were not Heisey's first project with The Longaberger Company. In 1995, the Heisey Tour Plates (left) debuted in Longaberger stores throughout Dresden.

1997 Green

The 1995 Pink Plate originally sold for $21 and was limited to 2,200 pieces. In the next years, production was increased to 5,500 for both the 1996 Blue Plate and the 1997 Green Plate. The series ended in 1998 when due to its unique color, production problems halted sales of the Yellow Plate. There were only 618 pieces made of this final plate.

1998 Yellow

There have been reports of some counterfeit Yellow Plates that resulted from plates that were production errors not destroyed at the factory. The faux pieces are more vibrant yellow and do not come with a product card and box, as the others did.

Fun Facts

Incentive/Award Jewelry

Consultants are given several opportunities throughout the sales year to earn incentives. When a consultant sells or sponsors the required amount or number then she may earn an incentive like a basket or other product. Recognition is somewhat different than an incentive because the purpose is to thank a consultant for their hard work throughout the year. Recognition usually takes place at The Bee and includes marches, special luncheons, and of course, exclusive products. In the past, Consultants have received baskets of all sizes, savings bonds, supply order items, jewelry and trips.

Shown here are just a few examples of jewelry that has been given to the sales force:

- **A.** 1992 Medallion necklace, Top Sponsors
- **B.** 1994 14K Peg Basket charm, matches Bee Basket, given to Top Sponsors
- **C.** 1995 14K Small Chore, matches Bee Basket
- **D.** 1992 14K gold bracelet has a unique basket weave design. Each link has "Longaberger" engraved on the back. Top Sponsors.
- **E.** 1993 white gold pin designed like the Top Sponsoring Award basket

Oak to Maple Handles
1989: Handles changed from Oak to Maple

Oak handles prior to 1989

Maple handles after 1989

Prior to 1989, all handles on Longaberger Baskets were made of Oak. This practice was handed down from J.W. himself. The smooth, worn finish of oak is a feature among most of his creations.

In March 1989, a concern arose that the core from the maple logs used for making the veneer splints for the basket were just being thrown out. Instead, they could be used to make handles. Test marketing started immediately to compare oak versus maple. Initially, these studies reported no real difference in durability, however the maple handles tended to be favored because they blended better with the baskets.

In May 1989, maple handles were implemented on all baskets, with the exception of the 1989 J.W. Banker's Waste™.

After the change, many wondered if the change was based on cost efficiency, rather than quality. Dave assured the Consultants that while there were many factors that affected the decision, the test studies eventually proved that maple handles were more durable than oak, not cracking with long term use, like oak has a tendency to do.

Fun Facts

Insurance
Tips from an Agent

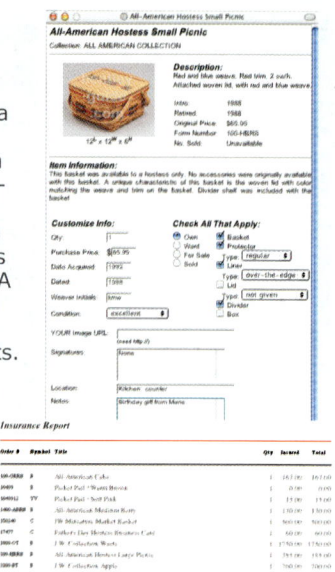

As your basket collection grows, it is a good idea to consider how best to insure it. A relatively small collection is usually not a problem under a typical homeowner's policy; however, any collection can be viewed as more than a hobby if it reaches a size or falls into a category where the insurance company views it as more than "items normal and incidental to a normal household." A hobby can be viewed as a business, even if you have never sold a basket, simply because the potential to some day make money from it exists.

The best person to consult with regarding this subject is your insurance agent. She may initially recommend scheduling your baskets onto your policy, which simply means they are insured separately under a floater from the items listed as unscheduled personal property in your policy. If you don't schedule your baskets, at least make sure you have a replacement cost endorsement so you will not have depreciation taken you may not recoup after a loss.

If you are a consultant, it is necessary to have a separate business policy since your homeowner's has a limit on the amount paid for business property. Your agent will be able to advise you on the best package for covering your business risk. He can also explain liability coverage because in today's legal climate, even casual statements about potential resale possibilities or product durability can come back to haunt salespeople. Many consultants have secured professional liability coverage to provide for defense if they find themselves in court.

If your home ever suffers smoke and/or fire damage, do not clean your baskets with normal household cleaners. Smoke has toxic chemicals that not only soil a basket, but interact with it chemically. It is necessary for items to be cleaned professionally and the sooner the better because after 24 hours, damage begins to get substantially worse.

Your insurance adjuster should not be upset if you have accrued reasonable expenses to protect your baskets from further damage before she is able to inspect the loss. You will have saved her the cost of replacing them or at least improved their salvage value somewhat, even if they will not clean completely. Again, your agent can advise you on who to call because she probably knows cleaning contractors who specialize in fire and smoke damage restoration.

Finally, as you should do with all your valuables, take photographs/videos in duplicate of each basket; identify it by noting type, age, unique characteristics, condition, original cost and current market value. Then keep a set of the photos/videos at a location other than your house. Give the duplicates to your agent to keep in your file. Like any objects, baskets can get damaged and be destroyed so you need to protect yourself from a potential loss and insurance is a good start.

Richard Gordon, Jr.
Insurance Adjustor

Fun Facts

Pottery History
The Other Collectible!

We all know someone who is positively basket crazy! But, do you know someone who is crazy for Longaberger Pottery? Since its introduction in 1990, Longaberger Pottery has had a following of dedicated collectors.

Roseville

The addition of pottery to the Longaberger product line was a natural progression for The Longaberger Company. Just like baskets, pottery has a rich history and was an important commodity in Ohio. In fact, J.W. Longaberger's Ware Baskets were crafted for local pottery companies.

As you begin building your collection of pottery, or as you add to your current collection, there are a couple of details to keep in mind to ensure you are getting an authentic Longaberger product.

1st Generation

First, Longaberger Pottery is easy to spot because of the distinct design. All pottery, except for Heirloom Ivory, has the colorful detail known as the four petal motif in Traditional Red, Classic Blue, or Heritage Green.

Second, all Longaberger Pottery is embossed with the woven "L" logo. Pottery that does not include these two attributes is not an authentic Longaberger product. We have heard of collectors purchasing what they thought was authentic pottery when, in fact, it was not. This includes items that are seconds. Contrary to popular belief, pottery that does not meet Longaberger's stringent quality standards, or seconds, is NOT more collectible, or worth more than first-quality pieces.

2nd Generation

You may notice slight differences in your pottery pieces especially if you have ones that were produced prior to 1992. From 1990 to late 1991 Friendship Pottery in Roseville, Ohio produced Longaberger Pottery. Available only in Classic Blue, each piece was dated and initialed. The unique embossment on pieces made in Roseville is actually molded into the bottom of each piece and the body of the pottery is a creamy white color.

Current

After problems ensued, Longaberger moved production to Sterling Pottery in East Liverpool, Ohio. These pieces are embossed with a woven L according to which color pottery you have and the body is a brighter white. It is important to note that these pieces are not dated and initialed.

Even though the pottery has been made in two different locations, there is absolutely no difference in its quality and attributes. Each piece can go from freezer to oven to table with ease.

When Longaberger Pottery was introduced it was promoted as bringing two great American classics back together again. We could not agree more! Longaberger Baskets and Longaberger Pottery are wonderful additions to any household and great collectibles!

Fun Facts

Basket Stain History

Dark Stain 1979-82

Dark Stain 1983-85

Classic 1986-02

Natural 1994-01

Whitewash 2002-03

Warm Brown 2002-P

Sunwash 2005

Throughout the years Longaberger has changed, modified and tweaked its stain for the baskets several times in several different ways. Sometimes the changes were not noticeable like when the durability or chemical make-up was modified. At other times, though, the changes were significant and created different categories of collecting.

In 2002 the Company made perhaps its biggest adjustment to the stain when they retired what has become known as Classic Stain and replaced it with Warm Brown. Warm Brown was met with both excitement and disappointment. Some collectors were ready for a change and welcomed the rich hue of the new color and others thought by retiring the classic color their collections would suffer.

Since Classic Stain is now available only through the secondary market, a new niche has emerged. Like those collectors who search for the unique gray color used in 1984 or for the dark stain used in the very early years, Classic Stain lovers are among those who are willing to pay a premium for the color they love!

Besides the traditional brown baskets, in the past Longaberger has offered unique colors, and even no color, as well. Whitewashed Baskets made their debut in 2000, a Sunwashed finished appeared in 2005 and of course, no stain, or natural baskets have been brought in and out of the line for many years.

Fun Facts

Original Weavers
Meet the Original 5

We were lucky enough to have the chance to sit down with the original five weavers for a chat. What a hilarious evening of reminiscing ... some stories can be shared and others can not! From stories of pranks and fool-around baskets to ones about Dave getting picked up on the way to his first home show or throwing baskets at Mary Ann when she told him she didn't like one of his ideas! We laughed and laughed and laughed.

We would like to introduce you to the ones who were there when the legacy started! And if you ever see one of them around Dresden or at the Longaberger Homestead, be sure to ask them to sign your basket or maybe even treat them to dinner ... it will be worth every minute!

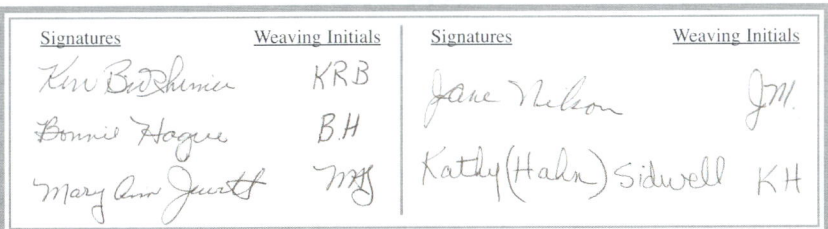

Weaving Techniques

Continuous Weaving
This is the practice of using the same splint to weave the entire basket. While it makes the basket very strong, it is a very time-consuming and difficult technique. It was one of J.W. Longaberger's trademarks and was a common feature for Longaberger Baskets until sometime after May 1989. It is evident on a basket by a split up-splint which was done to allow for the weave pattern to continue.

Left-handed Weaving
This feature is evident by looking at the trim strip. When you hold the basket in front of you, with the end of the trim strip facing up, look at which direction the trim turn is pointing. If it is pointing toward your left hand, it is a left-handed basket, meaning that a basketmaker who is left-handed made the basket. If the trim strip points towards your right hand, it was made by a right-hander.

Most Difficult to Make
According to a few basketmakers, the baskets most difficult to make are the small baskets with inverted bottoms, such as the Button or Tree-Trimming. The most difficult one, before the Founder's Basket, was the 1992 Discovery Basket. Because the basket was not made with double splints, if a mistake was made, it was difficult to correct.

Fun Facts

White House Easter Egg Roll

In 2001, Longaberger was commissioned by the Virginia Egg Council to make two large Easter baskets for the White House for their annual Easter Egg Hunt. There was no formal recognition, but the following year, they were invited back to the White House for an encore appearance.

In 2002, the 2002 Small Easter™ basket – whitewash with green accent weave – was given to each Congressmen and special guest of the President attending a special Easter reception.

Along with the basket, a very special hand-painted large Easter egg was tucked into each basket. They were not made or provided by The Longaberger Company. The smaller eggs shown here are the actual White House Egg Roll eggs that were also used during the event.

No word as to how many are in circulation. Without a question, a very special collectible!

Wood Loops

Loop handles, or "ears", seen here on the *Tea* and *Key Baskets*, were once made with wooden splints. Beginning in 1984, however, leather was used instead of wood. Loops on the Mini Cradle were removed altogether. In the market, this delicate feature has become very popular, sometimes paying twice the value of the basket for loops that are in good condition.

Quick Find

This quick-reference index was designed to help collectors find information quickly and easily regarding their baskets.

The "Quick Find" is divided into four columns: **Basket, Collections (Year), Form No. and Page in Guide.**

BASKET TITLE

Each basket is listed alphabetically by name, not by collection. For example, the *J.W. Corn* basket is found under *'C'* for *Corn*, <u>not</u> *"J"* for the *J.W. Collection*. If you want to see the baskets by collection, the front part of the Guide is what you should use. Also listed in this column are the basket's dimensions which is then followed by the name of the form used to make the basket.

COLLECTIONS

This column lists all the different collections of which the basket has been a part. The number in parenthesis represents the year(s) that the basket was available. The letter 'P' in the parenthesis stands for 'Present' and means that the item is still available directly from the Company.

FORM NO.

Listed is the basket's form number(s). If there is a subscript letter following a number, it is representing a color or feature to help distinguish the difference between the numbers. Common letters used for colors include **S** for **Stained**, **U** for **Unstained**, **WW** for **Whitewash**, **WB** for **Warm Brown**, **R** for **Red**, **B** for **Blue**, **G** for **Green**, etc... . If you have questions as to what a letter may represent, it might be helpful to locate the item within the Guide pages to read the description, which often lists the options that were available.

PAGE IN GUIDE

Refer to the listed page number in order to obtain additional information about the basket, such as its value or a picture of it. If "CL" is noted, the item is still available in the Regular Line and can only be found listed in the Collectors Inventory Checklist. If the page number is grey in color, a picture is not featured in the Guide.

<u>Disclaimer</u>
All basket names listed in this index are trademarks registered and owned by The Longaberger Company and J. Phillip Inc. has no interest therein.

Quick Find

BASKET	COLLECTION (YEAR)	FORM#	PAGE
Acorn	Shades of Autumn (91)	700-BGUBS	133
7^L x 5^W x 3.5^H (Tea)			
Address	Father's Day (96)	12611	47
	Incentive (00-P)	unknown	96
	Retired (98-04)	18546/17020^{WB}	123
	Retired, WWash (01-02)	10983	123
8.25^L x 6.25^W x 3.75^H (None)			
Advisor Recognition	Incentive (86)	2300-	94
14^L x 9^W x 4.5^H (Small Gathering)			
All In One Game	Feature (05-06)	10395	123
20.5^L x 15.75^W x 4.5^H (None)			
All-Star Trio	Feature (93)	64408	54
5.75^L x 3.75^W x 3^H (Rosemary)			
Aloha Hawaii	Incentive, Trip (02)	unknown	92
6.25^L x 5.25^W x 3^H (Horiz of Hope 99)			
Ambrosia	Booking (92-96)	10120	21
	Employ Christmas (95)	10120	45
5.5^L x 4^W x 4^H (Ambrosia)			
American Beauty	Incentive (97)	unknown	89
13.5^L x 8.25^W x 5.25^H (94 Easter)			
Apple	J.W. Collection (85)	3200-BT	99
13RD x 8.5^H (Large Fruit)			
Apple, Miniature	Collectors Club (98)	13749	27
5.25^{RD} x 3.25^H (None)			
Associate Homestead Tour	Incentive (00)	unknown	96
10RD x 6.25^H (Homestead)			
Associate Producer	Incentive (96)	unknown	89
5.5^{RD} x 2.5^H (None)			
Autumn Basket	Incentive (04)	unknown	97
4.75^L x 4.75^W x 2^H (Stuck On You)			
Autumn Pail	Autumn Reflections (02)	10068/12446	17
8RD x 6.75^H (Autumn Pail)			
Autumn Tote	Autumn Reflections (03)	10252	17
8.5^L x 5.5^W x 9^H (None)			
Back Porch	Employ Christmas (03)	unknown	46
	GOSummertime (02)	12381	65
13.25^L x 9.5^W x 3^H (None)			
Bagel	Retired (02-06)	10064	123
16^L x 7.5^W x 3.25^H (None)			

KEY:
See page 170 for a key to understanding the abbreviations and notations used in these p

Quick Find

BASKET	COLLECTION (YEAR)	FORM#	PAGE
Baguette 20.5^L x 6.5^W x 2.75^H (None)	Feature$^{(05)}$	10296	54
Baker's Bounty 10^L x 6.25^W x 3.75^H (None)	Shades of Autumn$^{(98)}$	11771	133
Bakery 14.5^L x 7.5^W x 3.75^H (Bread, New)	Feature$^{(87)}$ Heartland$^{(90-01)}$	4700-JO 4700-JCS/14711	54 66
Baking 14.5^L x 7.5^W x 3.75^H (None)	Crisco$^{(93)}$	14745	66
Baking Dish 11.5^L x 8^W x 2^H (None)	Feature, ACO$^{(03-04)}$	10586	54
Banker's Waste 12.5RD x 13.5^H (Banker's Waste)	Hostess$^{(99-02)}$ J.W. Collection$^{(89)}$	14761 1900-BBST	72 99
Banker's Waste Miniature 5.25RD x 5.25^H (None)	Collectors Club$^{(00-01)}$	16578	28
Barbeque Buddy 12^L x 5.25^W x 3^H (None)	GOSummertime$^{(00)}$ Retired$^{(01-02)}$	16284 10801	65 123
Barbeque Buddy Large 12.5^L x 6.25^W x 7^H (None)	Retired$^{(01-02)}$	16381	123
Barbeque Buddy Small 7.5^L x 3.75^W x 2.75^H (BBQ, Small)	Retired$^{(01-02)}$	10702	123
Barn Raising 7RD x 6.5^H (7" Measuring)	Special Event$^{(98)}$	222806	134
Basket Bin, Large 16.5^L x 12.5^W x 5^{FH} x 7.75^{BH} (None)	Retired$^{(00-03)}$	17850/17160^{WB}	123
Basket Bin, Small 12^L x 11.75^W x 3^{FH} x 5.5^{BH} (None)	Retired$^{(00-03)}$	17752/17117^{WB}	123
Basket Fest (05) 13^L x 8^W x 5^H (Medium Chore)	Special Event$^{(05)}$	unknown	137
Basket Fest (06) 13^L x 8^W x 5^H (Medium Chore)	Special Event$^{(05)}$	unknown	137
Basket O' Luck 5.5RD x 3.75^H (Laurel)	Feature$^{(90)}$	17000-AGS	52
Basket of Love 8.5RD x 4^H (Basket of Love)	Mother's Day$^{(95)}$	18805	103
Basket of Plenty 12RD x 5.75^H (Quilting)	Shades of Autumn$^{(95)}$	15563	133

Quick Find

BASKET	COLLECTION (YEAR)	FORM #	PAGE
Basket of Thanks 7^L x 5^W x 3.5^H (Tea)	Incentive$^{(93)}$	700-	95
Bayberry 9^L x 9^W x 4.5^H (Bayberry)	Christmas$^{(93)}$	11584^R/11592^G	25
Be Mine 8.5^L x 5^W x 3.5^H (Small Oval)	Sweetheart$^{(94)}$	18601	138
Be My Valentine 8RD x 4.25^H (None)	Sweetheart$^{(06)}$	10411^R/10415^{WB}	139
Beachcomber 10.5^L x 9^W x 8^H (Weekender)	GOSummertime$^{(99)}$	15342	65
Bed 11.5^L x 5^W x 3^H (Cracker)	Feature$^{(89)}$	4500-AO	54
Bee, Large (88) 14^L x 7.75^W x 5.25^H (Large Chore)	Bee$^{(88)}$	3600-AO	18
Bee, Medium (88) 13^L x 8^W x 5^H (Medium Chore)	Bee$^{(88)}$	3500-AN	18
Bee, 1989 8.75^L x 4.75^W x 6.5^H (Tour)	Bee$^{(89)}$	5600-B(R/G)ST	18
Bee, 1990 7RD x 6.5^H (7" Measuring)	Bee$^{(90)}$	3900-AO	18
Bee, 1991 8.5^L x 8.5^W x 5^H (Large Berry)	Bee$^{(91)}$	1500-	18
Bee, 1992 14^L x 9^W x 4.5^H (Small Gathering)	Bee$^{(92)}$	12335	18
Bee, 1993 13^L x 8^W x 5^H (Medium Chore)	Bee$^{(93)}$	13501	18
Bee, 1994 6.5^L x 6.5^W x 8^H (Large Peg)	Bee$^{(94)}$	unknown	18
Bee, 1995 10^L x 6^W x 4^H (Small Chore)	Bee$^{(95)}$	unknown	18
Bee, 1996 8.5^L x 8.5^W x 5^H (Large Berry)	Bee$^{(96)}$	unknown	18
Bee, 1997 5.5^L x 5.5^W x 6^H (Small Spoon)	Bee$^{(97)}$	unknown	19
Bee, 1998 5.25^L x 5.25^W x 4^H (None)	Bee$^{(98)}$	unknown	19
Bee, 1999 7^L x 3.5^W x 4.75^H (TourII)	Bee$^{(99)}$	unknown	19
Bee, 2000 5.5RD x 4^H (None)	Bee$^{(00)}$	unknown	19

KEY:
See page 170 for a key to understanding the abbreviations and notations used in these

Quick Find

BASKET	COLLECTION (YEAR)	FORM #	PAGE
Bee, 2001 7.5^L x 4.75^W x 2.5^H (Small Loaf)	Bee$^{(01)}$	10643	19
Bee, 2002 7.75^L x 5.5^W x 4.5^H (Little Market)	Bee$^{(02)}$	unknown	19
Bee, 2003 9.25^L x 5^W x 6.25^H (Small Boardwalk)	Bee$^{(03)}$	unknown	19
Bee, 2004 10.25^L x 8^W x 3.5^H (Vacation Keepsake)	Bee$^{(04)}$	unknown	19
Bee, 2005 7.5RD x 5.5^H (Golf 04)	Bee$^{(05)}$	unknown	19
Bee Attendance 9^L x 5.5^W x 6.5^H (None)	Incentive$^{(01)}$	unknown	96
Bee Facilitator 11^L x 6^W x 8.75^{FH} x 11^{BH} (Wall Pocket, Med)	Incentive$^{(05)}$	unknown	79
Bee, Speaker 11^L x 8^W x 5.5^H (Spring)	Incentive$^{(91\text{-}02)}$	900-	78-79
Bee, Speaker (88) 15^L x 10^W x 7.5^H (Medium Market)	Incentive$^{(88)}$	500-	78
Bee, Speaker (89) 5.75^L x 3.75^W x 3^H (Rosemary)	Incentive$^{(89)}$	unknown	78
Bee, Speaker (90) 16^L x 9^W x 6^H (Harvest)	Incentive$^{(90)}$	3700-	78
Bee, Speaker (03) 8.5^L x 8.5^W x 5^H (Large Berry)	Incentive$^{(03)}$	unknown	79
Bell 6.5RD x 7^H (None)	Christmas$^{(83)}$	4901-OO	24
Berry, Large 8.5^L x 8.5^W x 5^H (Large Berry)	Feature (1st/h)$^{(85,\ 88)}$ Feature (Natrl)$^{(99)}$ J.W. Collection$^{(90)}$ Retired (1sw/h)$^{(79\text{-}04)}$ Retired (no/h)$^{(79\text{-}99)}$ WTraditions$^{(92\text{-}97)}$	1500-AO 19844 1500-BBST 1500-BO/11517/17212^{WB} 1500-OO/11509 11533	55 50 99 123 123 148
Berry, Medium 7.5^L x 7.5^W x 3.5^H (Medium Berry)	All-American$^{(87)}$ Feature (1st/h)$^{(85,\ 88)}$ Feature$^{(96\text{-}97)}$ PAmerican$^{(04\text{-}05)}$ RLine (1sw/h)$^{(79\text{-}P)}$ Retired (no/h)$^{(79\text{-}99)}$	1400-ABRS 1400-AO 16241^B/25^G/33^R 10682 1400-AO/11428/17192^{WB} 1400-O/11410	15 53 54 121 CL 123
Berry, Mini 7^L x 5^W x 3.5^H (Tea)	renamed Tea as of May 1, 1992		123
Berry, Miniature 3.5^L x 3.5^W x 3^H (None)	Collectors Club$^{(01\text{-}02)}$	10842	28

Quick Find

BASKET	COLLECTION (YEAR)	FORM #	PAGE
Berry, Small	Employ Christmas [98]	unknown	46
	Feature (1st/h) [85, 88]	1300-AO	54
	Feature (Natrl) [00]	17841	50
	Retired (1sw/h) [79-04]	1300-AO/11312/17176[WB]	123
	Retired (no/h) [79-99]	1300-O/11304	123
6.5^L x 6.5^W x 3^H (Small Berry)			
Best Supporting Role	Incentive [96]	unknown	89
8.5RD x 4^H (Basket of Love)			
Beverage Tote	Regular Line [05-P]	10380	CL
5.75RD x 8^H (None)			
Binocular	CClub, Heartwood [05-06]	10388	31
10^L x 4.75^W x 7.25^H (None)			
Biscuit	Feature [04]	10009	55
7.5^L x 4.75^W x 2.5^H (Small Loaf)			
Bittersweet	Shades of Autumn [92]	10804	133
5.5^L x 5.5^W x 6^H (Small Spoon)			
Blackberry	Booking [05-06]	10236	21
6.25^L x 4.25^W x 3.5^H (None)			
Block Party	All-American [02]	12421	16
20.5^L x 12.5^W x 11.5^H (None)			
Blooms	Feature (AHG) [05]	10168	49
22.25^L x 11^W x 2.75^H (None)			
Blossoms	Feature (AHG) [05]	10257	49
13^L x 6.5^W x 2.25^H (None)			
Blue Ribbon Bread	All-American [99]	14346	16
10.5^L x 8.75^W x 4^H (None)			
Blueberry	Booking [04-05]	13060	21
6.5^L x 6.5^W x 3^H (Small Berry)			
Boardwalk, Large	GOSummertime [01]	10564	65
	Incentive, Trip [01]	unknown	92
	Regular Line [02-P]	10174	CL
17.75^L x 10.5^W x 12^H (None)			
Boardwalk, Little	Retired [03-04]	10578	123
6.75^L x 3.75^W x 4.5^H (None)			
Boardwalk, Medium	GOSummertime [01]	10552	65
	Incentive, Trip [03]	unknown	92
	Regular Line [03-P]	10261	CL
12.5^L x 6.75^W x 8.5^H (None)			
Boardwalk, Small	Employ Christmas [01]	unknown	46
	GOSummertime [01]	11393	65
	Retired [03-06]	10255	123
9.25^L x 5^W x 6.25^H (None)			
Bob and Dolores Hope	Special Events [89-96]	unknown	134
11^L x 8^W x 5.5^H (Spring)			

KEY:

175 See page 170 for a key to understanding the abbreviations and notations used in these p

Quick Find

BASKET	COLLECTION (YEAR)	FORM#	PAGE
Boo 11^L x 8^W x 5.5^H (Spring)	Feature (94)	10987	49
Book Keeper 15^L x 16^W x 3.5^{FH} x 10.25^{BH} (None)	Retired (00-02)	10516	123
Bountiful Harvest 10.25^L x 10.25^W x 4.5^H (None)	Shades of Autumn (97)	12254	133
Bouquet 6.75RD x 6^H (Daisy)	Retired (03-06)	10642	123
Bouquet Sweetheart 6.5RD x 6.5^H (Lilac)	Sweetheart (96)	11240	138
Bowl 10" 11.25RD x 5^H (None)	CClub, Heartwood (05-06)	10385	32
Bowl 11" 11.25RD x 5.5^H (None)	Regular Line (02-P)	10796	CL
Bowl 13" 13.25RD x 6.5^H (None)	Hostess (02-04) Regular Line (04-P)	10722 10722	72 CL
Bowl 9" 9.25RD x 4.75^H (None)	CClub, PAmerican (04) Regular Line (02-P)	10670 12785	33 CL
Bowl 7" 7.25RD x 3.75^H (None)	Regular Line (03-P)	10783	CL
Branch Award, Lg 7.75^L x 6.25^W x 2.75^H (Shaker Harmony #4)	Incentive (05)	n/a	86
Branch Award, Sm 7.5^L x 5.75^W x 2.75^H (02 Small Easter)	Incentive (05)	n/a	86
Branch Basket 15.75^L x 6.5^W x 11^H (Branch Basket)	Incentive (88-02)	unknown	90
Branch Basket II 17.75^L x 10.5^W x 12^H (Large Boardwalk)	Incentive (02-04)	unknown	91
Branch Bouquet 10.5^L x 6^W x 4^H (None)	Incentive (97)	unknown	85
Branch Excellence (98) 6.5^L x 6.5^W x 3^H (Small Berry)	Incentive (98)	unknown	85
Branch Excellence (99) 9.5^L x 6^W x 6^H (Small Purse)	Incentive (99)	unknown	85
Branch Leader 17.75^L x 10.5^W x 12^H (Large Boardwalk)	Incentive (04-P)	unknown	91
Branch Sales (00) 7.75^L x 3.75^W x 4.5^H (Branch Sales 00)	Incentive (00)	unknown	85

Quick Find

BASKET	COLLECTION (YEAR)	FORM #	PAGE
Branch Sales (01) 8^L x 7.75^W x 3.5^H (8" Generations)	Incentive$^{(01)}$	unknown	85
Branch Sales (02) 5.75^L x 5.25^W x 6.25^H (None)	Incentive$^{(02)}$	unknown	85
Branch Sales (03) 7.5^L x 4.75^W x 2.5^H (Small Loaf)	Incentive$^{(03)}$	10004	85
Branch Sales (04) 5.75RD x 4.25^H (Little Pumpkin)	Incentive$^{(04)}$	unknown	86
Branch Sponsoring (99) 7^L x 5^W x 3.5^H (Tea)	Incentive$^{(99)}$	unknown	85
Branch Sponsoring (00) 5.75^L x 3.75^W x 3^H (Rosemary)	Incentive$^{(00)}$	unknown	85
Branch Sponsoring (01) 7^L x 6.75^W x 3^H (7" Generations)	Incentive$^{(01)}$	unknown	85
Branch Sponsoring (02) 5.25^L x 5.25^W x 4.5^H (None)	Incentive$^{(02)}$	unknown	85
Branch Sponsoring (03) 4.75^L x 3.75^W x 2.25^H (Business Card)	Incentive$^{(03)}$	unknown	86
Bread (new) 14.5^L x 7.5^W x 3.75^H (Bread, New)	Feature, WT (Natrl)$^{(00)}$ Feature, Seasons$^{(06)}$ Incentive$^{(86)}$ Regular Line$^{(88-P)}$ RLine, Heartwood$^{(06-P)}$ Retired (WWash)$^{(01-02)}$ Retired (Natrl)$^{(99-01)}$ WTraditions$^{(92-01)}$	18031 17231-12^P/19^G/21^W/16^B/22^R 4700-AO 14702/17231^{WB} 10454 10370 14974 14737	51 53 94 CL CL 123 123 148
Bread (old) 15^L x 8^W x 2.25^H (Bread, Old)	Retired$^{(82-88)}$	4600-OO	123
Bread & Milk 16^L x 8^W x 11^H (Magazine)	Feature$^{(81)}$ J.W. Collection$^{(87)}$ J.W. Originals	2100- 2100-ABT unknown	54 99 100
Bread & Milk Miniature 6^L x 3.25^W x 4.5^H (None)	Collectors Club$^{(00)}$	13391	28
Breakfast 14.5^L x 7.5^W x 3.75^H (Bread, New)	Feature$^{(89)}$	4700-AO	54
Brownie 11.25^L x 9^W x 2.5^H (None)	Retired$^{(04-06)}$	10543	124

KEY:
See page 170 for a key to understanding the abbreviations and notations used in these p

Quick Find

BASKET	COLLECTION(YEAR)	FORM#	PAGE
Bushel, Large 18RD x 11.25^H (None)	Hostess$^{(05)}$	10396^G/-97^{WB}/-98^{BK}	72
Bushel, Medium 12RD x 7.75^H (None)	Feature$^{(05)}$	10342^G/-02^{WB}/-29^{BK}	55
Bushel, Small 7.5RD x 4.75^H (None)	Feature$^{(05)}$	10341^G/-04^{WB}/-27^{BK}	55
Business Card 4.75^L x 3.75^W x 2.25^H (Business Card)	Father's Day$^{(94)}$ Incentive$^{(99-P)}$ Retired$^{(97-04)}$	17477 17361 17361/17257^{WB}	47 96 124
Button 7RD x 3^H (Button)	Booking$^{(xx-84)}$ Employee Christmas$^{(93)}$ Heartland$^{(94-01)}$ PAmerican$^{(03-05)}$ Regular Line$^{(84-P)}$ Retired (Natrl)$^{(99-01)}$ WTraditions$^{(99-01)}$	5400-JO 5400- 15423 10047 5400/15407/17273^{WB} 19526 12971	21 45 66 121 CL 124 148
Cake 12^L x 12^W x 6^H (Cake)	All-American$^{(88)}$ Employee$^{(92)}$ Employee Christmas$^{(88)}$ Feature (2sw/h)$^{(83-84)}$ Feature (Natrl)$^{(98)}$ Feature (Seasons)$^{(06)}$ Heartland$^{(99-00)}$ J.W. Collection$^{(92)}$ J.W. Originals RLine (2sw/h)$^{(85-P)}$ Retired (1st/h)$^{(79-94)}$ Retired (Natrl)$^{(94)}$ SEvent (GSales)$^{(03-05)}$ WTraditions$^{(96-00)}$	100-GBRS 11011 100- 100-CO 10481 1730012^P/-19^G/-21^W/-16^B/-22^R 15148 100-CBST n/a 100-CO/11011/17300^{WB} 100-A/100-GO/11002 16144 1734610^R/-20^B/-30^G/-40^{PR}/-50^{BK} 11657	15 44 45 55 51 53 66 99 100 CL 124 124 136 148
Cake, Miniature 4.75^L x 4.75^W x 2.5^H (None)	Collectors Club$^{(02-03)}$	11474	28
Cancun 12.5^L x 6.25^W x 7^H (Large BBQ)	Incentive, Trip$^{(01)}$	unknown	92
Candle 9^L x 5^W x 5^H (Medium Key)	All-American$^{(94)}$ Booking$^{(84-90)}$ Christmas$^{(81)}$ Employ Christmas$^{(89)}$ Retired$^{(99-02)}$	11134 1100-AO 1100- 1100- 19739	16 21 24 45 124
Candy Cane 5^L x 5^W x 4.5^H (Small Peg)	Christmas$^{(86)}$	14000-ART/AGT	24
Candy Corn 7.75^L x 4^W x 3.75^H (None)	Feature$^{(99)}$	14354	49

178

Quick Find

BASKET	COLLECTION (YEAR)	FORM #	PAGE
Canister, XLarge 9.25RD x 8.75^H (None)	Regular Line$^{(03-P)}$	10603	CL
Canister, Large 8RD x 7.75^H (None)	Regular Line$^{(03-P)}$	10368	CL
Canister, Medium 7RD x 7^H (None)	Regular Line$^{(03-P)}$	10371	CL
Canister, Small 5.5RD x 6^H (Small Canister)	Regular Line$^{(03-P)}$	10384	CL
Canister Set Set of 3 Baskets	Retired$^{(79-80)}$	unknown	124
Canning 13.75^L x 5.75^W x 5^H (None)	Blue Ribbon$^{(03)}$	10164	20
Card File 7.25^L x 6^H x 4^H (None)	Feature (WWash)$^{(05)}$ Retired$^{(04-06)}$	10247 10696	51 124
Card Keeper 10.75^L x 9^W x 5^{FH} x 7^{BH} (None)	Feature$^{(01)}$	12195	55
Caroling 7.5RD x 5^H (None)	Christmas$^{(03)}$	10465	26
Carry Along 5.5^L x 5.5^W x 6^H (Small Spoon)	All-American$^{(95)}$	21091	16
Carry Along II 15.5^L x 9^H x 5.5^H (None)	Feature (WWash)$^{(05)}$ Retired$^{(05-06)}$	10043 10042	51 124
Carry-n-Caddy 12.75^L x 10.5^W x 4^H (None)	Regular Line$^{(06-P)}$	10443	CL
Casserole 10.25RD x 3.5^H (Casserole)	All-American$^{(02)}$	12144	16
Casserole, ACO 9^L x 7.5^W x 3^H (None)	Feature, ACraft$^{(03-04)}$	10585	54
Catalog 14.5^L x 7.5^W x 4.5^{FH} x 11.5^{BH} (None)	Regular Line$^{(04-P)}$	10698	CL
Catalog Caddy 12^L x 6^W x 4.5^{FH} x 11.5^{BH} (None)	Incentive$^{(00-P)}$	unknown	96
Catch-All, Large 12RD x 3.5^H (None)	Retired$^{(01-03)}$	15890/17389^{WB}	124
Catch-All, Medium 9RD x 3^H (None)	Retired$^{(01-03)}$	15792/17362^{WB}	124
Catch-All, Small 7.25RD x 2.25^H (None)	Retired$^{(00-03)}$ Retired (WWash)$^{(01-02)}$	15083 10382	124 124
Celebration 8.5RD x 8.5^H (None)	Collectors Club$^{(05-06)}$	60611	32

KEY:
See page 170 for a key to understanding the abbreviations and notations used in these p

Quick Find

BASKET	COLLECTION (YEAR)	FORM#	PAGE
Century Celebration Collectors Club[00] 10.5^L x 6.25^W x 4.75^H (None)		15385	32
Century Celebration Hostess Appreciation HAppreciation[00] 7.5^L x 4.5^W x 3.5^H (Cheers)		13498	77
Charitable Champ Employee[00-P] 9.5^L x 5^W x 9.5^H (Tall Key)		n/a	44
Checkerboard Father's Day[01] 15^L x 15^W x 6^H (None)		10036	47
Cheers Feature[00] 7.5^L x 4.5^W x 3.5^H (Cheers)		18945	55
Cherished Memories Sweetheart[98] 14.25^L x 6.25^W x 9.5^H (None)		17531[R]/16268[B]/16365[G] 16462[PR]/16560[C]	139
Chives Booking[96-01] Employee Christmas[97] 4^L x 4^W x 4^H (None)		15211 n/a	21 45
Chore, Large Feature[86] 14^L x 7.75^W x 5.25^H (Large Chore)		3600-CO	55
Chore, Medium Easter[87] Feature[85-86] Heartland[88-97] Retired[86-02] 13^L x 8^W x 5^H (Medium Chore)		3500-CX 3500-CO 3500-CCS/13528 13510	38 55 66 124
Chore, Mini Heartland[89-97] Mother's Day[89] 7^L x 5^W x 3.5^H (Tea)		700-ACS/10758 700-APS	66 103
Chore, Small Feature[86] Heartland[89-97] 10^L x 6^W x 4^H (Small Chore)		3400-CO 3400-ACS/13404	55 66
Christmas Sponsoring Incentive[97] 10^L x 9.25^W x 6.5^H (Snowflake)		n/a	93
Cilantro Booking[03-04] 5.5^L x 3.5^W x 1.75^{FH} x 3.25^{BH} (None)		10301	21
Clip Keeper Retired[04-06] 3^L x 3^W x 2.5^{BH} (None)		10292	124
Coaster Retired, ACraft[03-05] 5^L x 5^W x 2.5^{BH} (None)		10584	125
Coaster Tote Regular Line[05-P] 5.5^L x 5.5^W x 2.5^{BH} (Ivy)		19102	CL
Community Traditions[96] 14.75^L x 13.5^W x 6.25^H (None)		19119	143
Compote Collectors Club[05] 13.25^{RD} x 6.75^H (None)		10258	32

Quick Find

BASKET	COLLECTION (YEAR)	FORM #	PAGE
Cookie 7RD x 3^H (Button)	Christmas(85)	5400-AR/AG	24
Cookie, Crisco 10RD x 4^H (Darning)	Crisco(92)	10081	66
Cookie Jar 10RD x 8^H (None)	Regular Line(06-P)	60720	CL
Corn 17RD x 11.5^H (None)	Hostess(95-99) J.W. Collection(91) J.W. Originals Retired(79-94)	14443 4400-JBST n/a 4400-O/14401	72 99 100 125
Corn, Miniature 7.75RD x 4.25^H (None)	Collectors Club(01-02)	11466	28
Corner 11.25^L x 8.5^W x 5^H (None)	Retired(02-06)	12470	125
Corner Hamper 17.25^L x 17.5^W x 20.75^H (None)	Retired(03-06) Hostess(03)	10333 10333	125 72
Corner, Small 8^L x 6^W x 3^H (None)	Retired(03-05)	10282	125
Coverlet 16^L x 16^W x 8^H (None)	Incentive(86,88)	n/a	83
Cracker 11.5^L x 5^W x 3^H (Cracker)	Employ Christmas(96) PAmerican(03-05) Regular Line(82-P) Retired (Natrl)(94) WTraditions(92-00)	4500- 10039 4500-OO/14508/17401^{WB} 17198 14532	45 121 CL 125 148
Cradle, Doll 19^L x 12^W x 6^H (Large Gathering)	Feature(91) Hostess(86-90) Retired(79-86)	2500-LO 2500-LO 2500-LO	55 72 125
Cradle, Large (Infant) 30^L x 20^W x 10.5^H (Large Laundry)	Hostess(86-90) Retired(79-86)	2800-M 2800-MO	72 125
Cradle, Medium 28.5^L x 17.75^W x 9.75^H (Medium Laundry)	Retired(79-83)	2700-M	125
Cradle, Mini 7^L x 5^W x 3.5^H (Tea)	Retired(79-93)	700-K/10715	125
Cradle, Small 24^L x 17^W x 10^H (Small Laundry)	Retired(79-80)	2600-M	125
Craft Keeper 18^L x 13.75^W x 9.25^H (None)	Hostess(02-04) Retired(04-06)	12535/18954^{WB} 12535/18954^{WB}	72 125
Crafting 19.25^L x 11.75^W x 8^H (None)	Blue Ribbon(04)	10648	20

KEY:
See page 170 for a key to understanding the abbreviations and notations used in these pages

Quick Find

BASKET	COLLECTION (YEAR)	FORM #	PAGE
Cranberry 8.5^L x 8.5^W x 7^H (None)	Christmas$^{(95)}$	19500^R/19518^G	25
Crocus 14^L x 10.5^W x 6^H (None)	Feature$^{(06)}$	10434^{WB}/1043421^{SW}	55
Crocus, Little 7^L x 5^W x 3^H (None)	RLine, Booking$^{(06-P)}$	10487	CL
Cupcake 5.5RD x 3.5^H (Discovery)	Collectors Club$^{(06)}$	unknown	31
Dad's Valet 10^L x 6.75^W x 3.75^H (None)	Father's Day$^{(04)}$	10679	48
Daddy's Caddy 8^L x 6.75^W x 5.25^{FH} x 7^{BH} (Daddy's Caddy)	Father's Day$^{(02)}$	11854	48
Daily Blessings, Lg 12.75^L x 9.75^W x 5.25^H (None)	Autumn Reflections$^{(01)}$	10656	17
Daily Blessings, Sm 10^L x 7.25^W x 3.75^H (None)	Autumn Reflections$^{(01)}$	11404	17
Daisy 10RD x 4^H (Darning)	Feature (Stained)$^{(86, 87)}$ Feature (Natrl)$^{(86)}$	5500-AO 5500-AN	55 55
Daisy (new) 6.75RD x 6^H (Daisy)	May$^{(99)}$	13056	101
Darning 10RD x 4^H (Darning)	Feature (Natrl)$^{(99)}$ Heartland$^{(96-01)}$ PAmerican$^{(03-04)}$ Retired$^{(83-06)}$ Retired (Natrl)$^{(94)}$ WTraditions$^{(94-01)}$	19640 15598 10207 15504/17427^{WB} 15521 15539	51 66 121 125 125 148
Dealer's Choice 10^L x 10.25^H x 5.5^H (None)	Regular Line$^{(05-P)}$	10394	CL
Dash Away Sleigh 7.75^L x 4.5^W x 2.25^{FH} x 4.5^{BH} (Summertime)	Feature$^{(98-99)}$	13943	50
Deck the Halls 8.5^L x 8.5^W x 6^H (None)	Christmas$^{(00)}$	17639^R/17736^G	26
Desktop, Large 14.25^L x 10.75^W x 3.75^{FH} x 9.25^{BH} (None)	Regular Line$^{(03-P)}$	12225	CL
Desktop, Small 6^L x 6^W x 4.25^{FH} x 5.25^{BH} (Finder's Keepers)	Retired$^{(03-04)}$	10229	125
Director Award (02) 8^L x 7.5^W x 10.5^H	Incentive$^{(02)}$	unknown	90
Director Award, XLg 11.25RD x 9^H (Large Pumpkin)	Incentive$^{(04)}$	unknown	90
Director Basket 15.75^L x 6.5^W x 11^H (Branch Basket)	Incentive$^{(88-02)}$	unknown	91

Quick Find

BASKET	COLLECTION (YEAR)	FORM#	PAGE
Director Basket II 17.75^L x 10.5^W x 12^H (Large Boardwalk)	Incentive (02-04)	unknown	90
Director Sales Excellence (98) 12^L x 12^W x 4^H (Pie)	Incentive (98)	unknown	89
Director Sales Excellence (99) 16^L x 11^W x 9^H (Large Market)	Incentive (99)	unknown	89
Director Sponsoring Excellence (98) 12^L x 12^W x 4^H (Pie)	Incentive (Natrl) (98)	unknown	89
Director Sponsoring Excellence (99) 16^L x 11^W x 9^H (Large Market)	Incentive (Natrl) (99)	unknown	89
Director Sponsored (00) 14.5^L x 5.5^W x 9.5^H (None)	Incentive (00)	unknown	90
Director Award (03) 15^L x 9.5^W x 5.5^H (Small Market)	Incentive (03)	unknown	90
Directorship Leadership 14^L x 12.75^W x 5^H (14" Generation)	Incentive (01)	unknown	90
DirectorshipTeam(00) 9.5^L x 4.5^W x 5^H (None)	Incentive (00)	unknown	90
DirectorshipTeam(01) 12^L x 11^W x 4.5^H (12 Generations)	Incentive (01)	unknown	90
DirectorshipTeam(02) 6.5^L x 6.5^W x 8.5^H (None)	Incentive (02)	unknown	90
DirectorshipTeam(03) 12^L x 8^W x 4.25^H (None)	Incentive (03)	unknown	90
DirectorshipTeam(04) 9.25^{RD} x 7.25^H (Pumpkin)	Incentive (04)	10616	90
Discover the Gift(01) 10RD x 8^H (None)	Incentive (01)	unknown	96
Discover the Gift(02) 8.5^{RD} x 10.25^H (None)	Incentive (02)	unknown	97
Discover the Gift(03) 15RD x 7^H (None)	Incentive (03)	unknown	97
Discovery 5.5^{RD} x 3.5^H (Discovery)	Special Event (92)	5700-AO	137
Diskette 6^L x 6^W x 4.25^{FH} x 5.25^{BH} (Finder's Keepers)	Incentive (00-P)	16276	96
Dresden Basket see also **Tour** 8.75^L x 4.75^W x 6.5^H (Tour)	Tour (88-99)	5600-BO/15601	140

KEY:
See page 170 for a key to understanding the abbreviations and notations used in these pages

Quick Find

BASKET	COLLECTION (YEAR)	FORM#	PAGE
Dresden Basket (99-02) see also **Tour** (99-02) 7^L x 3.5^W x 4.75^H (Tour)	Tour$^{(99-02)}$	15814	140
Dresden Basket (03-04) 4.75^L x 5^W x 3.25^H (Let It Snow)	Tour$^{(03-04)}$	unknown	140
Dresden Basket(05) 5.5RD x 3.75^H (Lily of Valley)	Tour$^{(05)}$	unknown	140
Dresden Basket(06) 5.25^L x 4^H x 5.5^H (04 Horizon of Hope)	Tour$^{(06)}$	10502^C/10484^S/10485^{PR}	140
Dresden Basket II see also **Tour II** 7^L x 3.5^W x 4.75^H (TourII)	Tour$^{(96-99)}$	15814	140
Early Blossoms 11^L x 7.25^W x 2.75^H (None)	Mother's Day$^{(00)}$	19682	104
Easter (1989) 10RD x 4^H (Darning)	Easter$^{(89)}$	5500-ABS/APS/AO	38
Easter (1992) 10.5^L x 7.5^W x 4.5^H (None)	Easter$^{(92)}$	34000-APVCNK	39
Easter (1994) 13.5^L x 8.25^W x 5.25^H (94 Easter)	Easter$^{(94)}$	16926^S/-34^U/-00^{SC}/-18^{UC}	39
Easter (1995) 10.75^L x 8.75^W x 5.25^H (None)	Easter$^{(95)}$	18708	39
Easter (1996) 7.5^L x 5^W x 6^H (None)	Easter$^{(96)}$	12912^S/12939^U	39
Easter (2004) 11^L x 8^W x 5.75^H (None)	Easter$^{(04)}$	10630/10631^W	41
Easter (2005) 13^L x 8.5^W x 4^H (None)	Easter$^{(05)}$	10253/10249^W	41
Easter, Baby 7^L x 5^W x 3.5^H (Tea)	Easter$^{(88)}$ Retired (1st/h)$^{(79-87)}$ Retired (1sw/h)$^{(79-87)}$	700-AN 700-AO 700-BO	38 126 126
Easter,Customer(91) 11^L x 8^W x 5.5^H (Spring)	Easter$^{(91)}$	900-ATMS/ATMN	39
Easter, Hostess(91) 7^L x 5^W x 3.5^H (Tea)	Easter$^{(91)}$	700-ATMS/ATMN	39
Easter, Large 14^L x 7.75^W x 5.25^H (Large Chore)	Easter$^{(88)}$ Retired (1st/h)$^{(79-87)}$ Retired (1sw/h)$^{(79-87)}$	3600-AN 3600-AO 3600-BO	38 126 126
Easter, Large(90) 9.5RD x 5^H (Petunia)	Easter$^{(90)}$	41000-APVBS	38

Quick Find

BASKET	COLLECTION (YEAR)	FORM#	PAGE
Easter, Large(93) 10^L x 6^W x 4^H (Small Chore)	Easter$^{(93)}$	13439^S/13412^U	39
Easter, Large(97) 12^L x 7^W x 4.5^H (97 Large Easter)	Easter$^{(97)}$	13447^S/13455^U	39
Easter, Large(98) 9^L x 9^W x 4.5^H (Bayberry)	Easter$^{(98)}$	11851^S/11860^U	39
Easter, Large(99) 7.5^L x 7.5^W x 3.75^H (None)	Easter$^{(99)}$	14061^S/14265^U	40
Easter, Large(00) 12.5RD x 6^H (None)	Easter$^{(00)}$	19283^S/19186^U	40
Easter, Large(01) 12.75RD x 4^H (None)	Easter$^{(01)}$	10915^S/11016^U	40
Easter, Large(02) 12.5^L x 10.25^W x 4.25^H (None)	Easter$^{(02)}$	12233^S/12411^U	40
Easter, Large(03) 13.75^L x 10.75^W x 5.75^H (03 Large Easter)	Easter$^{(03)}$	10147^S/10151^U	40
Easter, Medium 13^L x 8^W x 5^H (Medium Chore)	Easter$^{(88)}$ Retired (1st/h)$^{(79-87)}$ Retired (1sw/h)$^{(79-87)}$	3500-AN 3500-AO 3500-BO	38 126 126
Easter, Medium(90) 8RD x 4.5^H (None)	Easter$^{(90)}$	40000-APVBS	38
Easter, Small 10^L x 6^W x 4^H (Small Chore)	Easter$^{(88)}$ Retired (1st/h)$^{(79-87)}$ Retired (1sw/h)$^{(79-87)}$	3400-AN 3400-AO 3400-BO	38 126 126
Easter, Small(93) 7^L x 5^W x 3.5^H (Tea)	Easter$^{(93)}$	10774^S/10766^U	39
Easter, Small(97) 8.5^L x 5^W x 3.5^H (Small Oval)	Easter$^{(97)}$	63541^S/63550^U	39
Easter, Small(98) 6^L x 6^W x 3^H (None)	Easter$^{(98)}$	11959^S/11967^U	39
Easter, Small(99) 5.75RD x 3^H (None)	Easter$^{(99)}$	14052^S/14168^U	40
Easter, Small(01) 6RD x 2.75^H (None)	Easter$^{(01)}$	10023^S/10125^U	40
Easter, Small(02) 7.75^L x 6.25^W x 2.75^H (None)	Easter$^{(02)}$	12093^C/-111^P/-101^G/-123^Y	40
Easter, Small(03) 10^L x 7.5^W x 4.25^H (03 Small Easter)	Easter$^{(03)}$	10106^S/10109^U	40
Envelope 12^L x 5.25^W x 3.75^{FH} x 5^{BH} (Envelope)	Regular Line$^{(99-P)}$	14311/17443^{WB}	126

KEY:
See page 170 for a key to understanding the abbreviations and notations used in these pa

Quick Find

BASKET	COLLECTION (YEAR)	FORM #	PAGE
Evergreen 15.5^L x 15.5^W x 12.25^H (None)	Holiday Hostess$^{(95)}$	19607^R/19615^G	69
Everything's Coming Up Roses (Small) see **Rose Bud**			89
Everything's Coming Up Roses (Medium) see **Rose Petal**			89
Everything's Coming Up Roses (Large) see **American Beauty**			89
Everyday Handbag 12.25^L x 5.5^W x 10.25^H (None)	Regular Line$^{(06-P)}$	10476/10475/10512	CL
Family 15.25^L x 11^W x 7.75^H (None)	Traditions$^{(95)}$	19101	143
Family Legacy 15^L x 9^W x 5.25^H (None)	Collectors Club$^{(04)}$	10718/10768	32
Fantasy of Paradise 5^L x 5^W x 2.5^H (Sweet Basil)	Incentive, Trip$^{(92)}$	n/a	91
Fellowship 12.5^L x 6.5^W x 7.75^H (None)	Traditions$^{(97)}$	15920	143
Ficus 16.25RD x 11.5^H (None)	Hostess$^{(04-06)}$	10681	72
Fiesta del Sol 5^L x 5^W x 2.5^H (Sweet Basil)	Incentive, Trip$^{(93)}$	n/a	91
File 20^L x 17.5^W x 12.5^H (None)	Hostess$^{(99-03)}$	12769	73
Finders' Keepers 6^L x 6^W x 4.25^{FH} x 5.25^{BH} (Finder's Keepers)	Father's Day$^{(98)}$	12777	47
$500 Million 10^L x 6^W x 4^H (Small Chore)	Incentive$^{(97)}$	unknown	95
5-Yr Anniversary 6^L x 5^W x 8.25^H (None)	CClub, Charter$^{(01-02)}$ CClub$^{(02-P)}$	17345 12020/18636	27 27
Flag 10.75^L x 5.75^W x 7.5^H (None)	Incentive$^{(89)}$	n/a	84
Flag, Miniature 6.25^L x 3.25^W x 4.5^H (None)	Collectors Club$^{(02)}$	10128/10500	32
Flag Recruit 7^L x 3.5^W x 4.75^H (TourII)	Incentive$^{(98)}$	unknown	144
Flag Sponsoring 7^L x 3.5^W x 4.75^H (TourII)	Incentive$^{(98)}$	unknown	144
Flora 8.5RD x 6.25^H (None)	RLine, AHG$^{(04-P)}$	10678	CL
Floral Vase 8.5RD x 6.25^H (None)	Collectors Club$^{(03)}$	10264	32

Quick Find

BASKET	COLLECTION (YEAR)	FORM#	PAGE
Flower Pot Basket 17^L x 7.5^W x 4.75^H (None)	Retired(94-98)	16306	126
Flower Pot Basket Small 14^L x 6^W x 3^H (Small Flower Pot)	Retired(96-01)	18414	126
Foliage 11.25RD x 8^H (None)	Retired, AHG(04-06)	10667	126
Fraternal Order of Police 7.25^L x 6^W x 4^H (Card File)	Special Event(05)	0440	137
Forever Yours 20.5^L x 15^W x 10.5^H (Gift Giving)	Sweetheart(94)	10367	138
Forget-Me-Not 5RD x 4.5^H (5" Measuring)	Booking(86-87)	3800-AO	21
Founder's 15^L x 10^W x 7.5^H (Medium Market)	Feature(00)	18791	56
Frame Handbag 14.5^L x 5.25^W x 9.25^H (Ivy)	Regular Line(06-P)	10469/10468	CL
Friendship 5.5^L x 5.5^W x 2.5^H (Ivy)	Feature(89)	13100-JO	56
Frosty 10RD x 4^H (Darning)	Feature(00)	10242	49
Frosty, Jr. 7RD x 3^H (Button)	Feature(00)	10230	49
Fruit, Large (Apple) 13RD x 8.5^H (Large Fruit)	Holiday Hostess(89) Incentive, NSales(93) Incentive, Recruit(88) Retired(79-05) Retired, Hanging(79-80)	3200-BGRS unknown 3200-BO 3200-B/13200/17516^{WB} 3200-P	68 84 92 126 126
Fruit, Medium 8RD x 6.5^H (Medium Fruit)	Incentive, NSales(93) Incentive, Recruit(88) Retired(79-04) Retired, Hanging(79-80)	unknown 3100-BO 3100-B/13102/17494^{WB} 3100-P	84 92 126 126
Fruit, Small 6.5RD x 5^H (Small Fruit)	Feature(Natrl) (00) Incentive, NSales(93) Incentive, Recruit(88) Retired (79-04) Retired, hanging(79-80)	17671 unknown 3000-BO 3000-B/13005/17470^{WB} 3000-P	51 84 92 126 126
Fruit, Tall 8RD x 9^H (Tall Fruit)	Retired, Hanging(79-80) Retired(79-95)	3300-P 3300-BO/13307	126 126
Game Duo 7.5^L x 7.5^W x 2.75^H (Tic-Tac-Toe)	Retired(05-06)	10393	126
Garden 15^L x 8^W x 2.25^H (Bread, Old)	Feature(86) Incentive(88)	4600-AO 4700-	56 95

KEY: See page 170 for a key to understanding the abbreviations and notations used in these pa

Quick Find

BASKET	COLLECTION (YEAR)	FORM #	PAGE
Garland 16.75^L x 16.25^W x 6.5^H (None)	Holiday Hostess$^{(05)}$	10338^R/10339^G/10366^{WB}	70
Gatehouse, XSmall 3.75RD x 3.75^H (None)	Retired$^{(01-04)}$	12433/17524^{WB}	127
Gatehouse, Large 6.5RD x 10.5^H (Large Gatehouse)	Retired$^{(01-04)}$	11763/17541^{WB}	127
Gatehouse, Small 4.75RD x 7.5^H (None)	Regular Line$^{(01-P)}$	11751/17532^{WB}	127
Gathering Event 12^L x 6.75^W x 3.5^W (None)	Collectors Club$^{(01-02)}$	11222	31
Gathering Event 6.5^L x 6.5^W x 8^W (Large Peg)	Collectors Club$^{(03-04)}$	10576	31
Gathering Event Pail 6RD x 4.75^H (None)	Collectors Club$^{(04-05)}$	10636	31
Gathering Event 5.5RD x 6^H (Small Canister)	Collectors Club$^{(05)}$	10028	31
Gathering, Large 19^L x 12^W x 6^H (Large Gathering)	Holiday Hostess$^{(90)}$ Hostess$^{(96-99)}$ Hostess$^{(05-P)}$ Incentive, NSponsor$^{(93-98)}$ Retired (1st/h)$^{(83-93)}$ Retired (2sw/h)$^{(79-94)}$	2500-CGRS 12564 10256 2500-A/12505 2500-C/12513	68 73 73 82-83 127 127
Gathering, Medium 18^L x 11^W x 4.5^H (Medium Gathering)	Feature (Natrl)$^{(87)}$ Holiday Hostess$^{(89)}$ Incentive, NSponsor$^{(93-98)}$ J.W. Collection$^{(88)}$ J.W. Original PAmerican$^{(03-05)}$ Retired (2sw/h)$^{(79-06)}$ Retired (1st/h)$^{(80-93)}$	2400-C 2400-AGRS 2400-ABT n/a 10061 2400-C/12416/17567^{WB} 2400-AO/12408	51 68 82-83 99 100 121 127 127
Gathering, Mini 7^L x 4.5^W x 2^H (None)	Collectors Club$^{(00-01)}$	18941	28
Gathering, Small 14^L x 9^W x 4.5^H (Small Gathering)	Easter$^{(87)}$ Employ Christmas$^{(90)}$ Feature (Natrl)$^{(98-00)}$ Incentive, N.Sponsor$^{(93-98)}$ Retired (2sw/h)$^{(79-06)}$ Retired (WWash)$^{(01-02)}$ Retired (1st/h)$^{(86-93)}$ Shades of Autumn$^{(91)}$	2300-AX 2300- 12572 2300-C/12319/17559^{WB} 11052 2300-AO/12301 2300-CGUBS	38 45 51 82-83 127 127 127 133
Gathering, XLarge 23^L x 15^W x 8^H (None)	Incentive$^{(96-98)}$	unknown	82-83
Generations, 7" 7^L x 6.75^W x 3^H (7" Generations)	Retired$^{(98-02)}$	13757	127

Quick Find

BASKET	COLLECTION (YEAR)	FORM #	PAGE
Generations, 8" 8^L x 7.75^W x 3.5^H (None)	Retired$^{(98-02)}$	13765	127
Generations, 10" 10^L x 9.25^W x 4^H (10"Generations)	Retired$^{(98-04)}$	13773/17583^{WB}	127
Generations, 12" 12^L x 11^W x 4.5^H (12"Generations)	Retired$^{(98-02)}$	13790	127
Generations, 14" 14^L x 12.75^W x 5^H (14"Generations)	Regular Line$^{(98-04)}$	13781/17613^{WB}	127
Generosity 19.25^L x 13.5^W x 7.75^H (None)	Traditions$^{(99)}$	13358	143
Geranium 10.25^L x 6.25^W x 7.5^H (None)	May$^{(02)}$	12373	102
Geranium, Miniature 4.5^L x 3^W x 3.5^H (None)	Collectors Club$^{(05)}$	60245	28
Get Together 12.25^L x 9.25^W x 5.25^H (None)	Christmas$^{(05)}$	10728^R/10729^G/10086^{WB}	26
Getaway 17^L x 14^W x 11^H (Large Picnic)	Heartland$^{(90)}$ Sweetheart$^{(90)}$ Sweetheart$^{(93)}$	300-CCS 300-CRS 10359	66 138 138
Gift Giving 20.5^L x 15^W x 10.5^H (Gift Giving)	Holiday Hostess$^{(92)}$	12700^R/12718^G	68
Gingerbread 10^L x 6^W x 4^H (Small Chore)	Christmas$^{(90)}$	3400-ARST/AGST	24
Glad Tidings 8.75^L x 6^W x 7.5^{FH} x 9^{BH} (None)	Christmas$^{(98)}$	12386^R/12394^G	25
Gold Nugget 4.5RD x 3^H (Thyme)	Incentive$^{(94)}$	n/a	88
Gold Rush 6.5RD x 4.75^H (Gold Rush)	Incentive$^{(94)}$	n/a	88
Golf 6.75RD x 6^H (Daisy)	Tour$^{(00-01)}$	16098	140
Golf, 2002 9RD x 5.5^H (None)	Tour$^{(02)}$	unknown	141
Golf, 2003 6.5RD x 6.75^H (Pumpkin Patch)	Tour$^{(03)}$	801361	141
Golf, 2004 5.5RD x 7.5^H (None)	Tour$^{(04)}$	unknown	141
Golf, 2005 10RD x 6.25^H (Homestead)	Tour$^{(05)}$	10087	141
Golf, 2006 10.5RD x 7^H (None)	Tour$^{(06)}$	10483	141

KEY:
See page 170 for a key to understanding the abbreviations and notations used in these p

Quick Find

BASKET	COLLECTION (YEAR)	FORM#	PAGE
Gourmet Gathering 18^L x 11^W x 4.5^H (Medium Gathering)	Sweetheart$^{(97)}$	15946^R/16055^G 16063^B/16071^{PR}	138
Gourmet Picnic 13.25^L x 11.25^W x 9^H (Gourmet Picnic)	Hostess$^{(92-95)}$	10413	73
Grandad's Sleigh 9.25^L x 5.5^W x 2^{FH} x 5.5^{BH} (None)	Christmas$^{(82)}$	4900-Z	24
Greetings 18^L x 14^W x 8^H (Greetings)	Holiday Hostess$^{(04)}$	10730^R/10733^G	69
Growing Great People 11.5^L x 9.25^W x 10.5^H (Small Oval Waste)	Incentive$^{(01)}$	n/a	96
Growing Strong Together 9.5^L x 5^W x 9.5^H (Tall Key)	Incentive$^{(96-97)}$ Incentive$^{(98-02)}$	n/a n/a	95 95
Gumdrop 7.5^L x 5.5^W x 3.5^H (None)	Tree Trimming$^{(04)}$	10735^R/10736^G	144
Hamper, Corner 17.25^L x 17.5^W x 20.75^H (None)	Retired$^{(03-06)}$ Hostess$^{(03)}$	10333 10333	125 72
Hamper, Large 16.5^L x 16.5^W x 21.5^H (None)	Feature$^{(86)}$ Feature$^{(93-94)}$ Feature, SOA$^{(91)}$ Hostess$^{(86-90)}$ Retired$^{(79-86)}$	1600-OO 11622 1600-DS 1600-DO 1600-DO	56 56 56 73 127
Hamper, Large (1995 – P) 17^L x 17^W x 22^H (None)	Hostess$^{(95-01)}$ Hostess$^{(01-04)}$ Regular Line$^{(04-P)}$	11631 11362/19055^{WB} 11362/19055^{WB}	73 73 CL
Hamper, Lattice 19.25^L x 12^W x 23^H (None)	Regular Line$^{(06-P)}$	10437	CL
Hamper, Medium 12^L x 12.25^W x 16.25^H (Medium Hamper)	Hostess$^{(86-90)}$ Retired$^{(79-86)}$	1700-DO 1700-DO	73 127
Hamper, Small 12^L x 12.25^W x 16.25^H (Medium Hamper)	Feature, SOA$^{(91)}$	1700-DS	56
Hanging, 5" Sq. Bottom 5RD x 4.5^H (5"Measuring)	Retired$^{(80-86)}$	3800-PO	127
Hanging, 7" Sq. Bottom 7RD x 6.5^H (7"Measuring)	Retired$^{(80-86)}$	3900-PO	127
Hanging, 9" Sq. Bottom 9RD x 8.5^H (9"Measuring)	Retired$^{(80-86)}$	4000-PO	127

Quick Find

BASKET	COLLECTION(YEAR)	FORM #	PAGE
Hanging, 11" Sq. Bottom 11RD x 10.5^H (11"Measuring)	Retired(80-86)	4100-PO	127
Hanging, 13" Sq. Bottom 13RD x 12.5^H (13"Measuring)	Retired(80-86)	4200-PO	127
Hanging, Woven Bottom 8.25RD x 7.75^H (None)	Retired(79-86)	3700-PO	127
Happy Halloween 5.75RD x 3.5^H (None)	Feature(04)	10709	49
Harbor 10^L x 8.25^W x 8.25^H (None)	Collectors Club(98)	10677	32
Hartville Basket see also **Tour** 8.75^L x 4.75^W x 6.5^H (Tour)	Tour(95-99)	15661	141
Hartville II see also **Tour II** 7^L x 3.5^W x 4.75^H (TourII)	Tour(96-99)	15814	141
Harvest 16^L x 9^W x 6^H (Harvest)	Hostess(90-92)	3700-AOS	73
Harvest (1993) 7^L x 4.75^W x 7.75^H (None)	Shades of Autumn(93)	14303	133
Harvest Blessings Large 19.5^L x 8^W x 3.25^H (None)	Autumn Reflections(00)	14397	17
Harvest Blessings Small 15.25^L x 5.75^W x 2.5^H (None)	Autumn Reflections(00)	18058	17
Hat Box 13RD x 6^H (None)	Hostess(05-06)	60092	73
Hawaiian Holiday 13RD x 6^H (None)	Incentive, Trip(94)	n/a	91
Hearthside 11.75RD x 6.5^H (None)	Hostess(90-92)	42000-AOS	73
Heirloom 15^L x 10^W x 7.5^H (Medium Market)	Hostess(90-92)	500-HOS	73
Herb 11.5^L x 5^W x 3^H (Bread, Old)	Feature(86) Incentive(87-88)	4500-AO 4500-	56 95
Heritage Days (03) 8RD x 6.75^H (Autumn Pail)	Special Events(03)	123814	134
Heritage Days (04) 12^L x 7^W x 4.5^H (97 Easter)	Special Events(04)	523670	135

KEY:
See page 170 for a key to understanding the abbreviations and notations used in these p

Quick Find

BASKET	COLLECTION(YEAR)	FORM#	PAGE
Heritage Days(05) 7.5RD x 5^H (Caroling)	Special Events(05)	unknown	135
High Achiever 12RD x 5.75^H (Quilting)	Incentive(95-96)	unknown	88-89
Holiday Cheer 12^L x 8^W x 4.25^H (None)	Christmas(96) Employee Christmas(00)	18511^R/18520^G n/a	25 46
Holiday Helper(03) 4.75^L x 4.75^W x 2^H (Stuck On You)	Feature(03)	10530	50
Holiday Helper(04) 7.75^L x 3.75^W x 4.5^H (00 Branch Sales)	Feature(04)	60043xxx	50
Holiday Helper(05) 5.5RD x 3.5^H (Discovery)	Feature(05)	60560166	50
Holiday Sleigh 13^L x 7.5^W x 3^{FH} x 8^{BH} (Medium Vegetable)	Feature(97-99)	16811	50
Holly 15^L x 8^W x 2.25^H (Bread, Old)	Christmas(84)	4600-AZ	24
Homecoming 15^L x 15^W x 7.5^H (Medium Picnic)	Holiday Hostess(93) Hostess(99-02)	12084/12092 13081	69 73
Homestead 10RD x 6.25^H (Homestead)	Collectors Club(99) Feature(99)	6609596 13871	32 56
Hope Chest 23^L x 14^W x 11.25^H (None)	Hostess(98-03)	18431	73
Horizon of Hope(95) 5.75^L x 3.75^W x 3^H (Rosemary)	Horizon of Hope(95)	17124	71
Horizon of Hope(96) 6.75^L x 4.75^W x 2.25^H (None)	Horizon of Hope(96)	15911	71
Horizon of Hope(97) 5.5^L x 4^W x 4^H (Ambrosia)	Horizon of Hope(97)	18724	71
Horizon of Hope(98) 4^L x 4^W x 5.5^H (None)	Horizon of Hope(98)	10472	71
Horizon of Hope(99) 6.25^L x 5.25^W x 3^H (None)	Horizon of Hope(99)	14150	71
Horizon of Hope(00) 7.75^L x 4.25^W x 2.75^H (00 Horizon of Hope)	Horizon of Hope(00)	17787^S/19194^{WW}	71
Horizon of Hope(01) 5.25RD x 4.25^H (None)	Horizon of Hope(01)	10591^S/11605^{WW}	71
Horizon of Hope(02) 4RD x 4.25^H (Pencil)	Horizon of Hope(02)	17213^S/17311^{WW}	71

Quick Find

BASKET	COLLECTION (YEAR)	FORM#	PAGE
Horizon of Hope(03) 5.5^L x 4.5^W x 2^H (None)	Horizon of Hope$^{(03)}$	10546^S/10547^{WW}	71
Horizon of Hope(04) 5.5^L x 4^W x 5.5^H (None)	Horizon of Hope$^{(04)}$	10660^S/10661^{WW}	71
Horizon of Hope(05) 6.75^L x 3.75^W x 3.5^H (None)	Horizon of Hope$^{(05)}$	10280^S/10295^{WW}	71
Hospitality 18.5^L x 13.5^W x 5.25^H (None)	Traditions$^{(98)}$	10669	143
Hostess Appreciation (94) 8^L x 4^W x 2^H (Lavender)	HAppreciation$^{(94)}$	unknown	77
Hostess Appreciation (96) 5.5^L x 5.5^W x 2.5^H (Ivy)	HAppreciation$^{(96)}$	unknown	77
Hostess Appreciation (98) 5.75^L x 3.75^W x 3^H (Rosemary)	HAppreciation$^{(98)}$	unknown	77
Hostess Appreciation (01) 5.5^L x 4^W x 4^H (Ambrosia)	HAppreciation$^{(01)}$	15873	77
Hostess Appreciation (03) 4RD x 3.25^H (None)	HAppreciation$^{(03)}$	10162	77
Hostess Appreciation (04) 6.25^L x 3^W x 4^H (None)	HAppreciation$^{(04)}$	10541	77
Hostess Appreciation (05) 5^L x 5^H x 3.25^H (None)	HAppreciation$^{(05)}$	10704	77
Hostess Appreciation (06) 7^L x 4^H x 3.5^{FH} x 5^{BH} (None)	HAppreciation$^{(06)}$	10390	77
Hostess Halloween 8.5RD x 4.5^H (None)	Feature$^{(04)}$	10716	49
Hostess Thank You see **Spring, Booking** 7.5^L x 4.25^W x 2.75^H (00 Horizon of Hope)		10691	23
Hostess Two-Pie 14^L x 13^W x 7.75^H (None)	Feature$^{(03)}$	19219	56
Household Caddy 18.25^L x 8.5^W x 4.25^H (None)	Hostess$^{(04-05)}$	10693	74
Housekeeper 26^L x 20^W x 13.75^H (None)	RLine, Hostess$^{(04-P)}$	10360	CL

KEY:
See page 170 for a key to understanding the abbreviations and notations used in these

Quick Find

BASKET	COLLECTION (YEAR)	FORM #	PAGE
Ice Bucket 9.25RD x 8.5^{H} (None)	Feature$^{(03)}$ PAmerican$^{(04)}$	10363 10638	56 121
Inaugural (89) 5RD x 4.5^{H} (5"Measuring)	Special Event$^{(89)}$	3800-ABRST	135
Inaugural (93) 5^{L} x 5^{W} x 4.5^{H} (Small Peg)	Special Event$^{(93)}$	11461	135
Inaugural (97) 5.5RD x 3.25^{H} (None)	Special Event$^{(97)}$	15326	135
Inaugural (01) 5.5^{L} x 4^{W} x 4^{H} (Ambrosia)	Special Event$^{(01)}$	16080	136
Inaugural (05) 7.25RD x 2.75^{H} (None)	Special Event$^{(05)}$	10737	136
Inverted Waste Large Round 14RD x 16^{H} (None)	Feature$^{(87)}$ Retired (no/h)$^{(79-84)}$ Retired (1sw/h)$^{(79-84)}$	2000-BO 200-OO 2000-BO	56 127 127
Inverted Waste Small Round 12.5RD x 13.5^{H} (Banker's Waste)	Retired (no/h)$^{(79-84)}$ Retired (1sw/h)$^{(79-84)}$	1900-OO 1900-BO	127 127
Ivy 5.5^{L} x 5.5^{W} x 2.5^{H} (Ivy)	Booking$^{(90-92)}$ Employee$^{(91)}$	13100-JOS 13100-	21 43
JAM (00) 5.5RD x 3.75^{H} (Lily of The Valley)	Incentive$^{(00)}$	n/a	96
JAM (02) 11^{L} x 9.75^{H} x 4.75^{H} (Small Storage Solutions)	Incentive$^{(02)}$	n/a	97
JAM (04) 6^{L} x 5.5^{H} x 7^{H} (Tiny Tote)	Incentive$^{(04)}$	n/a	97
JAM Facilitator unknown	Incentive$^{(02)}$	n/a	97
JAM Small Easter 7RD x 2.5^{H} (Button)	Incentive$^{(04)}$	10627/10628	97
Jelly Bean 5.5RD x 3.75^{H} (Lily of The Valley)	Easter$^{(00)}$	19488	40
Jingle Bell 8RD x 6^{H} (None)	Christmas$^{(94)}$	17906^{R}/17914^{G}	25
Joyful Chorus 12RD x 7.5^{H} (None)	Holiday Hostess$^{(03)}$	10501	69
June Hostess Bonus 5.75^{L} x 3.75^{W} x 3^{H} (Rosemary)	Feature$^{(04)}$	10016	56
Junior Recognition 8.75^{L} x 4.75^{W} x 6.5^{H} (Tour)	Employee$^{(xx-97)}$	n/a	43

Quick Find

BASKET	COLLECTION (YEAR)	FORM #	PAGE
Keepsake 5.75^L x 3.75^W x 3^H (Rosemary)	Booking$^{(88-90)}$	45000-IO	21
Key, Medium 9^L x 5^W x 5^H (Medium Key)	Feature$^{(94)}$ Heartland$^{(88-97)}$ Retired$^{(79-04)}$	15172^R/15199^B/15181^G 1100-ICS/11118 1100-I/11100/17656^{WB}	53 66 127
Key, Small 7^L x 5^W x 3.5^H (Tea)	Feature$^{(94)}$ Heartland$^{(94-97)}$ Retired$^{(79-04)}$	17078^R/17051^B/17060^G 10782 700-I/10723/17640^{WB}	53 66 127
Key, Tall 9.5^L x 5^W x 9.5^H (Tall Key)	Employ Christmas$^{(91)}$ Feature$^{(94)}$ Heartland$^{(88-97)}$ Holiday Hostess$^{(88)}$ Regular Line$^{(79-05)}$ Retired (Natrl)$^{(94)}$	1000- 14672^R/14699^B/14681^G 1000-ICS/11061 1000-IRGS 1000-I/11053/17711^{WB} 14630	45 53 66 68 127 127
Knick Knack 8.5^L x 5^W x 3.25^H (None)	Regular Line$^{(04-P)}$	10652	CL
Laundry, Large 30^L x 20^W x 10.5^H (Large Laundry)	Hostess$^{(86-90)}$ Retired$^{(79-86)}$	2800-O 2800-OO	74 127
Laundry, Lattice 27.5^L x 17.5^W x 10.75^H (None)	Regular Line$^{(06-P)}$	10441	CL
Laundry, Little 7.25^L x 5^W x 3.25^H (None)	Regular Line$^{(06-P)}$	10488	CL
Laundry, Medium 28.5^L x 17.75^W x 9.75^H (Medium Laundry)	J.W. Original Retired$^{(79-83)}$	n/a 2700-O	100 127
Laundry, Oval 21.25^L x 14.25^W x 10.5^H (None)	Feature$^{(01)}$ Hostess$^{(02-03)}$	10893 10893/18989^{WB}	56 74
Laundry, Small 24^L x 17^W x 10^H (Small Laundry)	Holiday Hostess$^{(88)}$ Retired$^{(79-98)}$	2600-ORGS 2600-O/12602	68 127
Laurel 5.5RD x 3.75^H (Laurel)	Booking$^{(90-92)}$	17000-JOS	22
Lavender 8^L x 4^W x 2^H (Lavender)	Booking$^{(92-99)}$	10138	22
Leadership Excellence (Large) 13.75^L x 10.75^W x 5.75^H (03 Large Easter)	Incentive$^{(03)}$	unknown	92
Leadership Excellence (Small) 10^L x 7.5^W x 4.25^H (03 Small Easter)	Incentive$^{(03)}$	unknown	92
Leadership Vase 6.75RD x 6^H (Daisy)	Incentive$^{(04)}$	unknown	97
Leading Strong Together 6.5^L x 6.5^W x 8^H (Large Peg)	Incentive$^{(02)}$	unknown	97

Quick Find

BASKET	COLLECTION (YEAR)	FORM #	PAGE
Let It Snow 4.75^L x 5^W x 3.25^H (Let It Snow)	Tree-Trimming$^{(00)}$	18147^R/18155^G	144
Let Me Call You Sweetheart 6RD x 5.5^H (None)	Sweetheart$^{(04)}$	10644	139
Letter Tray 15^L x 12^W x 4^H (None)	Regular Line$^{(04\text{-}P)}$	10699	CL
Liberty 11.5^L x 5^W x 3^H (Cracker)	All-American$^{(93)}$	14541	16
Lightship 7.5RD x 5.75^H (None)	Collectors Club$^{(06)}$	10505	32
Lilac 6.5RD x 6.5^H (Lilac)	May$^{(94)}$	16209	101
Lily of the Valley 5.5RD x 3.75^H (Lily of The Valley)	May$^{(93)}$	15717	101
Little Bin, Bottom 7.25^L x 8^W x 2.5^{FH} x 3.75^{BH} (None)	Retired$^{(00\text{-}03)}$	16586/17079^{WB}	128
Little Bin, Top 7.25^L x 7.5^W x 2^{FH} x 3^{BH} (None)	Retired$^{(00\text{-}03)}$	16489/17052^{WB}	128
Little Elf 3.75RD x 3.75^H (XSm Gatehouse)	Feature$^{(02)}$	19179	50
Little Joy 5^L x 3.75^W x 4.5^H (None)	Hostess Appreciation$^{(99)}$	19445	77
Little Love 6.25^L x 4.75^W x 2.25^H (None)	Sweetheart$^{(00)}$	17728^R/10874^B/18062^G 10850^{PR}/10885^S	139
Little Membership(02) 6^L x 3.5^W x 5.75^H (None)	Incentive $^{(02)}$	16187	97
Little Membership(03) 7.5^L x 4^W x 3.5^H (None)	Incentive $^{(03)}$	10577	97
Little Star 7.5^L x 8^W x 3^H (None)	Feature$^{(01)}$ PAmerican$^{(03)}$	12202^R/12214^G 10617	50 121
Loaf, Small 7.5^L x 4.75^W x 2.5^H (Small Loaf)	Retired$^{(99\text{-}02)}$	12823	128
Loganberry 5^L x 5^W x 4.5^H (Small Peg)	Booking$^{(04\text{-}05)}$	10011	22
Lots of Luck 4.25^L x 4.25^W x 3^H (Lots of Luck)	Feature$^{(99)}$	18465	52
Love Letters 8.75^L x 7.75^W x 2.75^H (None)	Sweetheart$^{(99)}$	12963	139
Love Notes 5.75^L x 3.75^W x 5^H (None)	Sweetheart$^{(01)}$	12055^S/18026^R	139
Love Treasures 13.25^L x 12.5^W x 4.25^H (None)	Sweetheart$^{(99)}$	13064	139
Lucky Charm 5.25^L x 4.25^W x 1.75^{FH} x 3^{BH} (Lucky Charm)	Hostess Appreciation$^{(02)}$	11482	77

Quick Find

BASKET	COLLECTION(YEAR)	FORM#	PAGE
Lucky Twist 5.75^L x 5.75^W x 3^H (None)	Feature(06)	10498	53
Lucky You 4.75^{RD} x 3^H (None)	Feature(02)	11911	53
Lunch Box 12^L x 8.25^W x 6^H (Lunch Box)	Regular Line(05-P)	10213	CL
Magazine	Employee(92)	12106	44
	Holiday Hostess(89)	2100-CGRS	68
	Retired (2sw/h)(79-06)	2100-C/12106/17753^{WB}	128
	Retired (1sw/h, legs)(79-98)	2100-U/12122	128
16^L x 8^W x 11^H (Magazine)	Retired (1sw/h, legs, lid)(79-95)	2100-W/12114	128
Mail 12^L x 8^W x 11.5^H (None)	Hostess(92-96)	10600	74
Mail, Large 12^L x 8.75^W x 11^H (None)	Retired(00-02)	16373	128
Mail, Medium 10.75^L x 7.75^W x 10.25^H (None)	Retired(00-02)	16969	128
Mail, Small 9.75^L x 6.25^W x 8.5^H (None)	Retired(01-02)	11271	128
Make Your Dreams Come True 5.5^{RD} x 4.5^H (None)	Incentive, Recruit(99)	unknown	144
Management Excellence 19.5^{RD} x 10^H (None)	Incentive(93-96)	unknown	95
Maple Leaf 7RD x 6.5^H (7" Measuring)	Shades of Autumn(96)	13935	133
Market, Large	Feature(96-97)	16641^R/16624^B/11632^G	53
	Holiday Hostess(88)	600-ARGS	68
	J.W. Originals	n/a	100
	Retired (2sw/h)(83-04)	600-CO/10634/17869^{WB}	128
16^L x 11^W x 9^H (Large Market)	Retired (1st/h)(79-93)	600-AO/10626	128
Market, Little	Regular Line(02-P)	12500/17780^{WB}	128
7.75^L x 5.5^W x 4.5^H (Little Market)	SEvent (GSales)(03-05)	17780$10^R$/-20^B/-30^G/-40^{PR}/-50^{BK}	136
Market, Medium	Employ Christmas(87)	500-	45
	Feature (Natrl)(87)	500-A	51
	Feature (Natrl)(98)	10588	51
	Heartland(89-97)	500-ACS/10545	67
	Incentive(98)	unknown	96
	J.W. Collection(83)	500-AT	99
	J.W. Originals	n/a	100
	RLine (2sw/h)(83-P)	500-C/10537/17818^{WB}	CL
	Retired (WWash)(01-02)	11301	128
15^L x 10^W x 7.5^H (Medium Market)	Retired (1st/h)(79-98)	500-AO/10529	128
Market, Miniature 5.75^L x 4^W x 3^H (None)	Collectors Club(96)	150240	27

KEY:
See page 170 for a key to understanding the abbreviations and notations used in these page

Quick Find

BASKET	COLLECTION (YEAR)	FORM#	PAGE
Market, Small	All-American (92)	10707	15
	Retired (2sw/h) (93-02)	10430	128
	Retired (1st/h) (79-93)	400-AO/10421	128
15^L x 9.5^W x 5.5^H (Small Market)			
Master Employee	Employee (xx-97)	1900-	43
12.5RD x 13.5^H (Banker's Waste)			
Master Employee II	Employee (97-P)	n/a	43
8RD x 6.5^H (Medium Fruit)			
Master Employee II 15 Year	Employee (97-P)	n/a	43
8RD x 9^H (Tall Fruit)			
Master Employee II 20 Year	Employee (97-P)	n/a	43
13RD x 8.5^H (Large Fruit)			
MBA Basket	Incentive (88-03)	1000-FO	90
9.5^L x 5^W x 9.5^H (Tall Fruit)			
MBA II	Incentive (03-04)	n/a	90
12.5^L x 6.75^W x 8.5^H (Medium Boardwalk)			
Meadow Blossoms Pottery	Incentive (85)	n/a	94
Measuring, 5"	Booking (xx-84)	3800-BO	22
	Employ Birthday (88)	3800-	43
	Employ Christmas (92)	3800-	45
	Incentive, NSales (94-98)		84
	Retired (79-98)	3800-B/13803	128
	Retired (01-02)	11415	128
5RD x 4.5^H (5"Measuring)			
Measuring, 7"	Incentive, NSales (94-98)	84	
	Retired (79-98)	3900-B/13901	128
	Retired (00-02)	19861	128
7RD x 6.5^H (7"Measuring)			
Measuring, 9"	Incentive, NSales (94-98)	84	
	Retired (79-98)	4000-B/14001	128
	Retired (00-02)	19763	128
9RD x 8.5^H (9"Measuring)			
Measuring, 11"	Incentive, NSales (94-98)	n/a	84
	Retired (79-98)	4100-B/14109	128
11RD x 10.5^H (11" Measuring)			
Measuring, 13"	Holiday Hostess (90)	4200-CGRS	68
	Incentive, NSales (98)	n/a	84
	Retired (79-98)	4200-B/14206	128
	Retired (00-02)	19968	128
13RD x 12.5^H (13" Measuring)			
Media	Retired (04-06)	10697	128
11.5^L x 7.5^W x 7^{FH} x 9^{BH} (None)			
Melody	Tree-Trimming (03)	10452	144
5RD x 3^H (None)			

Quick Find

BASKET	COLLECTION (YEAR)	FORM#	PAGE
Membership 9.5^L x 5^W x 9.5^H (Tall Key)	CClub, Charter(95-96) Collectors Club(97-03)	62839 62847	27 27
Membership II 15^L x 8^W x 7.25^H (None)	CClub, Charter(03-P) Collectors Club(03-P)	10205 10085	27 27
Memory 8.75^L x 4.75^W x 6.5^H (Tour)	Christmas(89) Feature(88-89)	5600-BRST/BGST 5600-BBS	24 57
Mending 5.75^L x 5.75^W x 4.5^H (None)	Blue Ribbon(04)	10675	20
Mini Bee 5.75^L x 3.75^W x 3^H (Rosemary)	Incentive(02)	n/a	96
Mistletoe 7^L x 5^W x 3.5^H (Tea)	Christmas(87)	700-ART/AGT	24
Mom's Essentials 6RD x 4^H (None)	Mother's Day(04)	10668	104
Mom's Memories 9.5^L x 7.75^W x 6^H (None)	Mother's Day(02)	12136	104
Morning Glory 7.5^L x 7.5^W x 4.75^H (None)	May(00)	18899	101
Morning Glory Miniature 3.75^L x 3.5^W x 2^H (None)	CClub, Mini(06)	10349	29
Mother's Day (92) 10.5^L x 10.5^W x 4.5^H (None)	Mother's Day(92)	110-CPS	103
Mother's Day (93) 8.5^L x 8^W x 6^H (None)	Mother's Day(93)	12904	103
Mother's Day (94) 6.75^L x 9.25^W x 3.75^H (None)	Mother's Day(94)	16004	103
Muffin 11.5^L x 5^W x 3^H (Cracker)	Heartland(90-00)	4500-JCS/14516	67
Mulberry 4^L x 4^W x 3.5^H (Small Sweetest Gift)	Booking(05-06)	10381	22
Napkin 10.75^L x 9^W x 3.25^H (None)	Regular Line(05-P)	10130	CL
National High Sales	Incentive(99-P)	n/a	84-85
National Sales Leader 17.75^L x 10.5^W x 12^H (Large Boardwalk)	Incentive(04-P)	n/a	91
National Sales Leader 10.75^L x 9.75^W x 4.5^H (Shaker Harmony #1)	Incentive(05)	n/a	90
National Sponsoring	Incentive(99-P)	n/a	83

KEY:
See page 170 for a key to understanding the abbreviations and notations used in these pages

Quick Find

BASKET	COLLECTION (YEAR)	FORM #	PAGE
Newspaper 15.75^L x 10.5^W x 10.5^H (None)	Regular Line$^{(99-P)}$	17329/17907^{WB}	CL
Noel Bell 5.5RD x 5.5^H (None)	Feature$^{(00)}$	16845	50
Note Pal 7.5^L x 5.5^W x 2^{FH} x 3.5^{BH} (Paper)	Regular Line$^{(00-P)}$ Retired (WWash)$^{(01-02)}$	11606/17958^{WB} 11003	128 128
Nurses Inaugural 7RD x 3^H (Button)	Special Event$^{(99)}$	15423-ONA	137
October Fields 6.5RD x 9^H (None)	Feature$^{(00)}$	16951	49
Odds & Ends 18.75^L x 9^W x 12.75^{FH} x 5.25^{BH} (Odds & Ends)	Hostess$^{(95-02)}$	18902	74
Oregano 5^L x 3^W x 3.5^H (None)	Booking$^{(98-01)}$	13145	22
Original Easter 16^L x 9^W x 6^H (Harvest)	J.W. Collection$^{(93)}$	13722	99
Original Easter Miniature 6^L x 3.5^W x 2.25^H (None)	Collectors Club$^{(03)}$	10046	28
Our Business is Show Business (Small) see also **Associate Producer** 5.5RD x 2.5^H (None)			89
Our Business is Show Business (Medium) see also **Show Star** 7RD x 3^H (Button)			89
Our Business is Show Business (Large) see also **Best Supporting Role** 8.5RD x 4^H (Basket of Love)			89
Over the Rainbow (Small) see also **Gold Nugget** 4.5RD x 3^H (Thyme)			88
Over the Rainbow (Medium) see also **Pot of Gold** 5.5RD x 3.75^H (Lily of The Valley)			88
Over the Rainbow (Large) see also **Gold Rush** 6.5RD x 4.75^H (None)			88
Pail 8RD x 6.75^H (Autumn Pail)	Feature (AHG)$^{(05)}$	unknown	49
Paint the Town 5.75^L x 3.75^W x 3^H (Rosemary)	Incentive$^{(93)}$	n/a	88
Pansy 7RD x 4.5^H (Pansy)	May$^{(92)}$	10006	101

Quick Find

BASKET	COLLECTION (YEAR)	FORM#	PAGE
Pantry	Feature (85)	2300-JO	57
	Feature (96-97)	16446R/16420B/16438G	53
	Heartland (98-00)	13951	67
	Retired (86-02)	2300-JO/12327	128
	WTraditions (98-00)	13854	148
14L x 9W x 4.5H (Small Gathering)			
Paper	Father's Day (92)	16000	47
	Incentive (92-98)	16000-	95
	Incentive (99-00)	16000-	96
7.5L x 5.5W x 2FH x 3.5BH (Paper)			
Paper Tray, Bottom	Retired (99-04)	18961/18008WB	129
12L x 14.5W x 3H (None)			
Paper Tray Tapered	Incentive (99-00)	19062	96
	Retired (99-04)	19062/17133WB	129
12L x 14.5W x 3FH x 5.5BH (None)			
Parsley	Booking (99-02)	12882	22
6L x 4.5W x 2.5H (None)			
Patriot	All-American (97)	10651	16
7L x 5W x 3.5H (Tea)			
Peg, Large	Bee (88)	11000-AO	18
	Heartland (89-97)	11000-ACS/11177	67
	Mother's Day (87)	11000-BPS	103
	Retired (85-99)	11000-AO/11151	129
	WTraditions (95-99)	11142	148
6.5L x 6.5W x 8H (Large Peg)			
Peg, Medium	Bee (88)	10000-AO	18
	Feature (shaker) (84)	10000-AO	57
	Retired (85-99)	10000-AO/11070	129
5.5L x 5.5W x 6H (Small Spoon)			
Peg, Small	Bee (88)	14000-AO	18
	Retired (85-99)	14000-AO/11452	129
5L x 5W x 4.5H (Small Peg)			
Pen Pal	Regular Line (00-P)	11541/17991WB	CL
	Retired (WWash) (01-02)	10931	129
	SEvent (GSales) (03-05)	1799110R/-20B/-30G/-40PR/-50BL	136
4RD x 4.25H (Pencil)			
Pencil	Father's Day (92)	15000-	47
	Incentive (92-98)	15000-	95
	Incentive (99-00)	15000-	96
4RD x 4.25H (Pencil)			
Peony	May (01)	10184	102
12.75L x 6.25W x 2.75H (Peony)			
Peony, Miniature	CClub, Mini (05-06)	10199	29
5.75L x 2.75W x 1.25H (None)			
Peppermint	Tree-Trimming (99)	19364R/16837G	144
5.5RD x 2.75H (Peppermint)			
Perfect Attendance (94)	Employee (94)	n/a	44
6.5RD x 5H (Small Fruit)			

KEY:
See page 170 for a key to understanding the abbreviations and notations used in these pa

Quick Find

BASKET	COLLECTION (YEAR)	FORM#	PAGE
Perfect Attendance(95) Employee(95) 7RD x 4.5^H (Pansy)		n/a	44
Perfect Attendance(96) Employee(96) 9^L x 5^W x 5^H (Medium Key)		n/a	44
Perfect Attendance(97) Employee(97) 7RD x 6.5^H (7"Measuring)		n/a	44
Perfect Attendance(98) Employee(98) 6.5^L x 6.5^W x 8^H (Large Peg)		n/a	44
Perfect Attendance(99) Employee(99) 11^L x 8^W x 5.5^H (Spring)		n/a	44
Perfect Attendance(00) Employee(00) 14.5^L x 7.5^W x 3.75^H (Bread, New)		n/a	44
Perfect Attendance(01) Employee(01) 12^L x 5.25^W x 3.75^{FH} x 8^{BH} (Envelope)		12354	44
Perfect Attendance(02) Employee(02) 6.5RD x 10.5^H (Large Gatehouse)		n/a	44
Personal File 15.25^L x 12^W x 12^H (None)	Regular Line(04-P)	10700	CL
Personal Organizer 14^L x 6^W x 3^H (Small Flower Pot)	Father's Day(97)	13137	47
Petunia 9.5RD x 5^H (90 Large Easter)	May(97)	12947	101
Picket Pail 7.25RD x 6^H (None)	Easter(06)	10489^{WB}/-12^P/-11^{PR}/-13^B/-21^W	41
Picnic, Family 24^L x 17^W x 10^H (Small Laundry)	Retired(83-86)	2600-HO	129
Picnic, Family **Collectors Club** 20^L x 14^W x 9.5^H (None)	Collectors Club(99)	13561	33
Picnic, Family **Hostess** 21^L x 11.5^W x 9.75^H (None)	Hostess(06)	10509^R/10777^{CH}	74
Picnic, Large 17^L x 14^W x 11^H (Large Picnic)	All-American(87) Feature (Natrl)(99) Regular Line(79-P)	300-HBRS 19755 300-H/10324/18122^{WB}	15 51 CL
Picnic, Medium 15^L x 15^W x 7.5^H (Medium Picnic)	Retired(79-84)	200-H	129
Picnic, Oak Lid 12^L x 12^W x 6^H (Cake)	Feature(82)	n/a	57
Picnic, Oval XLg 21^L x 12.25^W x 11.25^H (None)	Hostess(03-04)	10007	74
Picnic Pal 9.5^L x 9.5^W x 2.75^H (Picnic Pal)	GOSummertime(98)	18643	65

Quick Find

BASKET	COLLECTION (YEAR)	FORM #	PAGE
Picnic, Small	All-American [88]	100-HBRS	15
	Feature (Natrl) [00]	18040	51
	PAmerican [03-04]	10069	121
12^L x 12^W x 6^H (Cake)	Retired [79-02]	100-H/11029	129
Picture Perfect	Sweetheart [98]	17523^R/16250^B/16357^G	139
7.25^L x 4^W x 4.5^H (None)		16454^{PR}/16551^S	
Pie	All-American [98]	12289	16
	Easter [87]	2200-AX	38
	Feature (Natrl) [99]	19941	52
	Feature [85]	2200-AO	57
	Retired [86-02]	2200-AO/12203	129
	Shades of Autumn [90]	2200-AGUBS	133
12^L x 12^W x 4^H (Pie)	Woven Traditions [94]	12211	148
Pie, Blue Ribbon	Blue Ribbon [05]	10270^{WB}/10328^B	20
13.25^L x 13.25^W x 4^H (None)			
Pie, Crisco	Crisco [91]	100-DBRS	66
12^L x 12^W x 6^H (Cake)			
Pie, Small	Feature [06]	10780^R/17092^{CH}/10807^{WB}	57
7RD x 2.25^H (None)			
Pineapple	Incentive, Trip [02]	n/a	92
6.5RD x 9^H (October Fields)			
Pinecone	Holiday Hostess [99]	15253^R/15164^G	69
13RD x 6.25^H (None)			
Planter, 10"	Feature (AHG) [06]	835714	49
unknown			
Planter,	Feature (feet) [88]	3200-RO	57
Large Fern	Retired (feet) [82-86]	3200-RO	129
	Retired (13") [79-86]	3200-SO	129
13RD x 8.5^H (Large Fruit)	Retired (20") [79-86]	3200-TO	129
Planter, Patio	Feature [84]	6000-R	57
10RD x 5.5^H (None)			
Planter, Sleeve	Incentive [91]	n/a	95
31.5RD x 18^H (None)	Incentive (25th) [98]	n/a	95
Planter	Feature (feet) [88]	2900-RO	57
Small Fern	Retired (feet) [82-86]	2900-RO	129
	Retired (13") [79-86]	2900-SO	129
8.5RD x 7.5^H (None)	Retired (20") [79-86]	2900-TO	129
Pocket Change	Father's Day [03]	10035	48
5.25^L x 4.75^W x 3^H (None)			
Poinsettia	Christmas [88]	3900-BRST/BGST	24
7RD x 6.5^H (7"Measuring)			
Pom Pom Peggy	Incentive [91]	n/a	88
12^H			
Pool	J.W. Originals	n/a	100
22^L x 14.5^W x 6.25^H (None)			

KEY:
See page 170 for a key to understanding the abbreviations and notations used in these pa

Quick Find

BASKET	COLLECTION (YEAR)	FORM#	PAGE
Popcorn 10.5RD x 5^H (None)	Christmas$^{(99)}$	15156^R/15351^G	25
Ports of Paradise 5.5RD x 3.75^H (Lily of The Valley)	Incentive, Trip$^{(95)}$	n/a	91
Pot of Gold 19.75RD x 12.5^H (Pot of Gold)	Feature$^{(02)}$	11903	57
Pot of Gold, Small 5.5RD x 3.75^H (Lily of The Valley)	Incentive$^{(94)}$	n/a	88
Potpourri 5^L x 5^W x 2.5^H (Sweet Basil)	Booking$^{(85-90)}$ Employee Birthday$^{(90)}$ Mother's Day$^{(91)}$	13000-AO 13000- 13000-APS	22 43 103
Pottery Ware 25RD x 13^H (None)	J.W. Originals	n/a	100
Precious Treasures 13.25^L x 11.25^W x 9^H (Precious Moments)	Sweetheart$^{(95)}$	10456	138
Pride 3.25RD x 5.25^H (None)	Blue Ribbon$^{(03)}$	10239	20
Pumpkin 9.25RD x 7.25^H (None)	Pumpkin$^{(95)}$	19402	122
Pumpkin, Large 11.25RD x 9^H (None)	Pumpkin$^{(97)}$	16039	122
Pumpkin, Little 5.75RD x 4.25^H (Little Pumpkin)	Pumpkin$^{(97)}$	16021	122
Pumpkin Patch 6.5RD x 6.75^H (Pumpkin Patch)	Feature$^{(01)}$	10621	49
Pumpkin, Small 7.25RD x 5.25^H (Small Pumpkin)	Pumpkin$^{(96)}$	16012	122
Purse, Kiddie 7^L x 5^W x 3.5^H (Tea)	Feature (Natrl)$^{(98)}$ Retired$^{(79-06)}$ Retired (Natrl)$^{(94)}$ Retired (WWash)$^{(01-02)}$	10898 700-E/10731/18211^{WB} 17019 11350	52 129 129 129
Purse, Medium 11^L x 8^W x 5.5^H (Spring)	Retired (1sw/h)$^{(79-97)}$ Retired (split lid)$^{(82-86)}$	900-E/10901 900-QO	129 129
Purse, Shoulder 9.5^L x 5.75^W x 7^H (None)	Retired$^{(96-99)}$	18210	130
Purse, Small 9.5^L x 6^W x 6^H (Small Purse)	Heartland$^{(88-98)}$ Mother's Day$^{(91)}$ Retired$^{(79-99)}$	800-ECS/10839 800-EPS 800-E/10821	67 103 130
Purse, Tall 9.5^L x 5^W x 9.5^H (Tall Key)	Retired$^{(79-89)}$	1000-EO	130
Quilting 12RD x 5.75^H (Quilting)	All-American$^{(89)}$	54000-ABRS	15

Quick Find

BASKET	COLLECTION (YEAR)	FORM#	PAGE
Raspberry 5.25^L x 4.25^W x 1.75^{FH} x 3^{BH} (Lucky Charm)	Booking$^{(05-06)}$	10234	22
Reach for the Stars (Small) see also **Star Bound** 4.75^L x 3.75^W x 2.25^H (Business Card)			88
Reach for the Stars (Medium) see also **Shining Star** 5.75^L x 3.75^W x 3^H (Rosemary)			88
Reach for the Stars (Large) see also **Star Team** 7^L x 5^W x 3.5^H (Tea)			88
Recipe	Heartland$^{(98-01)}$	10596	67
	Regular Line$^{(96-P)}$	17418/18253^{WB}	CL
	Retired (WWash)$^{(01-02)}$	10461	130
	Retired (Natrl)$^{(99-01)}$	19542	130
	Shades of Autumn$^{(94)}$	17400	133
	WTraditions$^{(98-01)}$	10499	148
8^L x 5.5^W x 4.5^{FH} x 6^{BH} (None)			
Recipe, Small	Retired$^{(01-02)}$	19496	130
	Retired (WWash)$^{(01-02)}$	10451	130
7^L x 5.25^W x 3.75^{FH} x 4.5^{BH} (Small Recipe)			
Recruit, 1999 5RD x 4.5^H (5" Measuring)	Incentive$^{(99)}$	n/a	144
Recruit, All-Star 8^L x 4^W x 2^H (Lavender)	Incentive$^{(93)}$	16101	142
Recruit **Flying High with Longaberger** 5RD x 4.5^H (5" Measuring)	Incentive$^{(92)}$	10154	142
Recruit **Pegged for Success** 5^L x 5^W x 4.5^H (Small Peg)	Incentive$^{(96)}$	n/a	142
Recruit **Rising Star** 12^L x 12.25^W x 16.25^H (Medium Hamper)	Incentive$^{(90-91)}$	1700-DST	142
Recruit **Share the Tradition** 5^L x 5^W x 2.5^H (Sweet Basil)	Incentive$^{(88-89)}$	13000-BBRS	142
Recruit **Together–We're Growing** 5.75^L x 3.75^W x 3^H (Rosemary)	Incentive$^{(90)}$	45000-ABRST	142
Red Pottery **Thank You** 11^L x 8^W x 5.5^H (Spring)	Feature$^{(93)}$	190xx	57
Red, White & You 5.5^L x 6^W x 2.25^H (Twinkle Twinkle)	Incentive, Recruit$^{(02)}$	n/a	144

KEY:
See page 170 for a key to understanding the abbreviations and notations used in these p

Quick Find

BASKET	COLLECTION (YEAR)	FORM#	PAGE
Region Award 7.25RD x 5.25^H (Small Pumpkin)	Incentive$^{(04)}$	n/a	87
Regional Basket 15.75^L x 6.5^W x 11^H (Branch Basket)	Incentive$^{(88-02)}$	n/a	91
Regional Basket II 17.75^L x 10.5^W x 12^H (Large Boardwalk)	Incentive$^{(02-04)}$	n/a	91
Regional Excellence (98) 8.5^L x 8.5^W x 5^H (Large Berry)	Incentive$^{(98)}$	n/a	87
Regional Sales (99) 15^L x 9.5^W x 5.5^H (Small Market)	Incentive$^{(99)}$	n/a	87
Regional Sales (00) 9.25^L x 5^W x 6.5^H (None)	Incentive$^{(00)}$	n/a	87
Regional Sales (01) 10^L x 9.25^W x 4^H (10"Generations)	Incentive$^{(01)}$	n/a	87
Regional Sales (02) 6.5^L x 6.5^W x 6.5^H (None)	Incentive$^{(02)}$	n/a	87
Regional Sales (03) 10^L x 6^W x 4^H (Small Chore)	Incentive$^{(03)}$	n/a	87
Regional Sponsored (91) 10^L x 6^W x 4^H (Small Chore)	Incentive$^{(91)}$	n/a	86
Regional Sponsored (92) 8.5^L x 5^W x 3.5^H (Small Oval)	Incentive$^{(92)}$	33000-	86
Regional Sponsored (93) 5^L x 5^W x 2.5^H (Sweet Basil)	Incentive$^{(93)}$	11321	86
Regional Sponsored (94) 9.5^L x 6^W x 6^H (Small Purse)	Incentive$^{(94)}$	n/a	86
Regional Sponsored (95) 7.5^L x 7.5^W x 3.5^H (Medium Berry)	Incentive$^{(95)}$	n/a	86
Regional Sponsored (96) 10RD x 4^H (Darning)	Incentive$^{(96)}$	n/a	86
Regional Sponsored (98) 4.25^L x 4.25^W x 3^H (Sweet Sentiments)	Incentive$^{(98)}$	n/a	87
Regional Sponsored (99) 15^L x 9.5^W x 5.5^H (Small Market)	Incentive$^{(99)}$	n/a	87
Regional Sponsored (00) 9.25^L x 5^W x 6.5^H (None)	Incentive$^{(00)}$	n/a	87

Quick Find

BASKET	COLLECTION (YEAR)	FORM#	PAGE
Remembrance 10.5^L x 9^W x 8^H (Weekender)	Feature$^{(96-97)}$ Hostess$^{(90-92)}$	16748^R/16721^B/16730^G 200-YOS	53 74
Renewal, 1997 9^L x 5^W x 5^H (Medium Key)	Collectors Club$^{(97)}$	105702	29
Renewal, 1998 8.5RD x 4^H (Basket of Love)	Collectors Club$^{(98)}$	13340	29
Renewal, 1999 6.75^L x 5.75^W x 4.75^H (None)	Collectors Club$^{(99)}$	12998	29
Renewal, 2000 6.75^L x 5.25^W x 3.25^H (None)	Collectors Club$^{(00-01)}$	18783	29
Renewal, 2001 5RD x 6^H (None)	CClub, Charter$^{(01-02)}$ Collectors Club$^{(01-02)}$	10273 10813	29 29
Renewal, 2002 6.25^L x 5^W x 1.75^H (None)	Collectors Club$^{(02-03)}$	12081	29
Renewal, 2003 4.5^L x 3.25^W x 4^H (None)	Collectors Club$^{(03-04)}$	10116	29
Renewal, 2004 5.5RD x 4.75^H (None)	Collectors Club$^{(04-05)}$	10633	29
Renewal, 2005 6.75^L x 3.75^W x 4.5^H (Little Boardwalk)	Collectors Club$^{(05)}$	10029	29
Resolution 5RD x 4.5^H (5" Measuring)	Feature$^{(87)}$	3800-ABS	57
Rings & Things 7RD x 3^H (Button)	Mother's Day$^{(98)}$	10383	104
Rose 14.5^L x 7.5^W x 3.75^H (Bread, New)	May$^{(91)}$	4700-CSS	101
Rose Bud 8^L x 4^W x 2^H (Lavender)	Incentive$^{(97)}$	n/a	89
Rose Garden 12^L x 7^W x 4.5^H (97 Easter)	Incentive$^{(97)}$	n/a	86
Rose Petal 8.5^L x 5^W x 3.5^H (Small Oval)	Incentive$^{(97)}$	n/a	89
Rosemary 5.75^L x 3.75^W x 3^H (Rosemary)	Booking$^{(90-92)}$	45000-JOS	22
Round Serving 12RD x 3.75^H (Round Serving)	Feature$^{(04)}$	10684^{WB}/10713^I/-17^P/-14^S	58
Row Your Boat 13.5^L x 6.5^W x 4^H (None)	Retired$^{(02-05)}$	12494/18326^{WB}	130
Saddlebrook, Lg 9.5^L x 5.5^W x 9.25^H (None)	Collectors Club$^{(00-01)}$ Retired$^{(00-02)}$	15776 19764	33 130

KEY:
See page 170 for a key to understanding the abbreviations and notations used in these p

Quick Find

BASKET	COLLECTION (YEAR)	FORM #	PAGE
Saddlebrook, Med 7.25^L x 4.5^W x 6.5^H (None)	Feature$^{(01)}$	12306	58
Saddlebrook, Sm 5.5^L x 3.5^W x 4^H (None)	Collectors Club$^{(00-01)}$ Retired$^{(00-02)}$	15679 17698	33 130
Saffron 5.5RD x 2.75^H (Peppermint)	Booking$^{(02-04)}$	12524/19090^{WB}	22
Sage 5.75^L x 5.5^W x 2.5^H (None)	Booking$^{(01-03)}$	19585/19152^{WB}	23
Salt & Pepper 5.75^L x 3.75^W x 3^H (Rosemary)	CClub, PAmerican$^{(03)}$ Retired$^{(01-04)}$	10054/60162 12044/18369^{WB}	33 130
Santa's Helper 4.25RD x 6.25^H (None)	Feature$^{(02)}$	10053	50
Santa's Little Helper 5.75^L x 3.75^W x 3.5^H (None)	Feature$^{(99)}$	19721	50
Scalloped Boutique 14^L x 6.5^W x 3.5^H (None)	Feature$^{(06)}$ Regular Line$^{(06-P)}$	10446-12^P/-21^W/-19^G 10446	58 CL
Scalloped Pocket Large 12.5^L x 5.5^W x 6.5^H (None)	Feature$^{(06)}$ Regular Line$^{(06-P)}$	10449-12^P/-21^W/-19^G 10449	58 CL
Scalloped Pocket Small 7.75^L x 4.25^W x 4.5^H (None)	Feature$^{(06)}$ Regular Line$^{(06-P)}$	10447-12^P/-21^W/-19^G 10447	58 CL
Scalloped Waste 12RD x 12.5^H (None)	Feature$^{(06)}$ Regular Line$^{(06-P)}$	10450-12^P/-21^W/-19^G 10450	58 CL
Seashell 7.75^L x 5.75^W x 5^H (None)	GOSummertime$^{(99)}$	15296	65
Season's Greetings 9.5^L x 6^W x 6^H (Small Purse)	Christmas$^{(92)}$	10316^R/10219^G	24
Seedling 6^L x 6^W x 4.5^H (None)	RLine, AHG$^{(04-P)}$	10673	CL
Senior Employee 16^L x 9^W x 6^H (Harvest)	Employee$^{(xx-97)}$	n/a	43
Senior Employee II 6.5RD x 5^H (Small Fruit)	Employee$^{(97-P)}$	n/a	43
Senior Recognition 8.75^L x 4.75^W x 6.5^H (Tour)	Employee$^{(xx-97)}$	n/a	43
Serve Around 13.75RD x 4.25^H (None)	Feature$^{(05)}$	10202	58
Serve It Up 23^L x 13.25^W x 3.75^H (None)	RLine, Hostess$^{(02-P)}$	60895/18784^{WB}	CL

Quick Find

BASKET	COLLECTION (YEAR)	FORM #	PAGE
Serving Bowl 12.75^L x 9.25^W x 5.25^H (None)	RLine, Heartwood$^{(06-P)}$	10455	CL
Serving Solutions 8 x 8 9.5^L x 9.5^W x 2.75^H (Picnic Pal)	Retired$^{(99-02)}$	15393	130
Serving Solutions 9 x 13 14.5^L x 9.5^W x 2.75^H (None)	Retired$^{(99-02)}$	15491	130
Serving Tray 20^L x 14^W x 3.75^H (None)	All-American$^{(00)}$ Collectors Club$^{(99)}$ Hostess$^{(92-02)}$ Hostess (WWash)$^{(01-02)}$	18091 15849 60011 68586	16 33 74 74
Serving Tray Heartwood 18.75^L x 11.25^W x 3.25^H (None)	CClub, Heartwood$^{(05-06)}$	10387	32
Serving Tray, Small 16.5^L x 10^W x 2.5^H (None)	Regular Line$^{(02-P)}$	11878	CL
Serving Tray Small, (CClub) 11.5^L x 15.5^W x 3.75^H (None)	Collectors Club$^{(96)}$	12629	33
Sewing Circle 8.5RD x 5.5^H (None)	Collectors Club$^{(01)}$	10575	33
Sewing Notions 11.25^L x 9.25^W x 5.75^H (Timeless Memory)	Retired$^{(01-04)}$ Retired (WWash)$^{(01-02)}$	10424/18415^{WB} 10435	130 130
Sewing Rectangular 16^L x 11^W x 9^H (Large Market)	Retired$^{(78-83)}$	600-F	130
Sewing, Round 13RD x 8.5^H (Large Fruit)	Feature (no stand)$^{(85,87)}$ Hostess$^{(95-00)}$ Retired (no stand)$^{(78-86)}$ Retired (stand)$^{(78-86)}$	3200-EO 13234 3200-NO 3200-NO	58 74 130 130
Shaker Harmony No1 10.75^L x 9.75^W x 4.5^H (None)	Collectors Club$^{(00)}$	19089	33
Shaker Harmony No2 9.75^L x 7.75^W x 4^H (None)	Collectors Club$^{(01)}$	18988	33
Shaker Harmony No3 8.75^L x 6.75^W x 3.25^H (None)	Collectors Club$^{(01)}$	16870	33
Shaker Harmony No4 7.5^L x 5.75^W x 2.75^H (Shaker Harmony #4)	Collectors Club$^{(02)}$	16861	33
Shaker Harmony No5 6.75^L x 4.75^W x 2^H (None)	Collectors Club$^{(01)}$	18881	33
Shaker Taker 7.5^L x 3.75^W x 2.75^H (Shaker Taker)	GOSummertime$^{(00)}$	17469	65

KEY:
See page 170 for a key to understanding the abbreviations and notations used in these p

Quick Find

BASKET	COLLECTION (YEAR)	FORM#	PAGE
Shamrock 5^L x 5^W x 2.5^H (Sweet Basil)	Feature$^{(90)}$	13000-HGS	52
Shining Star 5.75^L x 3.75^W x 3^H (Rosemary)	Incentive$^{(95)}$	n/a	88
Shining Star, Large 13.5^L x 14.5^W x 4.75^H (None)	Holiday Hostess$^{(01)}$	10753^R/10761^G	69
Shining Star, Small 10.25^L x 11^W x 3.75^H (None)	Christmas$^{(01)}$	10734^R/10745^G	26
Shopping Cart 17^L x 14.75^W x 38.5^H (None)	Hostess$^{(04-05)}$	10344	74
Shoulder Bag 10^L x 4^W x 6^H (None)	Hostess$^{(04-06)}$	10705	75
Shoulder Bag, Med 11^L x 5.5^W x 9^H (None)	Incentive$^{(04)}$	n/a	98
Show Star 7RD x 3^H (Button)	Incentive$^{(96)}$	n/a	89
Silver Bells 11.5^L x 11.25^W x 4^H (None)	Christmas$^{(05-06)}$	10335^R/10336^G/10337^{WB}	26
Sleeve, Bushel (Med) 12RD x 7.75^H (None)	Feature $^{(05)}$	unknown	58
Sleeve, Sunroom 24.5^L x 20^W x 14^H (None)	Hostess$^{(99-02)}$	15261	75
Sleigh Bell 16.5^{RD} x 11.5^H (None)	Holiday Hostess$^{(94)}$	14427^R/14435^G	CL
Small Comforts 7.75^L x 5.25^W x 4.25^H (None)	Retired$^{(01-04)}$	17558/18512^{WB}	131
Small Oval 8.5^L x 5^W x 3.5^H (Small Oval)	Mother's Day$^{(90)}$	33000-JPS	103
Snapdragon 7.5^{RD} x 9.25^H (None)	May$^{(98)}$	10863	101
Snowflake, Large 14^L x 12.75^W x 11.5^H (None)	Holiday Hostess$^{(97)}$	12661^R/12653^G	69
Snowflake, Small 10^L x 9.25^W x 6.5^H (None)	Christmas$^{(97)}$	12645^R/12637^G	25
Sophomore Recognition 8.75^L x 4.75^W x 6.5^H (Tour)	Employee$^{(xx-97)}$	n/a	43
Spare Change 6.5^L x 6.5^W x 3^H (Small Berry)	Father's Day$^{(91)}$	1300-JCWS	47
Sparkler 11^L x 8^W x 5.5^H (Spring)	All-American$^{(00)}$	18694	16
Special Things 8.5^L x 4.5^W x 2^H (None)	Mother's Day$^{(03)}$	10021	104

Quick Find

BASKET	COLLECTION (YEAR)	FORM #	PAGE
Spin Organizer 12.75^L x 10^W x 7.25^H (None)	Regular Line$^{(05-P)}$	10375	CL
Spirit of Longaberger 9^L x 6^W x 6.75^H (None)	Incentive$^{(94-P)}$	n/a	95
Sponsor, Large **All-Star** 8.5^L x 5^W x 3.5^H (Small Oval)	Incentive$^{(93)}$	13323	93
Sponsor, Small **All-Star** 8^L x 4^W x 2^H (Lavender)	Incentive$^{(93)}$	n/a	93
Sponsor, Large **Flying High with Longaberger** 7RD x 6.5^H (7" Measuring)	Incentive$^{(92)}$	n/a	93
Sponsor, Small **Flying High with Longaberger** 5RD x 4.5^H (5" Measuring)	Incentive$^{(92)}$	n/a	93
Sponsor **Pegged for Success** 6.5^L x 6.5^W x 8^H (Small Spoon)	Incentive$^{(96)}$	n/a	93
Sponsor **Rising Star** 16.5^L x 16.5^W x 21.5^H (Large Hamper)	Incentive$^{(90-91)}$	n/a	93
Sponsor, Superstar **Rising Star** 12^L x 12.25^W x 16.25^H (Medium Hamper)	Incentive$^{(90-91)}$	n/a	93
Sponsor **Share the Tradition** 8.5^L x 8.5^W x 5^H (Large Berry)	Incentive$^{(88-89)}$	n/a	93
Sponsor **Together–We're Growing** 9^L x 5^W x 5^H (Medium Key)	Incentive$^{(90)}$	n/a	93
Spoon, Large 7.5^L x 7.5^W x 10^H (Mini Waste)	Retired$^{(82-02)}$ Retired (Natrl)$^{(00-01)}$	11258 17680	131 131
Spoon, Medium 6.5^L x 6.5^W x 8^H (Large Peg)	All-American$^{(90)}$ Feature (Natrl)$^{(99)}$ Feature$^{(96-97)}$ Retired$^{(82-02)}$ Retired (Natrl)$^{(00-01)}$	11000-OBRS 19658 16349^R/16322^B/16331^G 11000-OO/11169 19658	15 52 54 131 131
Spoon, Small 5.5^L x 5.5^W x 6^H (Small Spoon)	All-American$^{(90)}$ Booking$^{(xx-84)}$ Feature (Natrl)$^{(98,\ 00)}$ Heartland$^{(88-99)}$ Retired$^{(85-04)}$ Retired (Natrl)$^{(00-01)}$	10000-OBRS 10000-OO 10871 10000-OCS/11096 10000-CO/11088/18458^{WB} 10871	15 23 52 67 131 131

KEY:
See page 170 for a key to understanding the abbreviations and notations used in these p

Quick Find

BASKET	COLLECTION (YEAR)	FORM #	PAGE
Spring	Easter [87]	900-AX	38
	Feature (Natrl) [98-99]	10880	52
	Feature (Seasons) [06]	1849112[P]/-19[G]/-21[W]/-16[B]/-22[R]	53
	Heartland [90-97]	900-ACS/10936	67
	Mother's Day [88]	900-APS	103
	PAmerican [03-05]	10057	121
	Regular Line [83-P]	900-A/10928/18491[WB]	CL
	Retired (WWash) [01-02]	11283	131
	WTraditions [95-97]	19038	148
11[L] x 8[W] x 5.5[H] (Spring)			
Spring Booking	Booking [04-05]	10691	23
7.5[L] x 4.25[W] x 2.75[H] (00 Horizon of Hope)			
Spring Meadow	Collectors Club [00]	17655	33
16.25[L] x 10.75[W] x 4[H] (None)			
Star Bound	Incentive [95]	n/a	88
4.75[L] x 3.75[W] x 2.25[H] (Business Card)			
Star Team	Incentive [95]	n/a	88
7[L] x 5[W] x 3.5[H] (Tea)			
Statehouse	Special Event [96]	n/a	137
11[L] x 8[W] x 5.5[H] (Spring)			
Step It Up	Hostess [04-06]	10690	75
18.75[L] x 9[W] x 12.75[FH] x 5.25[BH] (Odds & Ends)			
Stitching	All-American [89]	5400-ABRS	15
7RD x 3[H] (Button)			
Storage Solutions Large	Regular Line [01-P]	11512/18555[WB]	CL
21[L] x 16.5[W] x 7.5[H] (None)			
Storage Solutions Medium	Regular Line [01-P]	11520/18539[WB]	CL
17.5[L] x 14[W] x 6.5[H] (None)			
Storage Solutions Small	Regular Line [01-P]	11544/18513[WB]	CL
11[L] x 9.75[W] x 4.75[H] (None)			
Strawberry	All-American [01]	10141	16
6.25[L] x 6.25[W] x 3.5[H] (None)			
Strawberry, Large	Feature [05]	10267[WB]/10265[R]	58
7RD x 7.25[H] (None)			
Strawberry, Small	Feature [05]	10266[WB]/10262[R]	58
4.5[RD] x 4.5[H] (None)			
Street Basket	Incentive [06]	n/a	98
26RD x 17.5[H] (None)			
Stuck On You	Retired [01-04]	11865/18590[WB]	131
4.75[L] x 4.75[W] x 2[H] (Stuck On You)			
Sugar and Spice	Booking [88]	45000-AO	23
5.75[L] x 3.75[W] x 3[H] (Rosemary)			

Quick Find

BASKET	COLLECTION (YEAR)	FORM #	PAGE
Summertime 7.75^L x 4.5^W x 2.25^{FH} x 4.5^{BH} (Summertime)	All-American$^{(96)}$	18911	16
Sunburst 22RD (None)	Booking$^{(80)}$	7000-O	23
Sunsational Celebration 6.5^L x 6.5^W x 3^H (Small Berry)	Incentive, Trip$^{(96)}$	n/a	92
Sweet Basil 5^L x 5^W x 2.5^H (Sweet Basil)	Booking$^{(92-94)}$	10146	23
Sweet Pea 8.25RD x 7^H (Sweet Pea)	May$^{(96)}$	14915	101
Sweet Sentiments 4.25^L x 4.25^W x 3^H (Sweet Sentiments)	Sweetheart$^{(95)}$	19046	138
Sweet Treats 8^L x 5^W x 3^H (None)	Sweetheart$^{(97)}$	159-38^R/-54^G/-62^B/-71^{PR}	138
Sweetest Heart 8^L x 8.5^W x 2.5^H (None)	Sweetheart$^{(05)}$	10192^{WB}/10240^{WW}	139
Sweetest Gift, Lg 10.5^L x 10.5^W x 9^H (None)	Sweetheart$^{(02)}$	10300	139
Sweetest Gift, Small 4^L x 4^W x 3.5^H (None)	Sweetheart$^{(02)}$	10288	139
Sweetheart (90) 5.75^L x 3.75^W x 3^H (Rosemary)	Employee Birthday$^{(89)}$ Sweetheart$^{(90)}$	45000- 45000-ARS	43 138
Sweetheart (93) 5^L x 5^W x 2.5^H (Sweet Basil)	Sweetheart$^{(93)}$	11347	138
Tarragon 5.5^L x 5.5^W x 2.5^H (Ivy)	Booking$^{(01-04)}$	11830/19102^{WB}	23
Tea 7^L x 5^W x 3.5^H (Tea)	Employ Christmas$^{(94)}$ Feature (Natrl)$^{(98)}$ Feature (Seasons)$^{(06)}$ PAmerican$^{(04)}$ Regular Line$^{(79-P)}$ Retired (Natrl)$^{(99-01)}$ WTraditions$^{(95-99)}$	700- 10847 1860312^P/-19^G/-21^W/ -16^B/-22^R 10732 700-J/10740/18603 10847 10710	45 52 53 121 CL 131 148
Tea for Two 7.75^L x 5.75^W x 3.25^H (None)	Mother's Day$^{(99)}$	14931	104
Tea Tray 15.5^L x 11.5^W x 2.75^H (None)	Collectors Club$^{(04)}$	10724	34
Team Excellence(98) 8.25^L x 8.25^W x 3.5^H (None)	Incentive$^{(98)}$	n/a	89

KEY:
See page 170 for a key to understanding the abbreviations and notations used in these pa

Quick Find

BASKET	COLLECTION (YEAR)	FORM#	PAGE
Team Excellence(99) 15^L x 10^W x 7.5^H (Medium Market)	Incentive$^{(99)}$	n/a	89
Teaspoon 5^L x 5^W x 4.5^H (Small Peg)	Retired$^{(97-04)}$ Retired (Natrl)$^{(00-01)}$	11665/18432^{WB} 17868	131 131
Tee 5.25^L x 5^W x 3^H (None)	Father's Day $^{(99)}$	14940	47
10th Anniversary 15^L x 10^W x 7.5^H (Medium Market)	Incentive$^{(87)}$	500-A	94
Thanks-A-Million 5.5^L x 4^W x 4^H (Ambrosia)	Incentive$^{(99)}$	n/a	96
Thyme 4.5RD x 3^H (Thyme)	Booking$^{(95-98)}$ Collectors Club$^{(98)}$	19003 19224	23 34
Tic-Tac-Toe 7.5^L x 7.5^W x 2.75^H (None)	Father's Day$^{(01)}$	10346	47
Timeless Memory 11.25^L x 9.25^W x 5.75^H (Timeless Memory)	Mother's Day$^{(97)}$	13030	103
Tinsel 6.5^L x 6.5^W x 2.75^H (None)	Tree Trimming$^{(05)}$	10331^R/10334^G/10372^{WB}	144
Tiny Tote 6^L x 5.5^W x 7^H (Tiny Tote)	Employ Christmas $^{(02)}$ Regular Line $^{(02-05)}$	n/a 12512/18628^{WB}	46 131
Tissue 6.5^L x 6.5^W x 6.25^H (None)	Employ Christmas$^{(99)}$ Father's Day$^{(94)}$ Feature(Seasons)$^{(06)}$ Regular Line$^{(97-P)}$ Retired (WWash)$^{(01-02)}$ Retired (Natrl)$^{(99-01)}$	n/a 18490 6875712^P/-19^G/-21^W/ -16^B/-22^R 15831/18652^{WB} 10473 14184	46 47 53 CL 131 131
Tissue, Long 12^L x 7.25^W x 5.75^H (None)	Retired$^{(00-02)}$	10412	131
Top Performer 10.5^L x 9^W x 8^H (Weekender)	Incentive$^{(88-94)}$	n/a	87-88
Tour 8.75^L x 4.75^W x 6.5^H (Tour)	Employee Birthday$^{(92)}$ Tour$^{(88-99)}$	10022 5600-BO/15601	43 140
Tour II 7^L x 3.5^W x 4.75^H (TourII)	Tour$^{(96-99)}$	15814	43
Tour With Me (06) 26RD x 17.5^H (None)	Incentive$^{(06)}$	n/a	98
Traditions 9.75^L x 6.25^W x 4.5^H (None)	Christmas$^{(02)}$	10008^R/10018^G	26
Tray 14^L x 9^W x 4.5^H (Small Gathering)	Holiday Hostess$^{(87)}$	2300-JGRS	68

Quick Find

BASKET	COLLECTION (YEAR)	FORM#	PAGE
Treasure 20.25^L x 13.75^W x 7.5^H (Yuletide Treasures)	Hostess$^{(98-01)}$	18716	75
Treasure Chest 5.75^L x 3.75^W x 3^H (Rosemary)	Incentive$^{(92)}$	45000-	88
Treasures 19^L x 11.25^W x 8.75^H (None)	Holiday Hostess$^{(02)}$	10030^R/10041^G	69
Treats 6.25^L x 4^W x 3^H (None)	Tree-Trimming$^{(02)}$	10438^R/10448^G	144
Tree-Trimming 12.5RD x 13.5^H (Banker's Waste)	Holiday Hostess$^{(91)}$	1900-BRGS/BGRS	68
Tulip 14.25^L x 6.25^W x 3.25^H (None)	May$^{(95)}$	14648	101
TV Time 8^L x 6.75^W x 5.25^{FH} x 7^{BH} (Daddy's Caddy)	Regular Line$^{(04-P)}$	10665	CL
Twelve Days of Christmas 13^L x 13^W x 8.75^H (None)	Holiday Hostess$^{(00)}$	17833^R/17931^G	69
20th Century 8.75^L x 4.75^W x 6.5^H (Tour)	Tour$^{(97-99)}$	17575	142
25th Anniversary 8.75^L x 4.75^W x 6.5^H (Tour)	Special Events$^{(98)}$	17612	137
25th Anniversary, Lg 16^L x 8^W x 11^H (Magazine)	Collectors Club$^{(98)}$	12297	34
Twinkle Twinkle 5.5^L x 6^W x 2.25^H (Twinkle Twinkle)	Tree-Trimming$^{(01)}$	10664^R/10672^G	144
Two-Pie 12^L x 12^W x 10^H (None)	Feature (G.Bonnie)$^{(98)}$ J.W. Collection$^{(86)}$	19241 4800-BT	59 99
Two-Pie, Miniature 4.75^L x 5^W x 4^H (None)	CClub, Mini$^{(99)}$	19356	27
Two Pint 8.25^L x 5^W x 3.75^H (None)	Feature$^{(06)}$	10508^R/10779^{CH}	58
Two-Quart 9.5^L x 5^W x 9.5^H (Tall Purse)	All-American$^{(91)}$ Feature$^{(85, 87)}$	1000-CBRS 1000-CO	15 59
Umbrella 10RD x 17.5^H (None)	Hostess$^{(98-04)}$ J.W. Collection$^{(94)}$ Retired$^{(79-94)}$	11282/18822 11215 1200-OO/11207	75 99 131
Umbrella, Miniature 4RD x 6.5^H (None)	CClub, Mini$^{(03-04)}$	11933	28
Vacation Keepsake 10.25^L x 8^W x 3.5^H (Vacation Keepsake)	Feature$^{(03)}$	10244	59

KEY:
See page 170 for a key to understanding the abbreviations and notations used in these pag

Quick Find

BASKET	COLLECTION (YEAR)	FORM#	PAGE
Vanity 14.5^L x 7.5^W x 4.5^{FH} x 6.5^{BH} (None)	Mother's Day$^{(96)}$ Retired$^{(98-06)}$	14753 18449/18679^{WB}	103 131
Vase 5.75RD x 11.25^H (None)	RLine, Hostess$^{(05-P)}$	10402	CL
Vase, Apology 4.5RD x 4.5^H (None)	Collectors Club$^{(05)}$	n/a	34
Vase, Floral 8.5RD x 6.25^H (None)	Collectors Club$^{(03)}$	10264	32
Vase, Heartwood 7.25^W x 10.75^{FH} x 12.25^H (None)	CClub, Heartwood$^{(06)}$	10403	32
Vegetable, Large 16^L x 9^W x 3.5^{FH} x 9^{BH} (Large Vegetable)	Feature (Natrl)$^{(99)}$ Feature$^{(96-97)}$ Retired$^{(87-00)}$	19551 16543^R/16527^B/16535^G 5200-CO/15202	52 54 131
Vegetable, Medium 13^L x 7.5^W x 3^{FH} x 8^{BH} (Medium Vegetable)	Feature (Natrl)$^{(00)}$ Heartland$^{(97-99)}$ Retired$^{(82-02)}$ Retired (Natrl)$^{(94)}$	18333 16713 5100-C/15105 15113	52 67 131 131
Vegetable, Small 10.5^L x 6.5^W x 3^{FH} x 7^{BH} (None)	Retired $^{(82-02)}$ Shades of Autumn$^{(90)}$ WTraditions$^{(95-99)}$	5000-O/15008 5000-CGUBS 15016	131 33 148
Vintage Blossoms 7.5^L x 5.75^W x 6.5^H (None)	Mother's Day$^{(01)}$	10222	104
Violet 5^L x 5^W x 4.5^H (Small Peg)	May$^{(90)}$	14000-BVS	101
VIP Baskets 12^L x 7^W x 10^H (None)	Incentive$^{(86-P)}$	n/a	80-82
Wall Pocket, Med 11^L x 6^W x 8.75^{FH} x 11^{BH} (None)	Regular Line$^{(05-P)}$	10165	CL
Wall Pocket, Sm 9^L x 4.5^W x 5.75^{FH} x 7.5^{BH} (None)	Regular Line$^{(05-P)}$	10195	CL
Wall Vase 10.5^L x 5.75^W x 6.75^H (None)	RLine, AHG$^{(05-P)}$	10655	CL
Ware 9.5RD x 4.75^H (None)	Collectors Club$^{(04)}$	10058	34
Wash Day, Medium 18.75^L x 18.25^W x 9.5^H (None)	Feature (WWash)$^{(05)}$ Hostess$^{(00-04)}$ Regular Line$^{(04-P)}$	10248 19372/18938^{WB} 19372/18938^{WB}	52 75 CL
Wash Day, Small 16.25^L x 15.75^W x 8.5^H (None)	Hostess$^{(00-04)}$ PAmerican$^{(03-05)}$	15695/18842 10073	75 121

216

Quick Find

BASKET	COLLECTION (YEAR)	FORM #	PAGE
Waste, Medium (Large Waste) 13.5^L x 13.5^W x 16^H (None)	Feature (Natrl)(98) Retired(79-00)	11789 1700-O/11703	52 132
Waste, Medium II 16.5^L x 11.75^W x 18^H (None)	Regular Line(05-P)	10377	CL
Waste, Mini (Large Spoon) 7.5^L x 7.5^W x 10^H (None)	All-American(90) Father's Day(95) Incentive(99-00) Retired(82-99)	12000-OBRS 11266 11258 12000-OO/11258	15 47 96 131
Waste, Oval (Lg) 16.25^L x 13^W x 16^H (None)	Retired(00-04)	19666/18725^{WB}	132
Waste, Oval (Med) 14.25^L x 11.5^W x 12.75^H (None)	Retired(00-04)	19568/18709^{WB}	132
Waste, Oval (Sm) 11.5^L x 9.25^W x 10.5^H (None)	Retired(00-06)	19461/18602^{WB}	132
Waste, Oval (XLg) 17.5^L x 15.5^W x 22^H (None)	RLine, Hostess(01-P)	45989/18903^{WB}	CL
Waste, Small 9.5^L x 9.5^W x 12^H (None)	All-American(90) J.W. Collection(84) Retired(79-00)	1800-OBRS 1800-OT 1800-O/11801	15 99 132
Waste, Small II 11.75^L x 8^W x 11.5^H (None)	Regular Line(05-P)	10376	CL
Waste, Small Miniature 3.75^L x 3.75^W x 4.75^H (None)	CClub, Mini(97)	17797	27
Watch Your Business Bloom 5RD x 4.5^H (5"Measuring)	Incentive(97)	n/a	142
Weekend Tote 16^L x 6.5^W x 11^H (None)	Mother's Day(04)	10701	104
Weekender 10.5^L x 9^W x 8^H (Weekender)	Feature(87-88) Holiday Hostess(88) Hostess(01-04) Retired(04-05)	200-YO 200-YRGS 10362/18857^{WB} 18857	59 68 75 132
Welcome Home 15^L x 9.5^W x 5.5^H (Small Market)	Collectors Club(97)	10464	34
Welcome Home Gathering 5.5^L x 5.5^W x 6^H (Small Spoon)	CClub, Event(05)	n/a	31
Whistle Stop 10.75^L x 6.25^W x 7.75^H (None)	Collectors Club(01)	10303	34
Wildflower 13.5RD x 8.5^H (None)	Hostess(92-98)	10111	75

KEY:
See page 170 for a key to understanding the abbreviations and notations used in these pa

Quick Find

BASKET	COLLECTION (YEAR)	FORM #	PAGE
Window Box 21.25^L x 9^W x 5^H (None)	Feature$^{(02)}$ Retired, AHG$^{(05-06)}$	16977 10181	59 132
Wine, Large 16^L x 9^W x 3.5^{FH} x 9^{BH} (Large Vegetable)	Retired$^{(83-86)}$	5200-CO	132
Winter Wishes 12.5^L x 8.25^W x 10.5^{FH} x 12^{BH} (None)	Holiday Hostess$^{(98)}$	12483^R/12491^G	69
Work A Round 19.75RD x 12.5^H (Pot of Gold)	Hostess$^{(03-04)}$ Regular Line$^{(04-P)}$	10228 10228	76 CL
Work Load, Large 24^L x 13.25^W x 8.75^H (None)	Retired$^{(01-04)}$	11776/18776^{WB}	132
Work Load, Small 19^L x 10.5^W x 8.25^H (None)	Retired$^{(01-04)}$	12032/18760^{WB}	132
Woven Memories 10^L x 6^W x 4^H (Small Chore)	Tour$^{(99-01)}$	n/a	141
Woven Memories(02) 7.5RD x 4.5^H (None)	Tour $^{(02)}$	n/a	141
Woven Memories(03) 6.5^L x 5^W x 4^H (None)	Tour$^{(03)}$	728812^{WB}/914887^R	141
Woven Memories(04) 6.5^L x 7.25^W x 4^H (None)	Tour$^{(04)}$	n/a	142
Woven Memories(05) 7.25^L x 4^W x 6.5^H (None)	Tour$^{(05)}$	10210^{WB}/10211^R	142
Woven Memories(06) 10.75^L x 7.5^W x 4.25^H (None)	Tour$^{(06)}$	1047-9^{WB}/-21^W/-92^P/ -91^B/-22^R/-99^G	142
Woven Pedestal Base 3.75RD x 4.5^H (None)	Regular Line$^{(05-P)}$	10378	CL
Woven Shallow Bowl 10.75RD x 2.25^H (None)	Regular Line$^{(05-P)}$	10379	CL
Woven Table Lamp 6.25RD x 25.75^H (None)	RLine, Hostess$^{(05-P)}$	10389	CL
Yuletide Traditions 13^L x 7.5^W x 3^{FH} x 8^{BH} (Medium Vegetable)	Christmas$^{(91)}$	5100-CRST/CGST	24
Yuletide Treasures 20.25^L x 13.75^W x 7.5^H (Yuletide Treasures)	Holiday Hostess$^{(96)}$	18619^R/18627^G	69

Dimensional Search

Many collectors are not always able to identify their baskets. The Dimensional Search was designed to help you determine which basket you may have by looking at its dimensions. ****NOTE**** This tool can also be used to identify plastic protectors or liners. Follow the same steps below, except add a 1/2" to an 1" to your accessories' dimensions when matching to the list basket dimensions.

STEP 1

Measure your basket. At the top, measure length and width. If round, measure the diameter across the basket. Next, measure its height. All measurements in this Guide are listed in standard form: **length^L x width^W x height ^{H}**. Baskets that are sloped will have both its **front height^{FH}** and its **back height^{BH}** listed.

STEP 2

Go to the shape section that your basket most closely resembles. Octagonal, star, heart and other odd shaped baskets are listed as *Unique*. The dimensions are in numerical order. Scan down the list to find your dimension. Because baskets are handmade, measurements may vary within a 1/2". Locate the measurement that is *closest* to your basket.

STEP 3

Once you have located your basket's dimensions, note the baskets that are listed under that dimension. These are the baskets that share this same form. This is the point where you want to make note of the special features your basket has and try to identify baskets in the list that have the same feaature. At any point, you can refer to the different baskets in the *Quick Find* section which will tell you:

- The different collection in which your basket has been featured. Now is a good time to note distinguishing characteristics of your basket, such as color weave or commemorative tags that may point you to a specific collection or series.

- Other baskets that use the same form

- Its location in the Guide

If you are still not able to determine which basket you have or have other questions, please feel free to contact us at 1-800-VERIFY IT.

Dimensional Search

SQUARE

Dimensions	Item
3^L x 3^W x 2.5^H	Clip Keeper
3.5^L x 3.5^W x 3^H	J.W. Miniature Berry
3.75^L x 3.75^W x 4.75^H	J.W. Miniature Waste
4^L x 4^W x 3.5^H	Small Sweetest Gift, Mulberry
4^L x 4^W x 4^H	Chives
4^L x 4^W x 5.5^H	98 Horizon of Hope
4.25^L x 4.25^W x 3^H	Lots of Luck, 98 Regional Sponsoring, Sweet Sentiments
4.75^L x 4.75^W x 2^H	Stuck on You, Autumn, 03 Holiday Helper
4.75^L x 4.75^W x 2.5^H	J.W. Miniature Cake
5^L x 5^W x 2.5^H	Sweet Basil, 85 Bee, Potpourri, Fantasy in Paradise, Fiesta del Sol, 93 Regional Sponsored, Shamrock, Share the Tradition Recruit, 93 Sweetheart
5^L x 5^W x 4.5^H	Small Peg, Candy Cane, 93 Inaugural, Violet, Teaspoon, Loganberry
5.25^L x 5.25^W x 4^H	98 Bee
5.25^L x 5.25^W x 4.5^H	02 Branch Sponsoring
5.5^L x 5.5^W x 2.5^H	Ivy, Tarragon, Coaster Tote, Friendship, 96 Hostess Appreciation
5.5^L x 5.5^W x 6^H	Small Spoon, Carry-Along, 97 Bee, Medium Peg, Bittersweet, Shaker Peg, Welcome Home Gathering
5.75^L x 5.75^W x 3^H	Lucky Twist
5.75^L x 5.75^W x 4.5^H	Mending
6^L x 6^W x 3^H	98 Small Easter
6^L x 6^W x 4.25^{FH} x 5.25^{BH}	Finder's Keepers, Diskette, Small Desktop
6^L x 6^W x 4.5^H	Seedling
6.25^L x 6.25^W x 3.5^H	Strawberry
6.5^L x 6.5^W x 2.75^H	Tinsel
6.5^L x 6.5^W x 3^H	Small Berry, Blueberry, 98 Branch Excellence, Spare Change, Sunsational Celebration
6.5^L x 6.5^W x 6.25^H	Tissue
6.5^L x 6.5^W x 6.5^H	02 Region Award
6.5^L x 6.5^W x 8^H	Large Peg, 94 Bee, 03 Gathering Event, 02 Leading Strong Together, Medium Spoon, 97 Perfect Attendance, Pegged for Success Sponsor
6.5^L x 6.5^W x 8.5^H	02 Directorship Team
7.5^L x 7.5^W x 2.75^H	Tic-Tac-Toe, Game Duo
7.5^L x 7.5^W x 3.5^H	Medium Berry, 95 Regional Sponsored
7.5^L x 7.5^W x 10^H	Mini Waste, Large Spoon

continued next page

Dimensional Search

SQUARE

Dimensions	Name
8.25^L x 8.25^W x 3.5^H	98 Team Excellence
8.5^L x 8.5^W x 5^H	Large Berry, 91 Bee, 96 Bee, 03 Bee Speaker, 98 Regional Excellence, Share the Tradition Sponsor
8.5^L x 8.5^W x 6^H	Deck The Halls
8.5^L x 8.5^W x 7^H	Cranberry
9^L x 9^W x 4.5^H	Bayberry, 98 Large Easter
9.5^L x 9.5^W x 2.75^H	Picnic Pal, 8x8 Serving Solutions
9.5^L x 9.5^W x 12^H	Small Waste, J.W. Waste
10.25^L x 10.25^W x 4.5^H	Bountiful Harvest
10.5^L x 10.5^W x 4.5^H	92 Mother's Day
10.5^L x 10.5^W x 9^H	Large Sweetest Gift
12^L x 12^W x 4^H	Pie, 98 Director Excellence
12^L x 12^W x 6^H	Cake, Small Picnic, Crisco Pie, Old Oak Lid Picnic
12^L x 12^W x 10^H	Two-Pie
12^L x 12.25^W x 16.25^H	Medium Hamper, Rising Star Recruit & Superstar, Small Hamper
13^L x 13^W x 8.75^H	Twelve Days of Christmas
13.25^L x 13.25^W x 4^H	Pie, Blue Ribbon
13.5^L x 13.5^W x 16^H	Medium Waste
15^L x 15^W x 6^H	Checkerboard
15^L x 15^W x 7.5^H	Medium Picnic, Homecoming
15.5^L x 15.5^W x 12.25^H	Evergreen
16^L x 16^W x 8^H	Coverlet
16.5^L x 16.5^W x 21.5^H	Large Hamper, Rising Star Sponsor
17^L x 17^W x 22^H	01 Large Hamper

end square

RECTANGLE

Dimensions	Name
4.75^L x 3.75^W x 2.25^H	Business Card, 03 Branch Sponsoring, Star Bound
4.75^L x 5^W x 3.25^H	Let It Snow, 03-04 Dresden Tour
4.75^L x 5^W x 4^H	J.W. Miniature Two-Pie
5.25^L x 4^W x 5.5^H	04 Horizon of Hope, 06 Dresden Tour
5.25^L x 4.75^W x 3^H	Pocket Change
5.25^L x 5^W x 3^H	Tee
5.5^L x 3.5^W x 1.75^{FH} x 3.25^{BH}	Cilantro

Dimensional Search

RECTANGLE

Dimensions	Item
5.5^L x 4^W x 4^H	Ambrosia, 97 Horizon of Hope, 01 Hostess Appreciation, 01 Inaugural, Thanks A Million
5.75^L x 3.75^W x 3^H	Rosemary, All-Star Trio, 89 Bee Speaker, Keepsake, Sugar & Spice, 02 Branch Advisor Mini Bee, 01 Branch Sponsoring, Employee Birthday Sweetheart, 95 Horizon of Hope, 98 Hostess Appreciation, 04 June Hostess Bonus, Paint the Town, Salt & Pepper, Shining Star, 90 Sweetheart, Together We're Growing Recruit, Treasure Chest
5.75^L x 3.75^W x 3.5^H	Santa's Little Helper
5.75^L x 4^W x 3^H	Miniature Market
5.75^L x 5.25^W x 6.25^H	02 Branch Sales
6^L x 3.25^W x 4.5^H	Miniature Bread & Milk, Miniature Flag
6^L x 3.5^W x 2.25^H	Miniature Original Easter
6^L x 3.5^W x 5.75^H	02 Little Membership
6^L x 4.5^W x 2.5^H	Parsley
6^L x 5.5^W x 7^H	Tiny Tote, 04 JAM Award
6.25^L x 3^W x 4^H	04 Hostess Appreciation
6.25^L x 4^W x 3^H	Treats
6.25^L x 4.25^W x 3.5^H	Blackberry
6.25^L x 5^W x 1.75^H	02 Renewal
6.5^L x 5^W x 4^H	03 Woven Memories
6.5^L x 7.25^W x 4^H	04 Woven Memories
6.75^L x 4.75^W x 2.25^H	96 Horizon of Hope
6.75^L x 5.25^W x 3.25^H	00 Renewal
6.75^L x 9.25^W x 3.75^H	94 Mother's Day
7^L x 3.5^W x 4.75^H	Tour II, 99 Bee, 99-02 Dresden Tour, Flag Recruit & Sponsor, Hartville Tour II
7^L x 4^W x 3.5^{FH} x 5^{BH}	06 Hostess Appreciation
7^L x 4.5^W x 2^H	Miniature Gathering
7^L x 4.75^W x 7.75^H	Shades of Autumn Harvest
7^L x 5^W x 3.5^H	Tea, Patriot, Baby Easter, 99 Branch Sponsoring, Mistletoe, 91 Easter Hostess, Mini Chore, Small Key, Holiday Basket of Thanks, Kiddie Purse, Mini Berry, Mini Cradle, Star Team, Acorn, 93 Small Easter
7^L x 5.25^W x 3.75^{FH} x 4.5^{BH}	Small Recipe
7.25^L x 4^W x 4.5^H	Picture Perfect
7.25^L x 4^W x 6.5^H	05 Woven Memories

continued next page

Dimensional Search

RECTANGLE

Dimensions	Item
7.25^L x 6^W x 4^H	Card File, Fraternal Order of Police
7.25^L x 7.5^W x 2^{FH} x 3^{BH}	Little Bin, Top
7.25^L x 8^W x 2.5^{FH} x 3.75^{BH}	Little Bin, Bottom
7.5^L x 4^W x 3.5^H	03 Little Membership
7.5^L x 4.25^W x 2.75^H	00 Horizon of Hope, Spring Booking
7.5^L x 4.75^W x 2.5^H	Small Loaf, 01 Bee, Biscuit, 03 Branch Sales
7.5^L x 5.5^W x 2^{FH} x 3.5^{BH}	Paper, Note Pal
7.75^L x 3.75^W x 4.5^H	00 Branch Sales, 04 Holiday Helper
7.75^L x 4^W x 3.75^H	Candy Corn
7.75^L x 4.5^W x 2.25^{FH} x 4.5^{BH}	Summertime, Dash Away Sleigh
7.75^L x 5.25^W x 4.25^H	Small Comforts
7.75^L x 5.5^W x 4.5^H	Little Market, 02 Bee
7.75^L x 5.75^W x 5^H	Seashell
8^L x 5^W x 3^H	Sweet Treats
8^L x 5.5^W x 4.5^{FH} x 6^{BH}	Recipe
8^L x 6.75^W x 5.25^{FH} x 7^{BH}	Daddy's Caddy, TV Time
8^L x 7.5^W x 10.5^H	02 Directorship Award
8.25^L x 6.25^W x 3.75^H	Address
8.25^L x 5^W x 3.75^H	Two-Pint
8.5^L x 4.5^W x 2^H	Special Things
8.5^L x 5.5^W x 9^H	Autumn Tote
8.75^L x 4.75^W x 6.5^H	Tour, Memory, 20th Century, 25th Anniversary, 89 Bee, 88-99 Dresden Tour, Sophomore/Junior/Senior Recognition
9^L x 5^W x 5^H	Medium Key, Candle, 95 Perfect Attendance, Together We're Growing Sponsor, 97 Collectors Club Renewal
9^L x 5.5^W x 6.5^H	01 Bee Attendance
9^L x 6^W x 6.75^H	Spirit of Longaberger
9.25^L x 5^W x 6.5^H	00 Region Award
9.25^L x 5.5^W x 2^{FH} x 5.5^{BH}	Grandad's Sleigh
9.5^L x 4.5^W x 5^H	00 Directorship Team
9.5^L x 5^W x 9.5^H	Tall Key, Two-Quart, Collectors Club Membership I, Growing Strong Together, MBA Basket, Tall Purse, Charitable Champ
9.5^L x 5.75^W x 7^H	Shoulder Purse
9.5^L x 6^W x 6^H	Small Purse, 99 Branch Excellence, Season's Greetings, Mother's Day Purse, 94 Regional Sponsored
9.5^L x 7.75^W x 6^H	Mom's Memories

Dimensional Search

RECTANGLE

Dimensions	Basket
9.75^L x 6.25^W x 4.5^H	Traditions
9.75^L x 6.25^W x 8.5^H	Small Mail
10^L x 4^W x 6^H	Signature Shoulder Bag
10^L x 6^W x 4^H	Small Chore, $500 Million in Sales, 95 Bee, Gingerbread, 93 Large Easter, 03 Regional Sales, 91 Regional Sponsored, Small Easter, 99-01 Woven Memories
10^L x 6.25^W x 3.75^H	Baker's Bounty
10^L x 6.75^W x 3.75^H	Dad's Valet
10^L x 7.5^W x 4.25^H	03 Small Easter, Small Leadership Excellence
10^L x 8.25^W x 8.25^H	Harbor
10.25^L x 8^W x 3.5^H	Vacation Keepsake, 04 Bee
10.5^L x 6.5^W x 3^{FH} x 7^{BH}	Small Vegetable
10.5^L x 7^H	06 Golf
10.5^L x 9^W x 8^H	Weekender, Beachcomber, Remembrance, Top Performer
10.75^L x 5.75^W x 7.5^H	Flag
10.75^L x 6.25^W x 7.75^H	Whistle Stop
10.75^L x 7.5^W x 4.25^H	06 Woven Memories
10.75^L x 7.75^W x 10.25^H	Medium Mail
10.75^L x 9^W x 3.25^H	Napkin
10.75^L x 9^W x 5^{FH} x 7^{BH}	Card Keeper
11^L x 5.5^W x 9^H	Signature Medium Shoulder Bag
11^L x 6^W x 8.75^{FH} x 11^{BH}	Medium Wall Pocket
11^L x 7.25^W x 2.75^H	Early Blossoms
11^L x 8^W x 5.5^H	Spring, Bob & Dolores Hope, Sparkler, 91-02 Bee Speaker, Boo, 91 Easter Customer, Medium Purse, Ohio Statehouse, 98 Perfect Attendance, Red Pottery Thank You
11^L x 9.75^W x 4.75^H	Small Storage Solutions, 02 JAM
11.25^L x 9^W x 2.5^H	Brownie
11.25^L x 9.25^W x 5.75^H	Timeless Memory, Sewing Notions
11.5^L x 5^W x 3^H	Cracker, Liberty, Bed, Muffin, Herb
11.5^L x 7.5^W x 7^{FH} x 9^{BH}	Media
11.5^L x 15.5^W x 3.75^H	Small Serving Tray (CClub)
11.5^L x 11.25^W x 4^H	Silver Bells
12^L x 5.25^W x 3.75^{FH} x 5^{BH}	Envelope
12^L x 6^W x 4.5^{FH} x 11.5^{BH}	Catalog Caddy
12^L x 6.75^W x 3.5^H	01 Gathering Event
12^L x 7^W x 10^H	VIP Baskets

continued next page

Dimensional Search

RECTANGLE

Dimensions	Name
12^L x 7.25^W x 5.75^H	Long Tissue
12^L x 8^W x 4.25^H	Holiday Cheer, 03 Directorship Team
12^L x 8^W x 11.5^H	Mail
12^L x 8.25^W x 6^H	Lunch Box
12^L x 8.75^W x 11^H	Large Mail
12^L x 11.75^W x 3^{FH} x 5.5^{BH}	Small Basket Bin
12^L x 14.5^W x 3^H	Paper Tray, Bottom
12^L x 14.5^W x 3^{FH} x 5.5^{BH}	Paper Tray, Tapered
12.75^L x 6.25^W x 2.75^H	Peony
12.75^L x 10.5^W x 4^H	Carry-N-Caddy
13^L x 6.5^W x 2.25^H	Blossoms
13^L x 7.5^W x 3^{FH} x 8^{BH}	Medium Vegetable, Holiday Sleigh
13^L x 8^W x 5^H	Medium Chore, 93 Bee, Medium Easter, Basket Fest, 88 Medium Bee
13^L x 8.5^W x 4^H	05 Easter
13.25^L x 9.5^W x 3^H	Back Porch
13.25^L x 11.25^W x 9^H	Gourmet Picnic, Precious Treasures
13.75^L x 5.75^W x 5^H	Canning
13.75^L x 10.75^W x 5.75^H	03 Large Easter, Large Leadership Excellence
14^L x 6^W x 3^H	Small Flower Pot Basket, Personal Organizer
14^L x 7.75^W x 5.25^H	Large Chore, 88 Large Bee, Large Easter
14^L x 9^W x 4.5^H	Small Gathering, Advisor Recognition, 92 Bee, Pantry, Tray
14^L x 13^W x 7.75^H	Hostess Two Pie
14.25^L x 6.25^W x 3.25^H	Tulip
14.25^L x 6.25^W x 9.5^H	Cherished Memories
14.25^L 10.75^W 3.75^{FH} 9.25^{BH}	Large Desktop
14.5^L x 5.5^W x 9.5^H	00 Director Sponsored
14.5^L x 7.5^W x 3.75^H	Bread (new)
14.5^L x 7.5^W x 4.5^{FH} x 6.5^{BH}	Vanity
14.5^L x 7.5^W x 4.5^{FH} x 11.5^{BH}	Catalog
14.5^L x 9.5^W x 2.75^H	9x13 Serving Solutions
15^L x 8^W x 2.25^H	Bread (old), Holly, Garden
15^L x 8^W x 7.25^H	Membership II
15^L x 9.5^W x 5.5^H	Small Market, Welcome Home, 03 Directorship, 99 Regional Sales/Sponsoring
15^L x 10^W x 7.5^H	Medium Market, 88 Bee Speaker, Founder's Basket, Heirloom, 98 JAM, 99 Team Excellence

Dimensional Search

RECTANGLE

Dimensions	Name
15^L x 12^W x 4^H	Letter Tray
15^L x 16^W x 3.5^{FH} x 10.25^{BH}	Book Keeper
15.25^L x 12^W x 12^H	Personal File
15.5^L x 9^W x 5.5^H	Carry Along
15.75^L x 6.5^W x 11^H	Branch/Region/Director Basket
15.75^L 10.5^W 10.5^{FH} 12.25^{BH}	Newspaper
16^L x 6.5^W x 11^H	Weekend Tote
16^L x 7.5^W x 3.25^H	Bagel
16^L x 8^W x 11^H	Magazine, 25th Anniversary, Bread & Milk
16^L x 9^W x 3.5^{FH} x 9^{BH}	Large Vegetable
16^L x 9^W x 6^H	Harvest, 90 Bee Speaker, Original Easter, Senior Employee Recognition
16^L x 11^W x 9^H	Large Market, 99 Director Sales/Sponsoring, Rectangular Sewing
16.25^L x 10.75^W x 4^H	Spring Meadow
16.25^L x 15.75^W x 8.5^H	Small Wash Day
16.5^L x 12.5^W x 5^{FH} x 7.75^{BH}	Large Basket Bin
16.5^L x 10^W x 2.5^H	Small Serving Tray (RLine)
16.75^L x 16.25^W x 6.5^H	Garland
17^L x 7.5^W x 4.75^H	Flower Pot Basket
17^L x 14^W x 11^H	Large Picnic, Getaway
17.5^L x 14^W x 6.5^H	Medium Storage Solutions
18^L x 11^W x 4.5^H	Medium Gathering, Gourmet Gathering
18^L x 13.75^W x 9.25^H	Craft Keeper
18.25^L x 8.5^W x 4.25^H	Household Caddy
18.75^L x 9^W x 12.75^{FH} x 5.25^{BH}	Odds & Ends
18.75^L x 18.25^W x 9.5^H	Medium Wash Day
19^L x 10.5^W x 8.25^H	Small Workload
19^L x 11.25^W x 8.75^H	Treasures
19^L x 12^W x 6^H	Large Gathering, Doll Cradle
19.25^L x 11.75^W x 8^H	Crafting
19.25^L x 12^W x 23^H	Lattice Weave Hamper
20^L x 14^W x 3.75^H	Serving Tray
20^L x 14^W x 9.5^H	Family Picnic (CClub)
20^L x 17.5^W x 12.5^H	File
20.25^L x 13.75^W x 7.5^H	Yuletide Treasures, Treasure
20.5^L x 12.5^W x 11.5^H	Block Party
20.5^L x 15.75^W x 4.5^H	All In One Game
20.5^L x 15^W x 10.5^H	Gift Giving, Forever Yours

continued next page

Dimensional Search

RECTANGLE

21^L x 11.5^W x 9.75^H	Hostess Family Picnic
21^L x 16.5^W x 7.5^H	Large Storage Solutions
21.25^L x 9^W x 5^H	Window Box
22.25^L x 11^W x 2.75^H	Blooms
23^L x 13.25^W x 3.75^H	Serve It Up
23^L x 14^W x 11.25^H	Hope Chest
23^L x 15^W x 8^H	XLarge Gathering
24^L x 13.25^W x 8.75^H	Large Workload
24^L x 17^W x 10^H	Small Laundry, Family Picnic, Small Cradle
26^L x 20^W x 13.75^H	Housekeeper
28.5^L x 17.75^W x 9.75^H	Medium Laundry, Medium Cradle
30^L x 20^W x 10.5^H	Large Laundry, Large (Infant) Cradle

end rectangle

ROUND

3.25RD x 5.25^H	Pride
3.75RD x 3.75^H	XSmall Gatehouse, Little Elf
4RD x 3.25^H	03 Hostess Appreciation
4RD x 4.25^H	Pencil, Pen Pal, 02 Horizon of Hope
4RD x 6.5^H	Miniature Umbrella
4.25RD x 6.25^H	Santa's Helper
4.5RD x 3^H	Thyme, Gold Nugget
4.5RD x 4.5^H	Apology Vase
4.75RD x 3^H	Lucky You
4.75RD x 7.5^H	Small Gatehouse
5RD x 2.5^H	Coaster
5RD x 3^H	Melody
5RD x 3.25^H	05 Hostess Appreciation
5RD x 4.5^H	5" Measuring, 5" Canister, 86 Bee, Forget-Me-Not, Flying High Recruit/Superstar, 89 Inaugural, Make Your Dreams Come True Recruit, Resolution, Watch Your Business Bloom, 99-02 National High Sales (Level1)
5RD x 6^H	01 CClub Renewal
5.25RD x 3.25^H	Miniature Apple
5.25RD x 4.25^H	01 Horizon of Hope
5.25RD x 5.25^H	Miniature Banker's Waste

Dimensional Search

ROUND

5.5RD x 2.5^H	Associate Producer
5.5RD x 2.75^H	Peppermint, Saffron
5.5RD x 3.25^H	97 Inaugural
5.5RD x 3.5^H	Discovery, Cupcake, 05 Holiday Helper
5.5RD x 3.75^H	Laurel, Basket O'Luck
5.5RD x 3.75^H	Lily of the Valley, 00 JAM Recognition, Pot of Gold, Jelly Bean, Ports of Paradise, 05 Dresden Tour
5.5RD x 4^H	00 Bee
5.5RD x 4.5^H	Woven Pedestal Base
5.5RD x 4.75^H	04 Renewal
5.5RD x 6^H	Small Canister, 05 Gathering Event
5.75RD x 3^H	99 Small Easter
5.75RD x 3.5^H	Happy Halloween
5.75RD x 4.25^H	Little Pumpkin, 04 Branch Sales
5.75RD x 8^H	Beverage Tote
5.75RD x 11.25^H	Hostess Vase
6RD x 2.75^H	01 Small Easter
6RD x 4^H	Mom's Essentials
6RD x 4.75^H	Gathering Event Pail
6RD x 5.5^H	Let Me Call You Sweetheart
6.5RD x 4.75^H	Gold Rush
6.5RD x 5^H	Small Fruit, 94 Perfect Attendance, Senior Employee II
6.5RD x 6.5^H	Lilac, Bouquet (Sweetheart)
6.5RD x 6.75^H	Pumpkin Patch, 03 Golf
6.5RD x 9^H	October Fields, Pineapple
6.5RD x 10.5^H	Large Gatehouse, 01 Perfect Attendance
6.75RD x 6^H	Daisy, Bouquet, 00-01 Golf, Inaugural Leadership Vase
7RD x 2.25^H	Small Pie
7RD x 3^H	Button, Stitching, Cookie, Frosty Jr, JAM Small Easter, Rings & Things, Nurses Inaugural, Show Star
7RD x 4.5^H	Pansy, 94 Perfect Attendance
7RD x 5.5^H	99-02 National High Sales (Level2)
7RD x 6.5^H	7" Measuring, 7" Canister, Barn Raising, 90 Bee, Poinsettia, Flying High Sponsor, 94-98 National High Sales, 96 Perfect Attendance, Maple Leaf
7RD x 7^H	Medium Canister
7RD x 7.25^H	Large Strawberry

continued next page

Dimensional Search

ROUND

Dimensions	Name
7.25RD x 2.25^H	Small Catch-All
7.25RD x 2.75^H	05 Inaugural
7.25RD x 3.75^H	7" Bowl
7.25RD x 5.25^H	Small Pumpkin, 04 Regional Award
7.25RD x 6^H	Picket Pail
7.5RD x 3.75^H	99 Large Easter
7.5RD x 4.5^H	02 Woven Memories
7.5RD x 4.75^H	Small Bushel
7.5RD x 5^H	Caroling, 05 Heritage Days
7.5RD x 5.5^H	04 Golf, 05 Bee
7.5RD x 5.75^H	Lightship
7.5RD x 9.25^H	Snapdragon
7.5RD x 11^H	Floral Vase
7.75RD x 4.25^H	Miniature Corn
8RD x 4.5^H	90 Medium Easter
8RD x 4.25^H	Be My Valentine
8RD x 6^H	Jingle Bell
8RD x 6.5^H	Medium Fruit, Master Employee II
8RD x 6.75^H	Autumn Pail
8RD x 7.75^H	Large Canister
8RD x 9^H	Tall Fruit
8.25RD x 4^H	03-05 National High Sales II (Level1)
8.25RD x 7^H	Sweet Pea
8.25RD x 7.75^H	Hanging Woven Bottom
8.5RD x 4^H	Basket of Love, 98 CClub Renewal, Best Supporting Role
8.5RD x 4.5^H	Hostess Halloween
8.5RD x 5.5^H	Sewing Circle
8.5RD x 6.25^H	Flora
8.5RD x 7.5^H	Small Fern Planter
8.5RD x 8.5^H	Celebration
8.5RD x 10.25^H	02 Discover the Gift
9RD x 3^H	Medium Catch-All
9RD x 5.5^H	02 Golf
9RD x 8.5^H	9" Measuring, 9" Canister, 94-98 National High Sales
9.25RD x 4.75^H	9" Bowl
9.25RD x 7.25^H	95 Pumpkin, 04 Director Team
9.25RD x 8.5^H	Ice Bucket
9.25RD x 8.75^H	XLarge Canister

Dimensional Search

ROUND

Dimensions	Description
9.5RD x 4.75^H	03-05 National High Sales II (Level2)
9.5RD x 5^H	90 Large Easter, Petunia
10RD x 4^H	Darning, 89 Easter, Crisco Cookie, Daisy, Frosty, 96 Regional Sponsored
10RD x 5.5^H	Patio Planter
10RD x 6.25^H	Homestead, 05 Golf, Associate Homestead Tour
10RD x 8^H	01 Discover the Gift
10^{BRD} x 6.75^{TRD} x 8^H	Cookie Jar
10RD x 17.5^H	Umbrella
10.25RD x 3.5^H	Casserole
10.5RD x 5^H	Popcorn
10.75RD x 2.25^H	Woven Shallow Bowl
11RD x 10.5^H	11" Measuring, 94-98 National High Sales
11.25RD x 5^H	Heartwood 10" Bowl
11.25RD x 5.5^H	11" Bowl
11.25RD x 8^H	Foliage
11.25RD x 9^H	Large Pumpkin, 04 Director Award
11.75RD x 6.5^H	Hearthside
12RD x 3.5^H	Large Catch-All
12RD x 3.75^H	Round Serving
12RD x 5.75^H	Quilting, High Achiever, Basket of Plenty
12RD x 7.5^H	Joyful Chorus
12RD x 7.75^H	Medium Bushel
12RD x 12.5^H	Scalloped Waste
12.5RD x 6^H	00 Large Easter
12.5RD x 13.5^H	Banker's Waste, Tree Trimming, Master Employee Recognition, Small Round Inverted Waste
12.75RD x 4^H	01 Large Easter
13RD x 6^H	Hat Box
13RD x 6.25^H	Pinecone
13RD x 8.5^H	Large Fruit, Master Employee (20yr), Apple
13RD x 8.5^H	Large Fern Planter, Sewing, Round Sewing
13RD x 12.5^H	13" Measuring
13.25RD x 6.5^H	13" Bowl
13.25RD x 6.75^H	Compote
13.5RD x 8.5^H	Wildflower

continued next page

Dimensional Search

ROUND

13.75RD x 4.25^H	Serve Around
14RD x 16^H	Large Inverted Waste
15RD x 7^H	03 Discover the Gift
16RD x 8.25^H	03-05 Natl Sponsoring III (Level4)
16.25RD x 11.5^H	Ficus
16.5RD x 11.5^H	Sleigh Bell
17RD x 11.5^H	Corn
18RD x 11.25^H	Large Bushel
19.5RD x 10^H	Management Excellence
19.75RD x 12.5^H	Pot of Gold, Work A Round
22RD	Sunburst
25RD x 13^H	Pottery Ware
26RD x 17.5^H	Street Basket
31.5RD x 18^H	Planter Sleeve

end round

OVAL

4.5^L x 3^W x 3.5^H	Miniature Geranium
4.5^L x 3.25^W x 4^H	03 CClub Renewal
5.25^L x 4.25^W x 1.75^{FH} x 3^{BH}	Lucky Charm, Raspberry
5.5^L x 3.5^W x 4^H	Small Saddlebrook
5.5^L x 4.5^W x 2^H	03 Horizon of Hope
5.75^L x 2.75^W x 1.25^H	Miniature Pansy
6^L x 5^W x 8.25^H	Five Year Anniversary
6.25^L x 5.25^W x 3^H	99 Horizon of Hope, Aloha Hawaii
6.75^L x 3.75^W x 3.5^H	05 Horizon of Hope
6.75^L x 3.75^W x 4.5^H	Little Boardwalk, 05 CClub Renewal
6.75^L x 4.75^W x 2^H	Shaker Harmony No.5
6.75^L x 5.75^W x 4.75^H	99 CClub Renewal
7^L x 5^W x 3^H	Little Crocus
7.25^L x 4.5^W x 6.5^H	Medium Saddlebrook
7.25^L x 5^W x 3.25^H	Little Laundry
7.5^L x 4.5^W x 3.5^H	Century Celebration, Cheers
7.5^L x 5^W x 6^H	96 Easter
7.5^L x 5.5^W x 3.5^H	Gumdrop

Dimensional Search

OVAL

Dimensions	Basket
7.5^L x 5.75^W x 2.75^H	02 Small Easter, 05 Small Branch, Shaker Harmony No.4
7.5^L x 5.75^W x 6.5^H	Vintage Blossoms
7.75^L x 5.75^W x 3.25^H	Tea for Two
7.75^L x 6.25^W x 2.75^H	02 Small Easter
7.75^L x 6.25^W x 2.75^H	05 Large Branch Award
8^L x 4^W x 2^H	Lavender, All-Star Recruit/Superstar, Rose Bud, 94 Hostess Appreciation
8.5^L x 5^W x 3.25^H	Knick Knack
8.5^L x 5^W x 3.5^H	Small Oval, All-Star Sponsor, Rose Petal, 92 Regional Sponsored, 97 Small Easter, Be Mine
8.5^L x 8^W x 6^H	93 Mother's Day
8.75^L x 6.75^W x 3.25^H	Shaker Harmony No.3
9^L x 7.5^W x 3^H	Casserole Basket
9.25^L x 5^W x 6.25^H	Small Boardwalk
9.5^L x 5.5^W x 9.25^H	Large Saddlebrook
9.75^L x 7.75^W x 4^H	Shaker Harmony No.2
10^L x 4.75^W x 7.25^H	Heartwood Binocular
10^L x 7.25^W x 3.75^H	Small Daily Blessings
10.25^L x 6.25^W x 7.5^H	Geranium
10.5^L x 6^W x 4^H	Branch Bouquet
10.5^L x 6.25^W x 4.75^H	Large Century Celebration
10.5^L x 7.5^W x 4.5^H	92 Easter
10.5^L x 8.75^W x 4^H	Blue Ribbon Bread
10.75^L x 8.75^W x 5.25^H	95 Easter
10.75^L x 9.75^W x 4.5^H	Shaker Harmony No.1, 05 National Sales Leaders
11^L x 8^W x 5.75^H	04 Easter
11.5^L x 8^W x 2^H	Baking Dish Basket
11.5^L x 9.25^W x 10.5^H	Small Oval Waste, Growing Great People
11.75^L x 8^W x 11.5^H	Small Waste
12^L x 7^W x 4.5^H	97 Large Easter, 04 Heritage Days, Rose Garden
12.25^L x 9.25^W x 5.25^H	Get Together
12.5^L x 6.5^W x 7.75^H	Fellowship
12.5^L x 6.75^W x 8.5^H	Medium Boardwalk, 03-04 MBA
12.5^L x 10.25^W x 4.25^H	02 Large Easter
12.75^L x 9.75^W x 5.25^H	Large Daily Blessings
13.5^L x 8.25^W x 5.25^H	94 Easter

continued next page

Dimensional Search

OVAL

Dimensions	Name
14^L x 9^W x 4.25^H	99-02 Small Natl Sponsoring II
14^L x 6.5^W x 3.5^H	Scalloped Boutique
14^L x 10.5^W x 6^H	Crocus
14.25^L x 11.5^W x 12.75^H	Medium Oval Waste
14.75^L x 13.5^W x 6.25^H	Community
15^L x 9^W x 5.25^H	Family Legacy
15.25^L x 5.75^W x 2.5^H	Small Harvest Blessings
15.25^L x 11^W x 7.75^H	Family
15.5^L x 11.5^W x 2.75^H	Tea Tray Basket
16.25^L x 13^W x 16^H	Large Oval Waste
16.5^L x 11.75^W x 18^H	Medium Waste (05)
17.5^L x 15.5^W x 22^H	XLarge Oval Waste
17.75^L x 10.5^W x 12^H	Large Boardwalk, Branch/National Sales Leader, 02-04 Branch/Regional/Director
18^L x 14^W x 8^H	Greetings
18.5^L x 13.5^W x 5.25^H	Hospitality
19.25^L x 13.5^W x 7.75^H	Generosity
19.5^L x 8^W x 3.25^H	Large Harvest Blessings
20.5^L x 6.5^W x 2.75^H	Baguette
20.75^L x 13^W x 2.25^H	99-02 Large Natl Sponsoring II
21^L x 12.25^W x 11.25^H	XLarge Oval Picnic
21.25^L x 14.25^W x 10.5^H	Oval Laundry
27.25^L x 17.5^W x 10.75^H	Lattice Weave Laundry

end oval

UNIQUE [INCLUDES OCTAGONAL, STAR, HEART & OTHER ODD SHAPES]

Dimensions	Name
3.75^L x 3.5^W x 2^H	Miniature Morning Glory
5^L x 3^W x 3.5^H	Oregano
5^L x 3.75^W x 4.5^H	Little Joy
5.5^L x 6^W x 2.25^H	Twinkle Twinkle, Red White & You
5.5RD x 5.5^H	Noel Bell
5.75^L x 3.75^W x 5^H	Love Notes
5.75^L x 5.5^W x 2.5^H	Sage
6.25^L x 4.75^W x 2.25^H	Little Love
6.5RD x 7^H	Bell
7^L x 6.75^W x 3^H	7" Generations, 01 Branch Sponsoring

Dimensional Search

UNIQUE

7.25^W x 10.75^{FH} x 12.25^{BH}	Heartwood Vase
7.5^L x 3.75^W x 2.75^H	Shaker Taker, Small Barbeque Buddy
7.5^L x 7.5^W x 4.75^H	Morning Glory
7.5^L x 8^W x 3^H	Little Star
7.75^L x 4.25^W x 4.5^H	Scalloped Small Pocket
8^L x 6^W x 3^H	Small Corner
8^L x 7.75^W x 3.5^H	8" Generations, 01 Branch Sales
8^L x 8.5^W x 2.5^H	Sweetest Heart
8.75^L x 6^W x 7.5^{FH} x 9^{BH}	Glad Tidings
8.75^L x 7.75^W x 2.75^H	Love Letters
10^L x 9.25^W x 4^H	10" Generations, 01 Regional Sales
10^L x 9.25^W x 6.5^H	Small Snowflake, Christmas Sponsoring
10^L x 10.25^W x 5.5^H	Dealer's Choice
10.25^L x 11^W x 3.75^H	Small Shining Star
10.5^L x 5.75^W x 6.75^H	Wall Vase
11.25^L x 8.5^W x 5^H	Corner
12^L x 5.25^W x 3^H	Medium Barbeque Buddy
12^L x 11^W x 4.5^H	12" Generations, 01 Directorship Team
12.25^L x 5.5^W x 10.25^H	Everyday Handbag
12.5^L x 5.5^W x 6.5^H	Large Scalloped Pocket
12.5^L x 6.25^W x 7^H	Large Barbeque Buddy
12.5^L x 8.25^W x 10.5^{FH} x 12^{BH}	Winter Wishes
12.75^L x 9.25^W x 5.25^H	Heartwood Serving Bowl
12.75^L x 10^W x 7.25^H	Spin Organizer
13.25^L x 12.5^W x 4.25^H	Love Treasures
13.5^L x 6.5^W x 4^H	Row Your Boat
13.5^L x 14.5^W x 4.75^H	Large Shining Star
14^L x 12.75^W x 5^H	14" Generations
14^L x 12.75^W x 11.5^H	Large Snowflake
14.5^L x 5.25^W x 9.25^H	Frame Handbag
14.5^L x 7.5^W x 3.75^H	Heartwood Bread
17^L x 14.75^W x 38.5^H	Shopping Cart
17.25^L x 17.5^W x 20.75^H	Corner Hamper
24.5^L x 20^W x 14^H	Sunroom Sleeve

end unique

Notes